AFRICAN ETHNOGRAPHIC STUDIES OF THE 20TH CENTURY

Volume 51

A TRIBAL SURVEY OF MONGALLA PROVINCE

A TRIBAL SURVEY OF MONGALLA PROVINCE

Edited by
L. F. NALDER

LONDON AND NEW YORK

First published in 1937 by Oxford University Press for the International African Institute.

This edition first published in 2018
by Routledge
2 Park Square, Milton Park, Abingdon, Oxon OX14 4RN

and by Routledge
711 Third Avenue, New York, NY 10017

Routledge is an imprint of the Taylor & Francis Group, an informa business

© 1937 International African Institute

All rights reserved. No part of this book may be reprinted or reproduced or utilised in any form or by any electronic, mechanical, or other means, now known or hereafter invented, including photocopying and recording, or in any information storage or retrieval system, without permission in writing from the publishers.

Trademark notice: Product or corporate names may be trademarks or registered trademarks, and are used only for identification and explanation without intent to infringe.

British Library Cataloguing in Publication Data
A catalogue record for this book is available from the British Library

ISBN: 978-0-8153-8713-8 (Set)
ISBN: 978-0-429-48813-9 (Set) (ebk)
ISBN: 978-1-138-59693-1 (Volume 51) (hbk)
ISBN: 978-0-429-48727-9 (Volume 51) (ebk)

Publisher's Note
The publisher has gone to great lengths to ensure the quality of this reprint but points out that some imperfections in the original copies may be apparent.

Disclaimer
The publisher has made every effort to trace copyright holders and would welcome correspondence from those they have been unable to trace.

Due to modern production methods, it has not been possible to reproduce the fold-out maps within the book. Please visit www.routledge.com to view them.

A TRIBAL SURVEY
OF MONGALLA
PROVINCE

by MEMBERS OF THE
PROVINCE STAFF

and

CHURCH MISSIONARY SOCIETY

Edited by
L. F. NALDER

Published for the
INTERNATIONAL INSTITUTE OF
AFRICAN LANGUAGES AND CULTURES

by the OXFORD UNIVERSITY PRESS
LONDON, NEW YORK, TORONTO
1937

OXFORD UNIVERSITY PRESS
AMEN HOUSE, E.C. 4
London Edinburgh Glasgow New York
Toronto Melbourne Capetown Bombay
Calcutta Madras
HUMPHREY MILFORD
PUBLISHER TO THE UNIVERSITY

PRINTED IN GREAT BRITAIN AT THE UNIVERSITY PRESS, OXFORD
BY JOHN JOHNSON, PRINTER TO THE UNIVERSITY

INTRODUCTION

THE framework of anthropological research in Mongalla Province has been laid down by Dr. Seligman, and all subsequent inquiries can only be extensions of his. His earlier studies, 'Little-known Tribes of the Anglo-Egyptian Sudan', 'The Bari', 'The Latuka', 'The Religion of the Pagan Tribes of the White Nile', have now been incorporated in his monumental *Pagan Tribes of the Nilotic Sudan*, to which continual reference is implicit in the following pages.

However, a certain amount of additional material has now been collected and there are advantages in having some source in which the new-comer to the province, be he missionary or government servant, can find in handy form a general description of the people and their principal institutions and a study in some detail of the particular tribes with which he will have to deal: the provision of these is the object of the following compilation.

It has been undertaken, as a piece of team work, by missionaries and district officers serving in the province; we are all amateurs only, but the book has this merit that the facts have been collected by those with a fluent knowledge of the native languages.

For reasons of space I have had to compress much of the material obtained; and in dealing with material from two or three sources dovetailing has been necessary. It is not therefore possible without an inconvenient number of footnotes to indicate to whom I am indebted for any particular statement. I can only enumerate here, with my grateful thanks, the principal collaborators. These are:

Dr. K. Fraser, C.M.S.	Moru.
Rev. W. L. Giff, C.M.S.	Fajulu, Kakwa, Kuku.
Captain G. R. King, O.B.E., M.C.	Topotha.
Lt.-Colonel Lilley, D.S.O. Mr. H. B. Arber	Latuka, Lango.
Mr. J. Winder	Kuku, Kakwa, Nyefu.
Capt. G. N. Cann	Acholi.
Mr. A. C. Beaton.	Bari, Mandari, Lokoiya, Luluba, Fajulu, Nyangwara.
Major D. Logan Gray, M.C.	Kakwa, Kaliko, Baka, Avukaiya, Mundu, Makaraka.
Major L. N. Brown, D.S.O.	Baka, Moru.
Mr. W. H. B. Mynors.	Moru.

INTRODUCTION

I am indebted to Dr. Seligman for reading a large portion of the manuscript and for valuable suggestions; and to Mr. Shackleton of the Kenya Political Service for permission to use his account of the Marille.

The book is divided into two portions: the first part is a general description and comparison of the tribes as a whole; the second a description of the individual tribes in some detail. Features mentioned in Part I are described in greater detail in Part II, but to avoid a mass of footnotes references have been omitted.

It will at once be noticed that certain tribes, particularly in sections ii and iii of Part II, have been only very superficially treated. In districts containing a 'minority' tribe differing in language from the bulk of the population a district commissioner can hardly be expected, in addition to his multifarious normal duties, to acquire the second language or to devote as much specialist attention to the small tribe as to the more important one; and this is generally the reason for the gaps to which reference has been made. Thus, in the Eastern District our attention has of recent years been of necessity concentrated on the Topotha rather than the Didinga, for which tribe we can add little to Mr. Driberg's articles in vols. v and viii of *Sudan Notes and Records*. He has also published a vocabulary and elementary grammar (*M.S.O.S.* xxxiv. 1, Berlin, 1931), while a short article has just been published by Father Molinaro (*Anthropos*, xxx. 3/4, pp. 421–31). Much the same is true of the Anuak of J. Lafon: there is little to add to Mr. Driberg's article (*S.N.R.* viii); we await Dr. Evans Pritchard's study of the Anuak in their own country. The Acholi and Madi in the Sudan are only small outlying fragments: their main home is in Uganda, where Father Crazzolara is now investigating them.

As regards the Abyssinian frontier tribes, apart from fleeting visits by Captains King and Whalley, we are not in direct contact with them at all. It is something to have disentangled their most confusing nomenclature and established their approximate position, and some of their affinities.

L. F. N.

CONTENTS

INTRODUCTION v

Part I. GENERAL AND COMPARATIVE

I. GEOGRAPHICAL 3

II. THE TRIBAL GROUPS 4
- Physical 5
- Linguistic 5
- Cultural 7
- Tribal History and Movements 9
- The Western Bari-speaking Tribes . . . 10
- Recent History 13

III. TRIBAL STRUCTURE 15
- The Clan 15
- The Village 17
- The Sections 17
- The Tribe 18
- Age Grades and Age Classes 18
- Chiefship 21
- Rain-making and Rain-makers 23
- The Earth Chief 25
- Servile Classes 27
- The Elephant Hunters (Liggo) 28

IV. RELIGIOUS BELIEFS 31
- God 31
- The Ancestral Spirits 32
- Other Spirits 33
- Tree and Stone Cults 34
- Fire Cults 34
- Drumming and Harvest 35
- Blood Purification 37
- Witchcraft 38
- The 'Allah Water' Cult 41

V. CRIME AND PUNISHMENT 43

VI. INDIVIDUAL LIFE 46
- Marriage 46
- Twins 50
- Burial 51
- Suicide 51

viii CONTENTS

VII. ECONOMIC LIFE 53
    CATTLE AND LIVE STOCK 53
    AGRICULTURE 54
    BEE KEEPING 55
    ARTS AND CRAFTS 55

VIII. VITAL STATISTICS 57

IX. IMPACT AND CHANGE 59

PART II. INDIVIDUAL TRIBES   63

I. NILO-HAMITIC GROUP 65
    TOPOTHA 65
    LATUKA GROUP 82
    LANGO 113
    LOKOIYA 114
    BARI 118
    MANDARI 139

II. OTHER TRIBES OF EASTERN MONGALLA . . 142
    DIDINGA-LONGARIM 142
    ANUAK OR BERRI (LAFON). 144
    ACHOLI 144

III. TRIBES OF THE ABYSSINIAN FRONTIER . . 148
    MARILLE 148
    NYANGATOM 150
    NYIKOROMA 150
    KICHEPO 151
    EPEITA OR MURULE 152

IV. MORU-MADI GROUP 153
    MORU 155
    KALIKO 183
    AVUKAIYA 184
    BAKA 185
    MADI 186
    LULUBA 188

V. WESTERN BARI-SPEAKING GROUP . . . 192
    NYANGWARA 193
    FAJULU 195
    KAKWA 206
    KUKU 216
    NYEFU 221

VI. MISCELLANEOUS 223
    MAKARAKA 223
    MUNDU 226

    INDEX 227

PART I
GENERAL AND COMPARATIVE

I. GEOGRAPHICAL

MONGALLA PROVINCE is the southernmost province of the Anglo-Egyptian Sudan; it is roughly bisected by latitude 5 N. and marches with Abyssinia, Kenya, Uganda, and the Belgian Congo. Its greatest width east to west is about 480 miles from the Abyssinian frontier to Maridi on the edge of the Zande country;[1] from north to south it measures some 200 miles. It is bisected by the Nile, which in the north is fringed by extensive marshes.

The highest land lies along the southern frontier, especially east of the Nile, where the three mountain masses, the Imatong, Dongotono, and Didinga Mountains, attain altitudes of 6,000–10,000 feet; thence the land slopes gradually downwards to the wide uninhabitable cotton-soil plains in the north, waterless in the dry weather and waterlogged in the rains. West of the river the Nile–Congo Divide attains no great height and would present no obstacle to tribal movement.

Rainfall varies greatly from 21 inches at Kapoeta and 40 at Torit to 60 at Yei and Maridi. The country between the Didinga Mountains and the Abyssinian frontier is semi-arid, being an extension of the desiccated Lake Rudolf region to the south, and the inhabitants are obliged to adopt a semi-nomadic existence; elsewhere the country is covered with forest, heavy or light according to the rainfall, and the population is stationary except for their periodic cultivation shifts as the soil becomes exhausted.

At the end of the rainy season the country is covered with high coarse grass which except in the regions of densest rainfall is burned off at the beginning of the dry season. This annual burning results in a lack of humus in the soil, and at the same time stunts forest growth.

Local rainfall varies universally from year to year, and semi-famine conditions due to lack of rain reoccur periodically, but generally only over restricted areas, especially east of the Nile; this goes far to explain the belief in the need for rain-makers.

The inhabitants are essentially plain dwellers; the high mountains are uninhabited, and one may guess that the hill-dwelling tribes became so by compulsion rather than by choice.

The country west of the Nile is an almost continuous tsetse-fly belt in which cattle cannot be kept; to the south this belt extends eastwards across the Nile.

[1] The Zande have since been included in Mongalla.

II. THE TRIBAL GROUPS

A LIST of the tribes with their numerical strength and a map showing their distribution will be found at the end of the book. They are extremely numerous, the list containing some thirty names, but they do nevertheless form a comparatively coherent pattern, falling into three main groups with close linguistic, physical, and cultural affinities within each.

These three groups are:

1. The Nilo-Hamitic group east of the Nile, comprising the Topotha, Latuka, Lango, Lokoiya, Bari, and Mandari, the two latter projecting west of the Nile.

2. The Moru-Madi group, which includes the Moru, Avukaiya, Kaliko, Lugbari, Madi, and Luluba. These are arranged in a crescent, curving round from the Moru to the north, living west of and some distance inland from the Nile, to the Madi who occupy both banks of the river; the Luluba lying north and slightly east of the Madi.

3. The western Bari-speaking group, Nyangwara, Fajulu, Kakwa, Kuku, and Nyefu, situated west of the Nile and inside the Moru-Madi crescent.

East of the Nile there are two unrelated elements: the Didinga and Longarim, related to the Beir of the Upper Nile Province and the Epeita (Murule) of the Boma Plateau; and the Nilotic-speaking Berri (Anuak) of Lafon, and the Acholi.

None of the three main groups is confined to Mongalla Province. The Karamoja tribes and the Turkana extend the Nilo-Hamitic group into Uganda and Kenya; the Lugbari and most of the Madi live in Uganda; and there are Kakwa in the Belgian Congo and in Uganda. But none of the groups projects north of the province frontier.

The Hamites, light-coloured, straight-nosed pastoralists of whom the Beja and the Galla are conspicuous representatives, are one of the most important racial factors in Africa. They may be taken to have entered at some point or points on the east coast at some very early date and to have spread westward, with an ever-increasing admixture of negro blood, in a series of waves. In his *Races of Africa* (p. 19) Dr. Seligman says: 'It would not be very wide of the mark to say that the history of Africa south of the Sahara is no more than the story of the permeation through the ages, in different degrees and at

THE TRIBAL GROUPS

various times, of the Negro and Bushman aborigines by Hamitic blood and culture.'

Mongalla Province would appear to be one theatre of such a process with the Moru-Madi representing a negro stock coming apparently from the west and south face to face with the Bari, the most westernly representatives of the Nilo-Hamites. There is strong reason to suppose that the western Bari-speaking group are an amalgam of the two.

The terms 'Half-Hamite' (e.g. the Masai), 'Nilo-Hamite' (such as the Latuka or Bari), Nilote (Dinka, Nuer, Shilluk) are used to indicate diminishing intensity of the Hamitic strain: there is no precise division between the first two, and it is difficult to say to which the Turkana and Topotha rightly belong.

We can now consider the characteristics of the different groups.

1. *Physical.*

There is a distinct physical antithesis between the two main groups, the Nilo-Hamitic being long-headed and tall as compared with the rounder-headed and shorter tribes of the Moru-Madi group. The following figures are given by Dr. Seligman (*Pagan Tribes*):

	Height	Cephalic index*		Height	Cephalic index*
Masai	1·7	73·21	Western Bari-speakers:		
Turkana	1·69	74·18	Fajulu and Nyangwara	1·63	75·6
Nilo-Hamites:			Kakwa	1·66	76·7
Lango†	1·72	74·25	Fajulu	1·63	76.2
Latuka	1·78	73·3	Moru-Madi:		
Lakoiya	1·72	73·3	Kaliko	1·66	78·1
Bari	1·72	73·5	Avukaiya	1·66	76·4
Mandari	1·75	75·1	Moru	1·70	76·9
			Madi	1·77‡	75·3

* The shape of the head is determined by the percentage ratio of the length and breadth $\left(\dfrac{B \times 100}{L} = \text{C.I.}\right)$. 75 or less is accounted long (dolichocephalic), from 75 to 80 medium (mesaticephalic), 80 and above round or short (brachycephalic).

† In this book the term Lango is used of the so-called Lango of the Latuka-speaking tribes, and has no reference to the Lango of Uganda.

‡ This figure seems to require confirmation; the Madi do not strike one as being exceptionally tall.

2. *Linguistic.*

Corresponding to the physical difference there is a very definite linguistic antithesis between the two main groups.

THE TRIBAL GROUPS

Dr. Seligman (*Races*, pp. 17, 18) characterizes the Hamitic and the Negro languages as follows:

'The Hamitic languages are inflected: nouns have grammatical sex-gender which with number and case is expressed by suffixes; verbs are conjugated by both prefixes and suffixes and have a number of derivative forms, e.g. intensive, reflexive, causative, &c. . . . The Negro languages, i.e. those spoken by the true Negro, and also by many other blacks (e.g. the Nilotes) are generally termed Sudanic. Attempting to define these we may say that all words are built up on a monosyllabic basis, that there is an absence of inflexion —including grammatical gender—and that the genitive is placed before its governing noun. None of these three criteria must be taken too absolutely— languages of a perfectly pure type are rare—but, broadly speaking, the Sudanic languages all tend to exhibit these three features . . . since the number of such (monosyllabic) combinations is limited, the languages of these (western) Africans have become tonic . . . the pitch of the voice being used to change entirely the meaning of a word.'

The Topotha, Latuka, and Bari languages all conform to the above definition of the Hamitic languages and exhibit so many similarities as to be obviously related. Discussing the Nilo-Hamitic languages, G. W. Murray (*J.R.A.I.* 1920) postulates a common (Sudanic) origin not only for Bari, which as aforesaid is clearly related to Latuka and Topotha, and Masai, but also for Nubian, and believes them to have been 'once Sudan languages but now so overlaid with a common foreign (Hamitic) influence as to have developed into a very characteristic sub-family'.

Turning aside for a moment to the 'intrusive' tribes, the Berri (Lafon) and the Acholi speak a Nilotic language closely related to Anuak and Shilluk. The affinities of the Didinga-Longarim-Beir-Epeita group are so far unknown; Mr. Beaton finds in Didinga a certain number of resemblances in vocabulary with Bari but complete dissimilarity in construction.

Pending publication of Dr. Tucker's researches and the appearance of Mr. Mynors's promised Moru grammar,[1] we know less at present about the languages of the Moru-Madi group, but their mutual similarity is very striking and their general conformity to the Sudanic type clear.

In the western Bari-speaking group the dialects spoken by the Kuku, Mandari, Nyangwara, and Fajulu are almost identical with Bari. There are a few dissimilarities in vocabulary and in Fajulu a tendency to substitute *gp-* for the Bari *kw-*. In Kakwa the dis-

[1] Now completed.

THE TRIBAL GROUPS

similarity is greater in vocabulary; there is a strong tendency to drop initial glottal consonants and all final consonants, *upi* for *dupi*, *olo* for *bolot*, which, with elision into the following syllables, makes it at first confusing; but vocabulary and construction are essentially the same and the Bari and the Kakwa find little difficulty in mutual converse.

3. *Cultural.*

In addition to these physical and linguistic differences the two groups exhibit strongly marked cultural contrasts as well. Some of these have been outlined by Dr. Seligman (*Pagan Tribes*, p. 89); it is now possible to amplify and extend the list.

Thus the westerners are predominantly agriculturalist with few cattle or none; the Nilo-Hamites are pastoralists who have probably only taken to agriculture comparatively recently. Not only do cattle far transcend any other form of wealth, but the life of the individual pivots round his personal bull which he almost identifies with himself. Caution is, however, needed here, as it is certain that though the Moru to-day have no cattle, until comparatively recent times they were extensive cattle-owners.

Amongst most of the Nilo-Hamites, except the Topotha, the rain-maker is an extremely important personage, holding almost a priestly position and using a particular form of rain-making technique in which the washing of the sacred rain-stones is the essential feature. The possession of rain-making powers is essential to chieftainship. The Madi and Luluba in this respect seem to have adopted the Nilo-Hamitic practice, but in the rest of the Moru-Madi group the rain-maker either hardly exists (Kaliko, Avukaiya) or, though important (Moru), is much more a wizard than a priest and uses a quite different technique. Rain-stones are unknown in the western part of the province; though the Bongo farther west again have them, the related Baka have not.

Another important Nilo-Hamitic functionary is the 'earth chief' (Bari, *monyekak*), whose business it is to procure the fertility of the land; in the Moru-Madi group he is not found, fertility ceremonial being performed by the heads of the clans.

All the tribes east of the Nile have a highly developed age-class system which among the Moru and kindred tribes is entirely absent.

Dress ornaments and weapons offer conspicuous contrasts. Among the Nilo-Hamites the men go stark naked; the women wear aprons, hide skirts, often of considerable size, covering the buttocks, and often

THE TRIBAL GROUPS

skin capes. In the western group the men cover the genitals, while the women's dress is typically confined to a bunch of leaves in front and behind. Elaborate hairdressing and head-dresses are almost universal among the Nilo-Hamites, except the Bari. The red bead 'skull caps' of the Topotha, the brass helmets of the Latuka, the enormous 'panaches' of ostrich feathers worn by the Lokoiya are obvious examples (the Didinga with their hair felted into bonnets and the Acholi with their tremendous 'busbies' of ostrich feathers resemble the Nilo-Hamites in this respect); this characteristic is entirely absent west of the Nile, where even at dances a feather or two stuck into the hair is the maximum adornment, and the painting of the warriors' bodies with clay, very common east of the river, is never seen. Weapons tell the same story. Except for the Bari, who are bowmen, the weapons of the Nilo-Hamites are spears and shields and the bow is not used; among the Moru-Madi, on the other hand, the typical weapon is the bow, and shields are unknown, as are the wrist and finger knives particularly characteristic of the Topotha.

Another striking contrast is afforded by the deep-seated Nilo-Hamitic prejudice against the sounding of drums between seed-time and harvest when the grain is growing lest heavy winds, locusts, or other calamities should injure the crops. There is no trace whatever of any such belief west of the Nile; and among the Moru it is just at this time when the maximum number of drums is used.

The use of red ochre affords another instance (the Luluba here conforming to the practice of their eastern neighbours). Amongst the Nilo-Hamites it is much appreciated both as an emollient and an adornment, and girls in particular will be seen so thickly covered that they resemble a newly painted pillar box. As far as my observation goes, I should say that this practice was entirely wanting among the Moru and kindred tribes, except the Madi, who were prone to use it.

Burial customs provide another pronounced contrast. Among the Moru, Avukaiya, and Kaliko there is a very strong prejudice, shared by the Baka, Mundu, and Makaraka as well, against the earth with which the grave is filled falling on the body. To avoid this a recess in which the corpse is placed is cut at the bottom of the shaft and sealed with wooden stakes before the grave is filled in (or sometimes a roof is made in the shaft over the body). East of the Nile funeral practice varies, but this particular prejudice does not exist and the recessed grave is not found. There is one exception, the Bari rain-maker being buried in a recessed grave.

THE TRIBAL GROUPS

It may be tentatively mentioned that while amongst the Nilo-Hamites God is always a sky-god, amongst the Moru he is believed to live under the earth (in the intermediate Bari he has both aspects).

4. *Tribal History and Movements.*

On the hypothesis of a general Nilo-Hamitic move from the east and south-east we should expect the Topotha to be the latest arrivals, the Bari the earliest. The Topotha have very definite memories of migrating from Karamoja in two stages, of which the first correlated with the age grades seems to have occurred 150 years ago, the second perhaps 60. Driberg puts the Didinga movement from the south-east 300 years ago; and the Topotha when they occupied their present habitat displaced the related Epeita, who were driven to their present location in the Boma Plateau.

The Latuka have no memories of migration, but their traditions make Iliu and Chalemni, in the extreme east of their country, the early centres of dispersion—perhaps indicating entry by the gap between the Lafit and Dongotono Mountains—and there are indications of an east-to-west movement across their present area. Their earliest remembered hero lived ten generations ago, which even if no steps have been omitted should indicate a period of some 200 years. It is at any rate a plausible hypothesis that the Lafit, Lango, and Koriuk had preceded them and were driven on to their present hills by the arrival of the Latuka main body. The Lokoiya have definite memories of an earlier home near the northern Lafit three generations ago. From Latuka tradition it would appear that the Anuak arrival at Lafon from the north was roughly synchronous with the appearance of the Latuka from the east, and the Lafon people say that they were in contact with their kinsmen to the north until the Beir intrusion cut their communications. The Anuak settlements near Opari are colonies from Lafon.

The Bari have no general memory of any movements from the east; but one such tradition collected by Dr. Tucker is quoted by Dr. Seligman, and an eastern movement may be taken for granted. The present Bari rain-maker is the fourteenth of his line, giving a period of some 300 years.

West of the Nile a suggestive salient is formed in the Moru-Madi group by the western Bari-speakers, and tradition bears out the suggestion. Ten generations ago the Shindiru Bari were outnumbered by their Nyangwara, Fajulu, and Luluba neighbours. They defeated

10 THE TRIBAL GROUPS

them by a stratagem of the Dunsinane Wood pattern: the Luluba took to their present hills, the others crossed the river in a series of migrations, the Nyangwara coming possibly first, followed by the Fajulu and Kakwa. The Kuku and Nyefu movement into Kajo Kaji may have been somewhat later.

Owing perhaps to the vicissitudes they have undergone in recent years tribal memory is much fainter in the Moru-Madi group, and for the Moru and Avukaiya the Zande and Manbettu invasions are almost their earliest memories. The general impression is of a movement from the Congo northwards and north-east. Moru and Avukaiya have a faint idea of an earlier home to the southward; the Kaliko say they emerged from the Congo at a comparatively recent date. Our Madi east of the Nile are presumably an offshoot from the main body on the west, while the Luluba are presumably the farthest extension of the process. The pedigree of our principal Madi chief goes back some ten generations, and they seem to have no memory of movement from elsewhere.

Junker describes the home of the Amadi, with whom he clearly associates the Moru, as being in the big bend of the Welle in which the name Amadi is shown on the present-day maps, and it is at least possible that the Moru, Avukaiya, and Kaliko came to their present areas as a result of dispersion from that centre: it is significant that the Kaliko call themselves Madi, while the same name occurs frequently among the Moru sections. Mr. Mynors suggests that the Baka and Bongo represent an earlier movement, also from the south, separated later by the northern thrust of the Avukaiya and Moru.

5. *Cultural affinities of the Western Bari-speakers.*

It has already been suggested that the western Bari-speakers may be an amalgam of the eastern and western groups, an hypothesis stated by Dr. Seligman (*P.T.*, p. 297) as follows:

'We know that the Bari reached their present home from the east and that their language in both vocabulary and grammar resembles that of the Masai and kindred tribes. If we regard them as a conquering incoming cattle people who succeeded in crossing the Nile, but whose victorious course was stayed soon after this by the mesaticephalic "aborigines" represented by the Moru and their conquerors, agriculturalists in whose life hunting played a considerable part but who knew nothing of cattle, we shall find it less difficult to understand the predominantly Bari institutions of the west bank whose physical characteristics are so much nearer to those of the Moru and similar

THE TRIBAL GROUPS

tribes than to those of the true Bari. This view also allows us to infer a reason for the existence of the submerged classes and the varying degrees of disability from which they suffer from tribe to tribe.'

All examinations of the cultural evidence seem to show that this is if anything an understatement, and that apart from the Bari language and a belief in the dual god of the Bari, the characteristics of this cluster of tribes show that they belong predominantly to the Moru or the Madi.

As regards dress and weapons, the typical woman's dress consists of bunches of leaves, quite foreign to the Bari and the east-bank tribes. The men of the Nyangwara, Fajulu, and Kakwa, on the other hand, cover the genitals: to judge from Junker they have always done so and it is not merely a modern borrowing. The Kuku man, on the other hand, until recently went quite naked.

Their typical weapon is the bow: they do not use shields—in this respect the Bari resemble them.

The age-class system so prominent a feature of all the Nilo-Hamitic tribes is entirely wanting; the extraction of teeth tends to be a private rather than a ceremonial affair.

All except the Nyangwara use the recessed type of grave so typical of the west, completely unknown on the east (with the exception of the Bari rain-maker).

The position of the chiefs, rain-makers, and *monyekak*s is, except among the Kuku, quite different from those of the Bari and other tribes and may be considered in some detail.

Among the Nyangwara the chief is the descendant of a migration leader and is entirely secular. Two rain-makers exist: they are not chiefs but Bari immigrants, having but one rain-stone between them. They bless the seed corn by stirring it in the baskets before it is sown, otherwise there are no *komonyekak*. There are no *dupi*.

Among the Fajulu, the chiefs are the secular descendants of migration leaders; they are called *komonyekak*, but have no fertility functions. There are rain-makers using the Bari technique, but these with one exception are private individuals, not chiefs. They are a very few *dupi*.

Among the Kakwa the chiefs are styled *komonyekak*, but perform no fertility or rain rites. Rain-makers are numerous and important, generally using the Bari technique of male and female rain-stones and assisted by *dupi*; but in some cases with a different procedure, stirring oil and water in a pot. The rain-makers also bless the seed corn by

THE TRIBAL GROUPS

stirring the baskets; there are other *komonyekak* who perform fertility rites, and some of the Congo Kakwa told Mr. Giff that the *monyekak*s were the original owners of the land (cp. Kuku, below). The social position of the *dupi* is very vague and difficult to elucidate.

Among the Kuku the aspect is somewhat different. At the top of the scale we find the Kasura class of rain chiefs, chiefs, and rain-makers, whose ritual, *dupi*, and burial correspond exactly to those of the Bari. *Monyekak*s, concerned with the fertility of the land, are numerous, but are apparently never members of the Kasura rain clan. The Kuku themselves recognize the existence of at any rate one earlier strain which they say is Madi, and we may assume with some certainty that we have here an original Madi stock whose chiefs are incoming Bari, welcomed because of their rain power, who have respected the fertility powers inherent in the people whose land they have taken over.

Among the Kakwa the coexistence of the two different rain rituals points to a similar admixture without the political ascendancy gained among the Kuku by the Bari, and in the rain-maker's burial there is particularly strong evidence for the existence of a Moru strain. To begin with, the generic Kakwa term for all rain-makers is *bura* or *bora*; amongst the Moru the important Moru Öndri rain-making clan is called Vora; but this may be only a coincidence. But Mr. Winder thus describes the burial of a Kakwa rain-maker: he is buried just outside his house; he is buried at night and in silence because if the people wail or lament his spirit will become a lion or a leopard; a thatched roof is erected over the grave. Compare this with Mr. Mynors's account of the Vora funeral: he is buried at night, without mourning or lamentation, in dead silence lest he turn into a leopard which will prey upon the living; a grass roof is set up over the grave. The similarity is complete, and it may also be added that the Moru practice of tying a string to the finger of the corpse and leading it out of the grave is practised by the Kakwa at the burial of children.

The cumulative effect of the evidence appears to form a strong case for the presence of a large Moru-Madi element in all these tribes. The argument may be tentatively carried a step farther. The Nyang-wara and Fajulu have vague traditions that they and the Luluba are 'brothers'. But the Luluba are a definitely Moru-Madi-speaking tribe, and Bari tradition has the Luluba and Fajulu living together round Shindiru ten generations back. In other words, there is a possibility that when the Bari arrived the Moru-Madi were in possession

THE TRIBAL GROUPS

of both banks of the Nile, and that those on the east bank had acquired the Bari language and a considerable degree of Bari culture before their expulsion across the river. Amongst the Kuku the amalgamation is less complete, and the Kasura would appear to be unmixed Bari imposing themselves on a Madi population. The same would be true of certain elements in the Kakwa.

It is convenient to mention here certain beliefs and customs shared by the Bari and the Bari-speaking tribes in contradistinction to all or most of the tribes each side of them.

Bari, Nyangwara, Fajulu, Kakwa, and Kuku all believe twins to be unlucky (amongst the Bari if they are of the same sex) and in former days one or both were exposed. The Madi and Acholi share this belief, which is, however, not found elsewhere in the province, east or west.

The dual aspect of God, God in the sky and God below the earth, shared with the Bari by the western Bari-speakers, is not found elsewhere. The Nilo-Hamitic god dwells in the sky; the Moru place him below the earth.

The professional elephant hunters, the *Liggo*, are found among the Bari, Nyangwara, Fajulu, and Kakwa and not, apparently, elsewhere.

6. *Recent History.*

The first European contact was made by Mohammed Ali's expedition of 1841 which was accompanied by Werne. They found the Bari extremely friendly. From their description there are indications of an indirect trade contact with either Abyssinia or the Zanzibar Arabs.

The missionaries led by Knoblecher followed soon afterwards, but owing to illness and lack of organization they were only able to hold on a few years.

On their heels came the Khartum ivory- and slave-traders whom Baker found in full activity on his first journey in 1861. On his second visit he formally annexed Equatoria to Egypt, and in fifteen years the whole province had been occupied as far east as the Lafit and Dongotono, and there were stations in Zande and Manbettu country in what is now the Belgian Congo.

In 1885 with Emin's withdrawal from Lado the Dervish rule, advancing from the west, succeeded that of the Egyptians and lasted till 1898, when Chaltin, the forerunner of the Belgians, stormed Rejaf and occupied what became the Lado enclave.

THE TRIBAL GROUPS

It would be impossible to exaggerate the destructiveness of the trading, Egyptian, and Dervish régimes: cattle were heavily reduced or in some districts completely wiped out, while famine and disease supplemented the removal of thousands of people as slaves to effect a marked reduction in the population. The physical and psychological effect on the people could not fail to be immense.

In the early days of the twentieth century the Uganda Government was pressing up the right bank of the Nile. They had a station at Gondokoro, but the interior was not administered till our advent in 1914. Mongalla was occupied by the Sudan Government in 1906; in 1910 on the expiration of the lease we took over the Lado enclave from the Belgians; and in 1914 the southern boundary with Uganda took approximately its present form.

III. TRIBAL STRUCTURE

(a) The Clan, Village, Section, and Tribe.

THE clans are, as it were, the bricks with which the tribal structure is built up, and in an analysis of the tribal organization it is convenient to consider them first.

The clan is an enlarged family, descended presumably from a common ancestor (often forgotten) and, in this province, reckoning descent in the male line. The Scottish clans are a convenient analogy, the clan Campbell being not merely the Campbell family in any particular locality but all the Campbells anywhere. The clan has its own individual name; its members are all 'brothers' bound together by common blood and common interests.

The clans are exogamous, that is to say, a man may not marry his fellow clanswoman but must find his bride from another group. Violation of the rule is not only wrong but is incest, an offence against the community which will bring misfortune and death upon all, not merely on the guilty pair. The prohibition is commonly extended to the mother's clan also and frequently to the grandparents' clans as well. It follows that when a marriage is being arranged the telling of the ancestry to ensure that there is no forbidden degree of relationship forms an important part of the preliminaries. Dr. Fraser mentions that the Moru have a special sign to indicate that the relationship of a couple has been challenged and found in order.

In a community which has grown very large and widespread the exogamy rule may obviously give rise to great practical difficulties, and accordingly we find the clans being split to allow of marriage between the subdivisions. This is probably the reason for the divisions of the very big Igago clan of the Latuka; in the Lafit, the Lesoba are definitely said to have been split off from the Imoru for this reason. All the larger Bari clans are subdivided either for this reason or owing to some ancient quarrel which led to secession. Similarly in cases of individual breaches of the rule there is a special ceremonial (Bari, Kakwa), symbolic of the splitting of the clan to regularize their position. Conversely it does not necessarily follow that where two groups do not intermarry they are regarded as related; the taboo may be due to some ancient quarrel or feud. Among the Moru if an accidental killing has been compounded and expiated by the customary purification ritual the two families concerned must strictly observe

TRIBAL STRUCTURE

the exogamy rule in the future. The Zande practice of blood-brotherhood, the artificial creation of relationship, is not believed to exist except among the Baka.

Though rather uncommon in this province the clans may be totemic, that is to say, have an animal associated with them, either the clan ancestor, 'brother', or special benefactor who may not be killed or eaten. Several of the Bari clans have animals, birds, and even trees thus associated with them, and one case is recorded from the Nyang-wara. The Latuka, Moru, and Baka are not only totemic to this extent but believe that after death the individual's soul passes into the clan animal. The Moru have in addition a highly complicated system of sub-totems which has not yet been worked out.

Originally, no doubt, each clan was a territorial unit, and in some tribes, e.g. the Kakwa and the Moru, they still to a great extent remain so. But generally speaking with the passage of time, and particularly owing to the convulsions of the past hundred years, they are becoming dispersed. In any one village two or three clans will be found, but even so in that village the clans retain their corporate existence to a surprising extent.

Cattle carry the clan marks, from which we may infer that they are regarded as the property of the clan. The clan is definitely the land-owner, with its own well-marked and well-known boundaries. It is the duty of the *monyekak* and of the clan head not only to ensure the fertility of the community's land by the appropriate ritual but to allocate land to the individuals inside the group.

The clans are usually numerous: in the Bari, for instance, Mr. Beaton enumerates 143. A curious exception is found in the Latuka, where there are apparently only five, of which one is subdivided into three: this must, one would imagine, make their marriage arrangements exceedingly difficult.

The Latuka are also exceptional in the way that their very complicated and very strong village organization has weakened the sense of the corporative clan bond. Elsewhere the more we investigate the clans the stronger they seem to be. There is not only the 'family' bond which makes for mutual assistance between individuals, but the sense of collective existence and responsibility under the clan head is so strong that in many tribes the clan can be made the unit for tax assessment and collection. In many other directions the clan seems likely to have a real value in modern life. Cotton clearing, coffee cultivation and ownership, the clearing of bush for restocking are

TRIBAL STRUCTURE

obvious examples of the need for communal endeavour and communal responsibility which was never more needed than at the present day and which the clans may be able to provide.

(b) The Village.

With the exception of one tribe villages in our sense hardly exist. We find instead a number of scattered homesteads, each belonging to a family. These are arranged generally in a semicircle; in the centre is the man's own hut, flanked on each side by those of his wives—each wife has her own—of the more or less grown-up children and of any other relations who have attached themselves. Opposite are the grain stores, each wife having her own, there being a separate bin for each kind of produce. The houses usually are close together, but amongst the western Mandari may be separated by a hundred yards.

A collection of such homesteads constitutes the 'village'. Its centre may be some large tree where the men sit and smoke and under which the village councils will be held.

The exception is provided by the Latuka, who have closely built villages in our sense of the word, divided into 'quarters', each with its own individual name, its social organization, its dancing place, and its drum house which is both its club and the centre of its activities.

The Topotha villages are closely built and so conform more to our idea of the village.

(c) The Sections.

After the clan the next unit we should expect to crystallize out is the section, not necessarily owing to clan dispersion, a collection of clans, but rather territorial. In this province we find it in different stages and forms.

Among the Topotha it is strongly marked: the sections were formed during their migration, have their own individual (topical) names, Magoth, Nikor, Peimong, &c., and their own territories. In the extreme west again the Moru are divided into territorial sections, Moru Misa, Moru Öndri, Moru Kodo, and the rest. The Latuka are divided into quite definite rain areas according to the different rain-makers on whose ministrations they depend; but these have no names of their own and are hardly self-conscious. Territorial groups also exist among the Bari, originally in most cases areas served by major or minor rain-chiefs, but in some cases at any rate the ruler's ancestors were laymen who owed their position to wealth or force of character.

TRIBAL STRUCTURE

These, however, have no names of their own except those given by us for administrative convenience. In the Nyangwara and Fajulu the old migration groups afford sections of a sort: in the Kakwa the faint traces of sections that have been recorded seem to derive from common ancestry and so are more akin to clans; the present administrative divisions are of our creation. Among the Kuku four families of the Kasura clan have divided the country between them.

(d) The Tribe.

From the fact that there is no name for 'tribe' in any of these languages, that one can only say: 'What is his tribe?' by a circumlocution, it seems a fair inference that the conception of the 'tribe-as-a-whole' is extremely vague. In past days intersectional fighting was just as common as an attack on a mutual enemy. It is indeed surprising that external threats to existence did not have a more unifying effect; one might have expected the Moru to unite against the Zande menace and the Lugbari to have rallied as a whole against the raids of the Kakwa. But the process simply did not happen, and one may suppose that it is only by some gifted and unscrupulous individual that clan and section prejudices can be overruled and the African tribe welded into a coherent whole as the Zande and the Zulu were welded.

Some tribes, e.g. the Luluba, enjoyed more than others the reputation of killing on sight any strangers they might catch. Quite recently some Didinga murdered some passing Acholi merely because they were foreigners, and among the Nilo-Hamites it was on a foreigner, man, woman, or child that you blooded your spear, On the other hand, where no specific feud exists, tribal intermarriage is almost surprisingly common. The Latuka rain-makers frequently find their rain-making wife outside the tribe: the Madi (in the Sudan) seem to have adopted Acholi language and custom to a great extent, and the Moru, intermarrying freely with the Nyangwara, the Mandari, and the Atwot Dinka, seem to be noticeably lacking in this kind of prejudice.

(e) Age Grades and Age Classes.

(i) *The Age Grades.* In all tribes, west of the Nile, as well as east, we find the males formally divided into grades according to their ages and resultant capabilities and duties. A typical series would be:

TRIBAL STRUCTURE

Children, who tend the goats.

Youths (uninitiated), who 'fag' for their elders and betters.

Warriors (initiated), who fight and hunt.

Elders, who talk and advise.

Dotards, who just sit.

Entry into manhood is signalized by initiation, which invariably takes the form of the extraction of two or more of the lower incisors. Circumcision is not practised by any tribe in the province except the Makaraka, who are cognate with the Zande who also practise it.[1] No 'reason' for tooth extraction can be given; it is vaguely said to be connected with fertility; several observers state that it seems to be dying out. The teeth of the Bari rain chief are not extracted.[2] Amongst the Nilo-Hamites it is generally ceremonial: all candidates, boys and girls, are done together; and it is a test of courage at any rate for the boys. In the western group it is generally done privately.

The important grades are the warriors and the elders, and the prestige of the latter is in some cases very great. The Topotha elders are the rulers of the tribe. Among the Moru entry into the elder grade was until recently marked by a special ceremonial, and the elders wore a strip of leopard skin round the forehead. Among the Kaliko they retain their importance; they wear an iron or ivory bracelet and are said to instruct the juniors in their duties. At a feast the Bari sit by grades, and each grade receives those joints of the beast traditionally apportioned to it.

(ii) *The Age Classes*. Amongst the Nilo-Hamites (and Didinga and Acholi) initiation is the preliminary to entry not only of the grade but of the age classes which supplement the grade system. The classes are no doubt in origin a fighting organization under which, generally at about four-year intervals, the oncoming young men are 'brigaded' into units, each of which has its own name and its own corporate existence.

It is seen at its simplest among the Bari, among whom every four years or so a new class is created and named, which, however, remains an independent unit and is not part of any larger whole. The Lokoiya practice is probably the same. The Topotha organization is more com-

---

[1] The Mandari on the east bank practise circumcision apparently as a supposed cure for pains. About 50 per cent. are circumcised: it is done at any age from childhood to 20 years or so.

[2] Werne (1841) mentions specifically that the chief Logono's teeth had not been extracted.

TRIBAL STRUCTURE

plicated. Here each class is regarded not as a unit in itself but as a subdivision of the main class which consists of (probably) three such sub-classes covering some fifteen or twenty years (the exact intervals are not yet precisely known). Moreover, probably because the candidate enters his class early in life before he has attained full manhood he does not become a warrior until he has also been initiated into a 'bull' or warrior class. Thus a man will belong to three classes, e.g. the Nyichuma bull class, the Merikopiri sub-class which is the senior unit of the Nyikaletho class. The new bull class has to find sponsors among the elders; arrangements are made to ensure that the *élite* of the class shall be its leaders and in due time its elders. On handing over to the class which succeeds it, the retiring warrior class becomes the ruling elder class of the country.

The Latuka system is even more elaborate. Here the young man is initiated first into his drum house; every four years the 'Father of the Village' initiates them into a village class; every sixteen years the rain-maker initiates the four classes of all villages in his rain area as the main class, on entry to which they become responsible for the safeguarding of the country. Thus a member of the *Naboro* (sand) main class will be a member of the (village) *Nyong* class which at Torit will also be called *Khima* (grain) and at Muragatika *Ibwoy* (lazy); he will belong to *Apotir* (wart-hog) the senior sub-class of *Ibwoy*, which in his own particular drum house will have a further subdivision, *Ikholo* (heron).

Amongst the Topotha the class covers the whole tribe: the class is initiated separately in each tribal section, but contemporaries of all sections belong to the same class. The Lango (who probably have the sixteen-year cycle) have the same arrangement, and also probably the Didinga. (Incidentally the class names of the Didinga and Lango have a large measure of correspondence.) The Latuka classes do not transcend the rain areas; among the Bari, and probably the Latuka also, the class is a village affair, and a big village may even have two class systems.

Class initiation takes various forms. Among the Bari it is confined to the teeth extraction; among the Latuka it is associated with an elaborate fire-making ritual; fire-making is practised by the Topotha, who also have a running-the-gauntlet ritual which is shared by the Didinga and Lango.

A picturesque feature of the Lokoiya classes is that each class has its own special dancing-kit, ranging from a few streaks of paint and a feather in the hair for the junior class to leopard skins, enormous head-

TRIBAL STRUCTURE

dresses of ostrich feathers, and strings of bells spiralled round the leg from ankle to thigh for the seniors. The Bari formerly did the same, but this has now lapsed. The Acholi classes have their special dancing dresses also: this is not seen among the Latuka, where the 'uniform' for all the *monyemiji* is the same, the brass helmet with the very tall plume of red feathers.

The bond between age fellows is a very strong one: all the members of a class are 'brothers' expecting and receiving mutual assistance in all crises and important occasions in life.

There are faint traces of age classes among the Nyangwara probably imitated from their Mandari neighbours. Otherwise the class system appears to be entirely confined to the tribes east of the Nile.

(f) *Chiefship.*

The weakness of the tribal as opposed to the clan or sectional conception has already been noted, and it is not therefore so surprising to find that the idea of a paramount tribal chief, so natural to our ideas, is completely absent. The position of the Bari rain chiefs of Shindiru approached most closely to it; they were, and are to-day, widely respected and feared not only among the Bari but by adjacent tribes as well. But there is an essential difference; their position was due to their powers in the magico-religious sphere, and to this sphere they largely confined themselves. In times of great crisis their wishes would command a wider hearing, but there is no evidence that they have ever wielded secular authority over the Bari as a whole.

The idea of the 'chief', so far as it existed at all, was confined to sections, groups, and clans. In many tribes the governance of the community was entirely in the hands of the elders. The Topotha are a case in point. Gifted individuals might owing to their prowess or prestige exercise a strong influence for a time, but on their death there was no question of their sons inheriting their position; the elders were, and remained, the ruling caste. The Didinga, in the same way, are emphatic that until the advent of the Abyssinians they had no chiefs. Where a recognized head of the community existed he was, except possibly the rain chief in his own area, far from autocratic. All matters of moment were deliberated by the elders, and their decisions could hardly be gainsaid. This democratic aspect of African society is very strong, and for the development of native administration extremely important. The petty affairs of the numerous small groups were dealt with by their own elders and headmen.

TRIBAL STRUCTURE

The idea of the secular, executive chief is entirely due to foreign influence. Almost the first thing which the foreigners did on arrival was to ask for 'the Chief'. Several things might then happen: they might single out the prominent rain chief and invest him with a variety of powers which he did not possess, or some complete nobody might be pushed forward to act as a go-between and as a whipping-boy, to bear the brunt of any trouble that might come. Some ingratiatory busybody might usurp the role: or the foreigner, finding nobody to act might frankly appoint one of his own people. The Bari term for the executive chief, *matat lo gela*, 'the foreigners' chief', is significant.

Tinged therefore to-day by this new idea of administrative office and duties, the basis of the chief varies greatly from tribe to tribe. He may be a Government appointee, an elder or some prominent individual, as among the Topotha. Among the Latuka, Lokoiya, Bari, Kuku rain powers are essential to chiefship. He may be, as amongst the Nyangwara and Fajulu, the descendant of an original migration leader. He may be a petty class or group headman. None of the Moru chiefs can trace their pedigrees more than two or three generations back, which raises a suspicion that they are merely Egyptian or Belgian appointees with no hereditary pretensions. The Acholi chief is a rain-maker and earth chief, the Madi chief is also a rain-maker with, according to Father Molinaro, great magical powers to reinforce his authority.

The tendency in the early days of the administration to deal direct with all the small groups led to a multiplicity of petty chieflings quite incompatible with any advance in native administration: in the Latuka District there were 76; in Yei 56. As opportunity offers they are being subordinated and the bigger sections are taking shape. But the next step, to the tribal chief, is a big and difficult one.

For the most part the chiefs are taking up their new responsibilities conscientiously and well, and are prompt to resent unauthorized interference. A Didinga, who having been ordered to pay compensation, went to a rain-maker to get him to bring magical pressure on the creditor to forgo his rights was drastically dealt with for contempt, though the court refrained from taking action against the rain-maker.

It is interesting to speculate on the future of the rain chief in those tribes where rain powers are regarded as essential to authority. Will he combine secular authority with his magico-religious powers? So

TRIBAL STRUCTURE 23

far the combination does not generally seem a success. Or will he, like Ikang, the Latuka rain-queen, exercise the political functions through a delegate? It is probable that there is a reluctance, a sense of impropriety, in having the religious 'aura' of the rain chief disturbed by secular cares, and cases are occurring on the rain chief's death of the powers being divided, the secular functions going to one son, the rain to another. The spread of Christianity will obviously complicate the problem if Christian education is to debar the chief's son from the essential qualification of his office. But such division of powers might obviously lead to a dangerous weakening of authority.

The customary prerogatives of all chiefs—though varying in detail —throughout the province are two or three days' work from all able-bodied men in hoeing and building, in return for which the chief provides a beer-party; one tusk of all elephants killed, and, very commonly, the skin of all leopards. Mr. Beaton notes that amongst the Lokoiya the free labour is the privilege of the rain chief and that a 'foreigners' chief' would not be so entitled.

It may be remarked that if only from the hereditary transmission of rain powers the hereditary principle is perfectly familiar, though not necessarily from father to son.

(g) *Rain-making and Rain-makers.*

The function and ritual of the Bari and Latuka rain chiefs have been very fully described by Dr. Seligman, and only a brief summary is requisite here.

Rain powers are essential to sovereignty. The ritual consists of sacrifice and the ceremonial washing with oil and water of the sacred rain-stones which are regarded as male and female and are sometimes ancient stone artifacts. Among the Bari the rain-maker is assisted by the *dupi*, serfs; sacred spears also have rain powers. The Acholi rain chiefs also have rain spears with very potent magical powers; also the Latuka.

The power is regarded as obtained originally from God, and it is to God that the prayers for rain are addressed. The rain-maker does not himself *make* the rain, but by the virtue of his ancestors is the intermediary with God for the people. An interesting point noticed by Mr. Bretherton at a recent Latuka ceremony was that the rain-maker's 'announcer', addressing the assembled crowds, stressed the need for every man present to believe that rain would result, as a single doubter might bring failure.

TRIBAL STRUCTURE

The powers are normally transmitted in the male line, not necessarily from father to son. Mr. Giff observes that among the Fajulu the powers can be transmitted to the grandson through the daughter, but only if she has a brother. Amongst the Lokoiya it is said that if the only possible successor is a small boy some female relative, preferably a sister, will act for him until he grows up. Among the Latuka and Acholi the rain-maker's mother must also have been possessed of rain powers.

Cases are on record among the Bari—and Lango—of rain-makers being killed by the people for failure, but as Dr. Seligman has recently pointed out, there is no suggestion—as with the Priest King of the Shilluks—that he must be killed before old age overtakes him so that the powers may pass unimpaired.

Among the Lokoiya the rain-maker is ceremonially installed by being anointed with spittle.

This rain-stone ritual is widely practised east of the Nile. The Topotha have no major rain-makers, resorting to Alukileng, the Didinga rain-maker who lives in the Boya Hills: the ritual he uses is not known. Latuka, Lokoiya, Bari, Acholi, and the Fajulu rain-making family of the Luluba all have it. The Lango many years ago killed their practitioners for failure and no one has taken their place. The Mandari 'have no rain' and resort to the Bari. According to Mr. Rogers (quoted by Dr. Seligman) the Madi rain chiefs use rain-stones, and their ceremonies are held in the sacred grove, *rudu*, in which the rain-makers are buried. They have a familiar spirit which can be used to punish their enemies.

In other words, on the east of the Nile, the rain-stone ritual is practically universal and is the only method of rain-making recorded.

Among the western Bari-speakers the Nyangwara have two 'imported' rain-makers, very unimportant: the Fajulu use the same technique, but the practioners are generally not chiefs. The Kuku resemble the Bari almost exactly: their rain-makers are the chiefs, the ritual is the same, the *dupi* assist, and the rain-maker's burial presents the same features; in addition, considerable importance is attached to the sacred grove, generally on some particular rain hill. The Kakwa have it, but among them a second ritual is found, of mixing oil and water in a pot and sprinkling it.

As soon as we come to the more western tribes we find a great diversity of practice. The Kaliko are emphatic that they have no rain-makers, because they do not need them. Amongst the Moru rain-

TRIBAL STRUCTURE

makers were important and greatly feared from their powers of turning into a leopard (cp. Madi); they sprinkle oil and water which has been mixed in a pot: but it seems probable that originally rain-making was not 'specialized' but practised by heads of clans when necessary. The Avukaiya have certain individuals who, if rain does not come, are tied up and ducked till it does. The Mundu practice seems similar. The Baka rain-makers are private individuals who bury certain roots in a pot under a tree and bring rain by blowing on a whistle: they can stop it by passing a burning torch around the pot. They know of the Bongo rain-stones but have nothing of the kind themselves. Among the Makaraka the rain is associated with the rainbow which in the form of a large python lives at the heads of streams. The rain-maker is its guardian who must keep it supplied with food. Should the rain fail a procession is formed and grain scattered in the stream.

Dr. Seligman has suggested that the rain-stone ritual came to the Bari from the west, and the fact that their rain-maker is buried in the western 'recessed' grave would seem to support this. On the other hand, it is difficult to see whence it can have come. On the east bank it is almost universal; west of the Bari-speakers, with the isolated exception of the Bongo, rain-stones are not found; what evidence there is points to the emergence of these tribes from the Congo, where rain-making would have little importance. There is also a suggestion (*vide* the Luluba and Kuku) that the Bari-speakers were the essential owners of these powers which made them welcome to Moru-Madi people who did not possess them.

(b) *The Earth Chief.*

Among the Nilo-Hamites and the tribes adjacent to them an important tribal functionary is the 'father of the land' (Bari, *moneyekak*), whose business it is to supervise the distribution and allocation of the clan lands, by sacrifice at seed-time and harvest to ensure its fertility, and by the appropriate ritual to give success to hunting parties. His functions do not bring him much into administrative view and he may thus pass almost unnoticed; he is essentially a clan functionary and his importance is therefore generally very local, but he may have great influence. Thus Stigand (*Equatoria*, p. 70), describing the Kuku 'owner of the country', says:

'As Lishaju takes no active part in anything and does not appear in any matter, a stranger might be months or even years in the country without discovering that he is practically the paramount chief of the Kuku, excepting

TRIBAL STRUCTURE

the Limi of Bulamatari. In reality no important decision is ever given without first referring to him and he is the final arbitrator in all matters and disputes which cannot be settled by the other chiefs.'

Full details as to the *monyekak*'s activities will be found in Part II: it is sufficient to note here that he is found among the Bari and Mandari; Luluba; Latuka (male and female), Lango and Lokoiya, Acholi; Kuku and Kakwa. Among the Fajulu and Nyangwara fertility ceremonies are performed by the rain-maker and the *monyekak* is not found.

Among the Latuka there is one case of a *lamonyekhari*, 'father of the river', whose permission must be obtained for fishing.

Among the Moru and other western tribes the specialized function disappears. Among the Kaliko there is a planting ceremony carried out probably by the clan head; the same is apparently true of the Avukaiya and Baka. Among the Moru the rain-maker has fertility powers and the clan heads also perform local ceremonies.

The suggestion has been made by Dr. Seligman that the *monyekak* may represent an older stock. This is almost certainly true of the Kuku, where the numerous *monyekak*s do not belong to the rain clans. Some of the Congo Kakwa told Mr. Giff that the *monyekak*s were the original owners of the land. Among the Luluba there is a strong presumption that the *monyekak*'s clan is one of the original Moru-Madi clans. For the Bari there is little evidence; there is one case where the *monyekak* belongs to a clan whose members are elsewhere serfs. Among the Latuka the *Lamonyefau*, 'father of the land', is only found in daughter villages thrown off by other communities. He is regarded as the descendant of the first settler, which would indicate that he is a Latuka.

A very similar functionary exists elsewhere, in central Africa. Thus Dr. Seligman (*Races*, p. 6) describing the Bambara, a branch of the West African Mandingo group, says that

'the religious and civil power is usually combined in one individual, the *dugutigi*, the "master of the land", traditionally the descendant of the first settler. He is the high priest of the village . . . and remains supreme in all matters concerning the allotment of land, as well as in spiritual affairs.'

So in a review of Rattray's *Tribes of the Ashanti Hinterland* (*Africa*, vol. iv, p. 514) it is stated of the Dagomba, where the original primitive people have been submerged by a more vigorous race, that

'the outstanding feature of the original tribal government had been the *tin'dana*, "lord of the land", who was priest and chief, but whose influence

TRIBAL STRUCTURE

and authority depended on moral and religious, not physical, sanctions. Under the new régime the *tin'dana* was either killed and replaced by the invading ruler, or, in the majority of cases, continued in his functions. The result was in a number of instances a dual government; there was the secular ruler . . . and . . . the former priestly rulers. A third class of "rulers" came into existence with the advent of the white man. When the first Europeans appeared and demanded to see "The king", the *tin'dana* tried to keep aloof . . . and some unimportant individual was thrust forward. . . .

'In course of time many of these individuals became so assured of their positions that the real ruler found himself becoming of less and less account, even in the eyes of his own people.'

(i) Servile Classes.

In most, if not all tribes there exist, or existed very recently, persons who were not fully free. These were either war captives taken in raids or, very frequently, tribesmen who from poverty or physical disability were unable to maintain their independence and were obliged to attach themselves to some rich man, as a rule more in the capacity of client to patron than of slave to master. Loss of independence was particularly caused by inability to find the necessary bride-price for marriage; this was provided by the patron who subsequently took to himself the bride-price of any daughters of the marriage, and again provided the bride-price for any sons.

Among the Makaraka such war captives (*jogo*) could attain considerable importance, even becoming their master's heir; similarly the *ganjibara* of the Mundu. Among the Kaliko the term is *batonge*. Among the Kakwa they are called *Kajua* or *dupi*, the latter term in this case connoting no special connexion with the rain-maker, and Mr. Giff notes that the wives found for them were free-born girls, while similarly Lugbari women captives married free-born Kakwa. Amongst the Fajulu they are known as *dupi wuri*, and are frequently Kakwa who were driven out of their own country by Bari raids early in the century. They are equally found among the Bari, where they are known as *dupi penna*.

With the modern facilities for earning wages, formerly completely non-existent, one may suppose that this class will disappear, as any able-bodied man is now in a position to earn money for the bride-price.

In negotiations between the Turkana and Topotha for the return of people who had been captured as children it was noted that the captors were entitled to compensation for having brought them up.

TRIBAL STRUCTURE

Among the Bari the term *dupi* has a more specialized meaning. The Bari divide society into freemen, *lui*, and serfs, *dupi*. The latter consist of fishermen, smiths, hunters, and the *dupi* proper, household menials. None of these may intermarry with freemen; and the *dupiet* has a particular association with the rain-maker, being his assistant in manipulating the rain-stones and, when he is buried, descending into his grave, a relic doubtless of the time when he was actually immolated with him. The *dupi* in this sense are only found among the Bari and the Bari-speakers: the Latuka are emphatic that there is no such class among them. Among the Kuku his position is exactly that of the Bari *dupi*. Among the Kukwa the term *dupi* or *dupi kana* (plain or simple *dupi*) is according to Major Gray applied rather to the first-mentioned 'client' category: the rain-maker's *dupi*, who manipulate the stones, descend into the grave, &c., are known as *kedi lo matat lo kudu*; they are regarded as rather superior to the *dupi kana* but are apparently in origin the same—people who through poverty have attached themselves to the rain-maker.

Whether *dupi* assist the Fajulu rain-makers is not clear: in one case (the Malari clan) the eldest son is the rain-maker and the next in age manipulates the stones. Smiths may have been a separate caste, but are now becoming free and marry free girls.

Among the Nyangwara there are no *dupi*, and smiths are free.

The theory has been advanced by Mr. Whitehead that the Bari *dupi*, who are said to differ physically from the ordinary Bari, being shorter, redder, and more hairy, are the representatives of an earlier stock submerged by the Bari. The fact that the present Shindiru rain-maker has a Makaraka *dupiet* would seem to show that nowadays at any rate the *dupiet* and the client are, as among the Kakwa, almost indistinguishable.

(j) *The Elephant Hunters (Liggo).*

An interesting contrast to the *yari*, the *dupi* hunting class, is provided by the *Liggo* (sing. *liggitot*), a professional caste of elephant hunters, apparently confined (with the exception of a few among the Luluba) to the Bari and the Bari-speakers. They can be, and mostly are, freemen; the craft is hereditary, but if the male line dies out can be acquired from the family by purchase.

A rough census in the Central District by Mr. Beaton gives the following numbers: Bari, 32, all free except 12; there is one group of 10 at Kogi, of whom only the leader is free; Luluba 9; Fajulu 29,

TRIBAL STRUCTURE

all except 4 being probably free; Nyangwara 64. There are a number among the Kakwa, and they thus appear to predominate on the west of the river.

Their particular weapon is the *dili*, the elephant spear, large of blade, thick and heavy in the handle and weighted with a lump of clay at the end; the overall length is about 5 feet and the spears sometimes have individual names. The average holding of spears is two.

The method is to drive the herd up to trees into which the hunters have climbed, and spear them from above as they pass. The *Liggo* are therefore divided into *karemak*, the spearman, and *kakepak*, the followers or beaters, the former enjoying the greater prestige.

There is an elaborate ceremony of blessing the spears before a hunt. They are placed on the ground tied together before the *bunit* (spirit doctor), who blesses them by sprinkling them with the blood of a goat or chicken, with cooked grain, with ochre, or merely by incantation. He then divines the issue of the hunt by throwing the leather strips (*kamuka*). If a successful issue is foretold the *kamuka* are placed on the spear-blades and the thong which binds them cut. If after repeated sacrifice to his father, mother, grandfather, and grandmother, the *bunit* is unable to obtain a favourable omen the hunt is abandoned.

After his first kill the hunter must go home, shave his head and hold a dance, otherwise in future he will not be able to kill another. In the case of ordinary kills his fellow hunters thrust his head first against that of the elephant and then against its posterior, otherwise he will die.

The meat is ritually divided in fixed proportions between the *bunit*, the slayer, and his relatives and companions.

Should the male line become extinct the widow among the Bari and most of the Fajulu may sell the spears, which carry the craft with them. The price is surprisingly low, 10 piastres or a goat or a couple of baskets of grain per spear, with another £E. 1 to follow after an elephant has been killed. Some of the Fajulu do not part with the spears, leaving them to rust away, believing that to sell them brings disaster.

Mr. Giff's account agrees substantially with Mr. Beaton's. He has concentrated on one particular group among the Fajulu, and instances as proof of their free status that the mother of the rain-chief Laila was a *liggitot*. In this group, the Somere, from the name of their former home, the headman is too old to function and his son Lubang acts; but he is not the 'father of the spear': this function belongs to one Buru, who not only holds the spears and trains the boys but is a smith

TRIBAL STRUCTURE

and acts, in Mr. Giff's words, as the 'armourer of the craft'. They frequent a special *bunit*, Tongkulya, for blessing the spears; these are placed on the ground and a pot of grain heated in their midst. Each of the *Liggo* beats two stones together and when the grain is heated throws them east and west.

The meat is divided as follows: the chief (Laila) is given one hind leg and the liver, carried to him by the *kakepak*; Lubang takes the other hind leg, Buru a front leg and part of the back; the *karemak* gets the solid meat, and the *kakepak* the ribs and jaws.

One of them, to substantiate their claim to be Fajulu, mentioned that the headman's father was buried in a plain grave with no recess, and when it was pointed out that the Fajulu use the recess-grave replied, 'Yes, nowadays, but long long ago we Fajulu buried our corpses in a plain grave with no recess.'

An interesting point is that to the Nyori clan the hunting or eating of elephant is taboo unless they get a special plant (*lugöyi*) from the *Liggo*: they give the *Liggo* a tusk or a cow and the *Liggo* spit on them, otherwise the *lugöyi* will lose its virtue.

Mr. Beaton is convinced that the *Liggo* have no connexion with the Liggi tribe mentioned by Emin and other early travellers, which in the upheavals of the past hundred years has been merged in the Kakwa, Fajulu, and Nyangwara and lost its identity.

The *Liggo* have their special elephant songs sung when an elephant has been killed. Mr. Giff and Mr. Beaton quote several, of which the following is typical:

Tome lo rime,	The elephant is speared:
Ku'de roba lo rime	Come avenge his death
Ti kule wökiwökun.	While others run away.
Mörö nikang na.	This is our fight.
Somere ti jara i roba marate.	The Somere are not backward in avenging a clansman's death.
Yi lo wai ku mero.	We are being scandalized by our enemies.

IV. RELIGIOUS BELIEFS

RELIGIOUS beliefs enter so largely into every department of life that this heading might cover a full description of the people and their activities. The rain-maker and the *monyekak* are 'religious' functionaries; initiation, agriculture, hunting, illness, all have their religious background. The present section deals in general with the individual's approach to the supernatural world, in dealing with which it is well to bear in mind Mr. Giff's reminder that the people's ideas are generally very vague and uncoordinated, and that our own habit of analysis and classification may produce a far too concrete and definite impression.

In general, the religious beliefs of all tribes and of all groups are so similar that one description will cover them all. They believe in a creator deity, not completely otiose but not greatly concerned with mankind. The souls of the dead persist, frequenting their old homes: they influence the fortunes of mankind for good or ill: illness and misfortune are generally due to their anger at neglect, when it is the duty of the spirit doctor to detect the offended spirit and prescribe how it may be placated. They are not subject to punishment and reward: it is left to us to instruct in the delights of Heaven or the terrors of an everlasting Hell. Nor do they lead mankind astray.

It is sometimes said that one great weakness of these religions is that they contain no positive sanctions for good conduct. There are, however, indications of a belief that the anger of the spirits may be caused not only by ritual neglect but by injustice and wrongdoing. Thus Father Molinaro describes how a sick man will be urged by the Madi to confess his misdeeds and compensate any one he has wronged; and Mr. Giff describes a Kuku spirit doctor eliciting that his patient had quarrelled with her father and ascribing to this the cause of her ill health.

(a) God.

The ideas of God are extremely vague: he is regarded as the Creator who now takes little interest in mankind. He kills or keeps alive at his will. He is not an object of worship; but it is to him that the Bari rain-maker's prayers for rain are directed, and the Moru will invoke his aid in a search for water.

Among the Nilo-Hamites God is generally thought of as living in

RELIGIOUS BELIEFS

the sky. Among the Moru he lives under the earth. Among the Bari, as was first pointed out by Dr. Seligman, he has a dual aspect, *Ngun-lo-ki*, God in the sky, associated with rain; and *Ngun-lo-kak*, God below the earth, concerned with the earth and agriculture, and in old time demanding human sacrifice. Among the Fajulu and Kuku he seems bound up with the ancestral spirits, almost the embodiment of their sum total. The Kakwa *Nguleso* living in the sky is opposed by the malignant *Ngulete*, a totality of malignant spirits. Among the Kaliko, according to Major Gray, God has two aspects: *Andragi-anyisi*, beneficent, living above; the shadow is his manifestation and its disappearance at night is a foretaste of death; and *Andragi-onje*, harmful and living below the earth.

There is a widespread belief that man originally lived with God in the sky and came down to earth by means of a rope which was subsequently broken, severing the connexion. It has been recorded among the Topotha, Fajulu, Bari, and Madi; the Kakwa have a faint belief that God threw a man down from the sky and taught him to cultivate.

(b) *The Ancestral Spirits.*

These are the active supernatural agency which for good or ill affects men's lives. The household shrine at which they are worshipped with offerings, especially of first-fruits, take many different forms. Spirit-houses, either small 'cromlechs' of stone or miniature huts, are erected just outside the house by the Lango, Acholi, Madi, Kuku, and Kakwa; the latter also erect a pole on which portions of animals killed and other offerings are hung (cp. the Lango *abila*).[1] Among the Fajulu the father's spirit lives in a tree or shrub; the mother's spirit lives in the head of the family's own house. Offerings of meat or food are made to it, which he subsequently eats; he will call a cow after her and will supplicate her for the children, saying, 'Mother, leave my children!' Among the Nyangwara the ancestral spirit lives in a small pot which is kept in the house.

By the Bari no spirit-houses are built, but each household has the three ceremonial cooking-stones on which twice a year a sacrifice is made to the spirits, the 'nephews of God' under the earth, and twice a year beans are cooked in honour of the grandmother, identified with the wagtail or the snake. The Lokoiya have such stones, and also

[1] The Lango shrine is a cromlech; the Madi and Kakwa make the miniature hut; the Kuku shrine may be either. The Acholi sometimes have the hut, but more usually a rough platform (*kak*).

RELIGIOUS BELIEFS

make 'peg shrines', groups of small stumps projecting a foot or two above the ground. Similar shrines are made by the Acholi. Among the Moru offerings are made on the grave itself; or for a sacrifice in a cultivation where no grave is present small notched pegs are driven into the ground and the sacrifice is made on them. Among the Kaliko the dead man's house is kept in repair and offerings placed therein. The Mundu erect a three-pronged stake outside the principal house.

Father Molinaro describes how according to Madi belief the ancestral spirits pass through two stages. As long as the *abila*, the miniature spirit-house, is kept in repair and offerings are made to it, the spirits live there; but when it becomes neglected and allowed to fall down, they go out into the bush and live in certain sacred trees or bushes which may not be touched or cut. Mr. Giff mentions that only two generations of spirits retain their powers among the Kakwa; the spirits of great grandparents need not be taken into account.

The need for a man to be buried in his proper grave is several times mentioned. Among the Madi, if a man die at a distance a special ritual is performed by the spirit doctor to bring his spirit to the spirit-house. By the Fajulu, if a man's body cannot be given due burial in the village the fruit of a sausage-tree is buried in its stead. The Madi half-bury a stone in the same way; but if a man has lost consciousness in apparent death and then recovers, a sausage-tree fruit is buried in the grave which has been prepared.

A peculiar feature of the Fajulu recorded by Mr. Giff is that each man is apparently believed to have two spirits, beneficent and malignant; after his death the bad spirit will seek to harm his family, but can be counteracted by the good spirit if it receives proper attention.

As may be imagined from much of the above, the moving of a village may be a serious matter as interfering with the cult of the ancestral spirits. Sacrifice may either continue in the old home (cp. Fajulu) or as among the Madi the *abila* will be erected on the new site.

(c) *Other Spirits.*

Little has been recorded of the existence of independent nature spirits, as contrasted with the ancestral spirits. The most conspicuous example is that of the Kakwa *Ngulete*, described by Mr. Giff, an evil spirit or rather plurality of spirits, male and female, contrasted with and yet even associated with *Nguleso*, God, inhabiting trees and streams and causing illness. They are the children of mothers called

34 RELIGIOUS BELIEFS

Jaguruba who live in the rivers, and the mother of all of them lives in the Nile. *Ngulete* has dealings with the ancestral spirits. There is also *Gong lo muko*, a spiritual attribute at the grave mound.

The Nyangwara also believe in a malignant spirit which inhabits the beds of streams and fastens on passers-by, inflicting sickness upon them.

The Acholi believe in malignant spirits, *cen*, which are caused when a man dies angry. The Acholi also have the *Jok* spirits inhabiting streams, and the *Lubanga*, a spirit that brings about freak births, &c. *Lubanga* is also apparently found as a spirit among the Madi.

West of the Nile the rainbow is frequently believed to be the belched-forth breath of a gigantic python (Fajulu, Kakwa, Moru, Luluba), near approach to which is dangerous and to point at which may cause leprosy. Ideas regarding the lightning are more vague than might be expected. Among the Fajulu it is regarded as almost personal, but not an agent of *Ngun*; it burns and strikes the perjurer and returns to the sky. The Kakwa lightning lives in the sky, has almost personal attributes, but the body of a calf with the face and teeth of a lion.

(d) *Tree and Stone Cults.*

These have been little investigated except among the Bari, whose sacred trees are frequent, regarded as the residence of *Ngun* and often having a snake associated with them. The sacred rocks at Juba have been described in detail by Mr. Richardson (see Part II under Bari). The idea that one rock may be the son or daughter of another recalls Jebel Keili in the Fung Province. Sacred trees are found among the Mandari and Lokoiya, in the latter case sacred rocks also. The rain-making of the Madi and Kuku is done in a sacred grove of trees (*rudu*).

The Koriuk have a black rock at Itoghom which is the scene of their initiation ceremonies. The Topotha have their sacred stone *Kwoto*, brought with them from Karamoja and set up on the banks of the Liyoro.

(e) *Fire Cults.*

These are found only among the Topotha and Latuka. The Topotha have a special fire-making clan. Before a raid a fire is kindled and the warriors must pass through it; at the initiation ceremonies a fire is made and the sacrificed bull is burnt therein. Among the

RELIGIOUS BELIEFS

Latuka fire-making is the central feature of the initiation ceremonies, all fires being extinguished and relighted from the new sacred fire.

There is no special fire-making clan, the fire being kindled by the 'father-of-the-village' or the rain-maker. A fire was also made before a raid.

It is of some interest that there is a well-developed fire cult among the Marille at the north of Lake Rudolf, as described by Mr. Shackleton, the extinguishing and relighting of fires being practised before war or at the time of an epidemic.

(f) *Drumming and Harvest.*

Among the Nilo-Hamites, and to a somewhat less degree among the Bari-speakers, there is a very definite prejudice against the use of drums from the time the grain has begun to sprout until after harvest. In some form, locusts or heavy winds, it is believed to bring disaster to the crops. Among the western tribes the prejudice does not exist; indeed, among the Moru it is precisely at this time that the maximum number of drums is used.

The following is a summary of the recorded information:

Topotha. These have no drums and do not hold funeral dances. But a dance is held when a man's personal bull dies, but if this occurs during the cultivation season the dance is postponed till after the harvest.

Latuka. Among the Latuka, and to a lesser extent the Koriuk, the use of the drum is regulated by the rain-maker. He holds two main ceremonies during the year: (1) the initial rain-making ceremony at the beginning of the cultivation season (May) when all the *monyemiji* go out to till the fields and a goat is sacrificed to bless the cultivation. Following this no drums may be used at all in ordinary dances and music is provided by the *natur*, a long trumpet, only. The only exception is that the drums may be used for the death of a *monyemiji*, but for the death of any one else their use is *odesa*, unlucky. (2) The *nalam*, or new year, hunt, at which the omens for the year are taken by the rain-maker from the entrails of the slaughtered game. This is usually held in October or November, after the harvest, and thereafter the *natur* is put away and drums may be used in all dances. In the interval between the harvest and the *nalam* four beats may be sounded on a single drum as an invocation to the *Naijok*, which may be followed by a general cry and *lulu*-ing. In 1933 an important exception was made for the fire ceremony, *nongopira*. Following on

RELIGIOUS BELIEFS

the fire-making the drums were produced from the drum houses and that only for the four rounds of the *monyemiji*'s dance; they were then put away until the *nalam*. (Mr. Arber mentions that a peculiar significance is attached by the Latuka to even numbers in all ritual of their social organization.)

The abstention from drumming probably holds good for the Koriuk, S. Lafit, and Logir, but not for the Logiri section of the Lango.

Lokoiya. These have no drumming between seed-time and harvest except only should a rain chief die, when a very small drum may be tapped three beats only lest the wind arise and beat down the corn. At an ordinary funeral in this season the mourners weep only very softly. A dance is held after the reaping.

Bari. There is a variation in practice in this tribe, but generally speaking drums may be beaten between seed-time and harvest only for the death of a rain chief.

Among the Nyangwara practice also varies, but drumming is not usual, though the drums are beaten at funerals.

No trace of the prejudice has been found among the Fajulu.

The Acholi and Madi old men apparently dislike it; in recent years it has been held to bring the locusts. Among the Kuku some youths who were tapping a drum to show the rhythm were stopped at once by a chief.

Moru. Amongst the Moru there is no prejudice, but different types of drums only are played at different seasons. There are six types of drums, three large and three small and high pitched; during the rains all are beaten, in the other seasons the biggest (*duje*) and one of the treble drums are not used. Each of the three seasons has its particular dance, and it may be significant that that of the rains, when all the drums are in use, is called *Di-Ago* (ancestors).

Where there is no rain-making clan, especially amongst the Kediru, the change is decreed by an elder. Where there is a rain-making clan, e.g. the Vora of the Moru Öndri, the change was made at a festival dance, the rain-maker's assistant (*kumari*) who was leading the song changing the tempo early in the morning to that of the new period, all the people following suit. With the decline of the rain-maker's importance this tends to be done merely by the rain-maker's decree that the time for alteration has come.

The Avukaiya, Mundu, and Baka have no feeling against drumming at this period; it may be suspected that the prejudice is essentially a Nilo-Hamitic one.

RELIGIOUS BELIEFS

(g) *Blood Purification.*

The belief that the slayer must be purified of the blood he has spilled seems to be universal on both sides of the Nile. The symbolism of the various rituals has not been investigated, and all that can be done at present is to catalogue the various ceremonies which have been recorded; but in several the idea of vicarious punishment seems to appear.

A party of Didinga who had murdered two strangers sacrificed an animal and smeared themselves with the entrails.

A Lango murderer who otherwise might have escaped detection made himself conspicuous by sacrificing a cock and painting his body.

Among the Bari the ritual varies as to whether the killing was accidental or intentional. In the former case the slayer ties a fillet of a special bark round his head; a spear (query: *the* spear) is driven into a mahogany tree, after which he wipes his body with the bark. In the latter event a red sheep is killed under a mahogany tree and eaten by the old men and women; the tree is speared and the slayer licks the spear-blade, and three days later his head is shaved.

Among the Madi a white animal is thrown which the killer and his kindred must then kick with their right foot; it is killed and the blood smeared on their chests and feet; it is not eaten.

Among the Fajulu for the accidental killing of one of his own kin a man merely shaves his head, as for his own relation. For intentional killing, after shaving his head he spears a *kiruet* bush; all then rush to their houses, the drum is beaten, and they make as if to repel an imaginary foe. If this is not done, leprosy will supervene. The same thing is done for the killing of a leopard.

Among the Moru a murderer drew attention to himself by tying some leaves of a plant to his bow. If two families agree to compound a killing, the man is shut up for three days with only uncooked grain and water; he is then led before the people, with the lethal weapon on the ground in their midst with a piece of special wood tied to it; an animal is killed (query: with *the* weapon), and the relations eat together of the uncooked liver; the man's head is shaved, and his forehead marked with charcoal. Thenceforward the two families may not intermarry.

Among the Mundu the elders and women strike the slayer's legs with sticks three times for a man, four times for a woman; a dance

RELIGIOUS BELIEFS

is held and food served in baskets. The slayer eats a little and it is then snatched away from him. The dance lasts for three days, and after it, for three days, he must wear a bark fillet.

Among the Makaraka he shaves his head and ties a strip of bark round it which he wears for three days, during which he may have no intercourse with his wife. A dance is held and a goat sacrificed; some of the blood is smeared over his heart, after which he washes his body and removes the bark.

(b) *Witchcraft.*

Belief in the power and influence of the spirits for good or ill inevitably leads to attempts to control the invisible world, to witchcraft. But in one sense the word is misleading: in native practice and estimation there is a very sharp distinction between the exponent of 'white' magic, the doctor and healer, and the maleficent and malignant wizard or sorcerer. For the former, in all but one of his functions, the word 'witchcraft' has too harsh a connotation.

In an analysis of Latuka beliefs Colonel Lilley divides the practitioners into four classes: the *leboni*, who heals both by suggestion and with medicinal drugs and ointments, who foretells future success or failure, and who traces death or misfortune either to the spirits, and indicates how they may be placated, or to the influence, conscious or unconscious, of the living; the *adiemani*, the 'evil eye', who consciously or unconsciously put an evil spell on others; the *lamomolani*, evil and anti-social, who causes death by putting spells on his enemy's hair or nails, or by wailing outside his hut at night, who by acts of bestiality causes his cattle to die; the *ladofani*, most feared of all, who with the aid of his magic bowl practises not only against his own enemies but for a fee against those of others.

If we count the two latter as really of one nature, the three classes are closely paralleled in every tribe we are considering.

The *leboni* is the Bari *bunit*, the Topotha *nyamorun*, the Moru *kwoso*. They may be male or female, and the function is almost always hereditary. Among the Kakwa, Mr. Giff tells us, the virtue is held to be transmitted not in the male line but through the daughter to the grandson. They are beneficent in intention and generally in fact. Though their stock in trade generally includes the sucking out of foreign objects from the patient's body, they often have a real knowledge of medicinal herbs and of massage; and their powers of suggestion are not to be despised. They may ascribe misfortunes to

RELIGIOUS BELIEFS

quarrelling or hatred and recommend the composing of differences as a remedy. And though we may smile at their identification of some particular spirit as the source of disaster or illness, it is highly probable that the resulting ceremonies give a sense of escape and release.

Their one function with which we are likely to quarrel is the smelling out of living persons as the 'evil eye' or the wizard or poisoner. Apart from the obvious probability of suffering to innocent victims, there is so great a danger of private malevolence. It can only be said that this is never urged in defence; and that in the native mind this function is as valuable and beneficent as any of his others.

The Latuka *adiemani*, the Bari *demanit*, the EVIL EYE, is a commonplace in every tribe. The power is inherited and innate and may be exercised unconsciously. The death of a man in his prime is always suspected of being due to unnatural causes; and a series of such deaths is certain to lead to charges of conscious or unconscious wizardry. A man so charged may be absolutely sincere in his protestations of innocence and willingly submit to ordeal; but if the ordeal convict him he will often be convinced of his guilt and the right of the community he has injured to destroy him. A peculiar form called *wuri*, wind, came to light recently among the Bari. The unfortunate possessor of the power was compelled periodically to kill something or somebody, otherwise it killed him. In this case the medicine chest provided a cure both for the evil eye and for one of his destined victims. Exorcism is in some cases regarded as possible.

The professional sorcerer who for spite or gain deals out illness or death to others is most dreaded of all, and in old days was killed without mercy. He acts in manifold ways; by dancing by night outside his enemy's house, by poison, by spells. By bestiality he may cause the cattle to die; the outraging of young children is in many tribes given a magical significance. The Kuku have an almost hysterical fear of women poisoners, who boil down snakes' heads and administer the resultant venom—probably innocuous taken in this form. The 'poisoner' may also attract lightning to his enemy's house. It is curious how often the sorcerer charged with his misdeeds will admit them.

The 'Evil Eye' and the sorcerer are commonly detected by divination and ordeal. These take various but widespread forms. On the west bank of the Nile a common form is to make a ring of stones or pegs, each of which is given the name of a group, an individual, or a spirit: a chicken tethered in the middle of the circle has its throat cut, and the stone against which it collapses denotes the responsible agency. In some cases a stone is named for 'God', thus giving a chance for a verdict of 'natural causes'. This is used often to give preliminary indication of the source of the trouble. As against the individual, the drinking of ivory powdered into water was a common test. Boiling water is a common form, particularly among the Longarim. The drinking of water in which some dust from the grave of the accused has been mixed is another common form. Very widespread is the drinking of water and a certain kind of bean. A person who is innocent will vomit and recover; the guilty will absorb the poison and die. At Kajo Kaji in 1932, when female poisoners were suspected, about a hundred women were subjected to ordeal by drinking a brew in which wood ash was, apparently, the only ingredient. Five died; the remainder vomited and were otherwise unhurt. The Acholi have the same practice.

Oaths generally take an ordeal form, being supposed, for instance, to bring death by lightning within a certain period if the oath is falsely taken. The Fajulu and Nyangwara have the queer habit of stabbing the mahogany tree to give sanctity to an oath, while the Fajulu, Nyangwara, Kaliko, Luluba, and Baka take oath by cutting the reddish feathers of a particular bird (*kongo*).

It is a general custom that the man who has undergone an ordeal at the plaint of an accuser and gone unscathed for a prescribed period is entitled to compensation from his accuser.

Secret societies, very numerous among the Zande, sometimes gain a temporary footing in the Maridi District, but are unknown elsewhere. A favourite form is *ruru* to which the Baka are particularly addicted; in essence it appears to be organized blackmail, persons being subject to illness or misfortune being informed that for a fee to the *Ruru* their troubles will be lifted.

The Lu cult is a hardy perennial in the Moru District.

Vagabond Dinka and Jur, especially from Rumbek District, are very apt to wander into the north of the province in search of a living. They range from the individual who on the strength of an infallible specific against locusts amasses large quantities of goats, to the pupil of Apur Mana, who was terrorizing the Moru and who claimed to have killed at least ten people.

RELIGIOUS BELIEFS

(i) *The Allah Water Movement.*

Mention of the Dinka and Jur recalls the Allah Water cult remarkable as the one movement of its kind which has spread from tribe to tribe and covers a very considerable area. It has been fully described by Driberg in *J.R.A.I.* 1931.

In 1919 serious disturbances broke out amongst the Lugbari of the west Nile District in Uganda. A police post of fourteen men was practically wiped out and many loyal natives killed. This was held to be due to the Allah Water cult. Following Driberg's account, sacred water, known as the water of Yakang, was dispensed by the chief of the cult to his devotees. Amongst other properties this water was believed to give immunity against disease, against rifles, and against Government punishment for disobedience of orders or refusing taxation. The participants were given imitation rifles which in due course would turn into real ones. The dispenser had a 'temple', generally square, in some secluded spot, in front of which was set up a long pole surmounted with a branch of the *niza* shrub.

A curious feature was the appearance of a sacred goat and later of a white calf, both ornamented with bracelets.

At the time of the outbreak the dispensers were said most definitely to be two Kakwa of Yei District, and they were eventually arrested and sent down to Mongalla. Yet oddly enough there was not the slightest suspicion of any unrest in the Yei District itself, and the District Commissioner regarded the dispensing of the water to be merely protection against sleeping sickness and influenza and stated that the same thing had been done in 1914, in the Loka neighbourhood. There is an account in *S.N.R.* xi. 227, by Castle Smith of the destruction in 1914 of the shrine of a god and goddess about seventeen miles south of Loka, which was presumably connected with the same cult; and there is a mention elsewhere of an epidemic of gods and goddesses distributing wooden rifles. Major Black detected wooden rifles among the Madi in 1917 and believed it to be the beginning of the same thing.

According to native accounts collected at the time of the Lugbari outbreak the first appearance of the cult was among the Agar Dinkas when they massacred Emin's garrison at Rumbek. It spread to the Bari—in 1907 the Uganda authorities expelled practitioners from Belinian—and appeared to have followed the line of Emin's soldiery.

RELIGIOUS BELIEFS

It was believed to have been at the root of the Uganda Mutiny and of the rebellion in German East Africa in 1905. It was also said that a Mundu chief named Magoro had obtained it from the Dinkas for protection against the Zande and the Dervishes. From Magoro it passed to the Moru, Avukaiya, Nyangwara, Fajulu, and Kakwa, and thence to the Lugbari.

It does not appear from the accounts that there is any connexion between the Allah Water cult and the holy lake of the Agar Dinkas at Khor Lait (*S.N.R.* v. 163).

V. CRIME AND PUNISHMENT

AS far as our inquiries go, ordinary crime, homicide, hurt, theft, adultery, are always looked on as wrongs against the individual, and the idea of crime as anti-social is conspicuously absent. There is one conspicuous exception, wizardry: the malignant wizard might not only practice against the individual but might by his machinations or even by his mere presence affect the whole life of the community by causing drought, barrenness, or death; the community killed him out of hand when detected, and in native eyes our refusal to sanction this had led to a definite increase in sorcery.

Within the group, although the wronged individual might take the law into his own hands, chiefs and headmen could, and did, act as mediators and assess the customary compensation prior to the coming of government. Compensation was commonly assessed by the headman and his elders: frequently as amongst the Bari and Acholi their decisions, in important cases at any rate, had to be reported to the chief, a practice which persists to-day in the Bari courts, where the parties address not the chief but the headmen who in their turn 'report' to the chief.

This is not the place for a general dissertation on customary law; but the practice regarding the payment of blood-money presents interesting points and may be summarized here.

Topotha.

Providing agreement could be reached the payment of blood-money has always been recognized and acceptable: it is paid in stock which is used for the purchase of wives. A girl might be handed over in place of cattle, but this was unusual, though a girl might be earmarked and part of her bride-price when she married handed over as blood-money. If a small boy was killed who was an only son, a boy of similar age might in some cases have been handed over.

Latuka.

Blood-money recognized and acceptable, originally paid in stock or by handing over a girl. Nowadays money as goods may be paid; if not otherwise forthcoming a girl's bride-price may be earmarked. Blood-money for a woman is the same as normal bride-price, for a man practically twice as much.

CRIME AND PUNISHMENT

Lokoiya.

Acceptable: the amount varies with the importance of the individual and there is no differentiation between men and women. A girl might be handed over instead.

The Luluba practice is the same.

Bari.

Paid in stock: the amount varies with the individual, might be up to 80 cattle; a woman might have been handed over in lieu; no difference between man and woman.

A curious point is that originally the blood-money was always paid to the rain chief, who would pass a little on to the dead man's brother; nowadays it is paid to the brother, but he sometimes passes it all to the rain chief. The idea is apparently that receipt of blood-money may bring illness in its train.

Mandari.

Acceptable: no difference as between a man and a woman.

Fajulu, Kakwa, Kaliko.

Inside the group accidental killing could be expiated by the provision of a few animals for sacrifice: for intentional killing a girl would have been handed over or, among the Kakwa, if a man had been killed a boy would have been handed over who when he grew up would have had to call his eldest son by the dead man's name. Intergroup killing in the old days invariably resulted in a blood-feud and could not be settled by blood-money, and to-day there is a general very strong dislike to accepting blood-money as likely to bring leprosy in its train. One chief has expounded the view that no harm ensues if the money is used for marriage purposes; but this is not generally held.

The Fajulu (and Nyangwara) of the Central District accept blood-money to-day, but remember that in the past it was regarded as tainted.

Moru.

Formerly accidental killing might be compounded, and there is a special rite uniting the families and preventing future marriage between them (i.e. they are regarded as becoming of one blood). Intentional killing invariably resulted in a blood-feud, and we may suppose that there is an underlying reluctance to accept blood-money

CRIME AND PUNISHMENT

to-day. Major Brown notes that the husband or parents will often pass it to a distant relative. No difference is made between a man and a woman.

Avukaiya (Yei).

Blood-money is now accepted at the rate of 20 hoes and 20 spears: formerly, though killing within the group might be compounded by payment of a girl, an outside killing always meant a blood-feud.

Mundu (Yei).

Was always compoundable within the group by payment of a girl, but outside a feud resulted. To-day blood-money may be accepted, but cases occur in which it is refused, not apparently as bringing leprosy or disease, but as bringing ridicule.

Makaraka (Yei).

Acceptable: now paid in spears, &c., but formerly a girl was handed over.

Baka (Yei).

In the old days a girl was handed over: nowadays 100 arrows and 5 spears are paid for a man, 200 arrows and 20 spears for a woman.

Certain interesting points emerge from the above. (1) The almost universal custom in the past of paying a girl as compensation, no doubt that she might bear children to the group in place of the member they had lost. This has now been commuted to a property payment which by a logical extension is in most cases regarded as a girl's bride-price. Among some tribes, e.g. Acholi (not quoted above), it is definitely stated to have been introduced at the instance of government, a rather good instance of how a to us barbarous custom can be humanized. The cattle-owning tribes always paid in stock, as for bride-price. (2) The sharp contrast drawn by some of the western tribes between killing inside or outside the group; and the very strong prejudice still existing in some tribes against the acceptance of blood-money in the latter case. (3) For marriage purposes daughters are an asset, sons a liability, for this and other reasons we might have expected the blood-money to be higher for a girl or woman than for a man. Actually only one mention of this is made (Baka); generally no difference exists, while in the case of Latuka the payment for a man is very much higher than that for a woman.

VI. INDIVIDUAL LIFE

(a) *Marriage.*

THE general ideas concerning marriage show considerable similarity among all the tribes.

To begin with, polygamy is the universal ideal. Its practice is, however, limited by two factors: the wealth of the individual and the proportion of adult men and women. According to sleeping-sickness census figures for Yei and Kajo Kaji the excess of women over men is about 10 per cent. which now that intertribal fighting is a thing of the past is probably a fair average for the whole province, with the exception of Maridi, where there appears to be a marked deficiency in women, only 80 to 100 men. Again, although chiefs may have seven or eight wives, few individuals are wealthy enough to find the bride-price for a plurality of brides. Mr. Beaton has made a detailed investigation of the position among the Bari and finds that 36·8 per cent. of the adult males are unmarried, 52·3 per cent. have one wife only, and only 10·9 per cent. have more than one wife. The same sort of proportion is probably true for most other tribes, Maridi being again exceptional for a high polygamy rate, no doubt in imitation of the Zande.

Moreover, of the comparatively few polygamists, a high proportion have become so as a result of the levirate, the universal custom which decrees that on a man's death his wife or wives shall pass to his sons or brothers. They generally have some freedom of choice as to which relative they shall go, and if a widow wishes to remarry out of the family she can generally do so providing the bride-price is forthcoming. It is to be observed that their inheritors have duties as well as rights in regard to them; and the institution has the merit of eliminating the problem of destitute women. It is over this custom of the levirate that the Christian ban on polygamy is most at variance with the social system.

It should hardly be necessary to remark that to regard restricted polygamy as here exhibited as a device to secure unlimited sexual indulgence is completely wide of the mark. It is in fact largely dictated by biological and economic needs. In the first place, with the very prolonged lactation period during which there is frequently no intercourse, and with a child mortality rate rising to 50 per cent. the chance for the monogamist to leave children behind him is small. Secondly, in a land where hired labour is unknown, polygamy is

INDIVIDUAL LIFE

practically the only way in which the family's wealth can be increased; owing to the additional labour power the polygamist is bound to be better off than the monogamist. Prostitution and illegitimacy are unknown at present; should the ban on polygamy become effective they would doubtless, as in other African countries, result.

The essential feature of the marriage contract, which distinguishes between a licit and an illicit union, is the payment of the bride-price. Among the cattle-owning tribes this is essentially made in cattle; by the others traditionally in iron bars, but everywhere cash payments are tending to become part of the price. Amounts vary from tribe to tribe, and, in the tribe, according to the wealth and status of the individual, a chief paying considerably more for his bride than a commoner. Among the Bari two or three cows and 50 goats is an average payment for a commoner; among the Kakwa 25 sheep or goats seem a typical minimum, 3 cows, a bull, and 8 sheep a fair average. With modern opportunities for earning money there is a tendency to hard bargaining and demands for higher payments than the family's status would justify.

The bride-price is not a cash payment for the delivery of a chattel but might be more truly regarded as a mutual guarantee between the families. It is paid traditionally not by the bridegroom but by his family and does not all go to her father but is divided among her family. But again, with modern opportunities for earning money it is becoming individualistic: a man may set to work to earn his own bride-price without assistance from his father or family.

As a man in poor circumstances may have to depend on his daughter's bride-price for his son's marriage, or to make a second marriage himself, a daughter is inevitably regarded as a source of wealth and, especially among tribes which practice infant betrothal, a girl's refusal to enter into a marriage which has been arranged for her leads to great complications if the father, as is frequently the case, has spent in this way the bride-money he has received for her. Formerly, even when the girl's consent was technically necessary, she had in fact little or no freedom of choice, and extreme physical coercion might be used on the recalcitrant, with the result that suicides of girls who were being forced into distasteful marriages were not uncommon and are not unknown to-day. Nowadays the native courts are bound to uphold such a refusal and the right to do so is becoming generally known.

In addition to the payment of the bride-price the bridegroom is expected in most tribes to work for one or two seasons for the bride's

48 INDIVIDUAL LIFE

people, hoeing and building; the girl similarly will generally weed her husband's crops before the marriage takes place.

The bride-price is frequently paid in instalments and the man is generally allowed to take his bride to his home when a reasonable proportion has been paid. In most tribes she goes straightway to her husband's house; but among the Acholi she will remain for some months with her own people, visiting her husband in the bachelors' 'barracks'. The Moru girl may remain up to two years with her own people, visiting her husband at intervals for a few days at a time.

Should a bride die childless most tribes give the husband the right to the return of the bride-price or another girl in her place. In other tribes he may expect such treatment but cannot claim it as of right. If one or two children have been born the bride-price is returnable with proportionate reductions. Exactly the same procedure obtains should the wife run away either to another man or, on account of ill treatment, to her father. If she is obdurate in refusing to return the bride-price must be repaid: the result is that considerable pressure may be put on a girl by her own people to fulfil her obligations.

By a woman divorce is generally obtained in this way, by running away. The man is entitled, for repeated unfaithfulness, to send the woman back to her people and recover the bride-price, but seldom does so. In the old days a man would take the law into his own hands for adultery, killing his rival if he caught him and savagely punishing the wife. Nowadays he may demand compensation; but our discouragement of private vengeance and the comparative leniency of our penalties is criticized by many chiefs as encouraging adultery, which is particularly rife among the tribes of the south-west. At Maridi this is no doubt occasioned by the shortage of women and the high polygamy rate.

Amongst some tribes, e.g. Topotha and Mandari, a man who fails to get a child will sometimes call in a relative.

Young children frequently indulge in erotic games and as a result physical virginity may be exceptional. Leakey (*J.R.A.I.* lxi) states that amongst the Kikuyu restricted forms of sex indulgence were not only permissible but even proper for young unmarried people: and the same may be true among some of our tribes. Be that as it may, there is no doubt that premarital pregnancy is gravely disliked and discouraged, and that its increase is greatly deplored: and that in all tribes marriage is regarded as the normal result.

In making the inquiries the points were raised whether, if no

INDIVIDUAL LIFE

marriage took place, the child suffered in status and whether the girl's bride-price was liable to reduction on her subsequent marriage. The following is a summary of the replies received (A. being the girl, B. her father, C. the seducer).

Topotha. Fairly frequent: as a common rule marriage follows. The father may refuse the marriage if C. is poor or undesirable. If C. refuses to marry, he has to pay compensation and the child belongs to B. until A.'s marriage (for normal bride-price), when the child belongs to her new husband.

Latuka. Fairly frequent, generally followed by marriage unless the man is debarred by clan relation or lack of bride-price. If C. refuses he is somewhat condemned and must pay compensation (*nebuto*) to the father: this payment entitles him to take the child if a boy, but if a girl it goes to B. A.'s subsequent bride-price is not reduced.

Lokoiya. Very rare owing to a healthy fear of tribal disapproval (though it does not prevent young people from sleeping together without sexual intercourse). There are special names for such children (*lomiang*, m.; *ipuxe*, f.) If C. refuses marriage the child belongs to B. and men will point the finger of scorn at it (*olonyi lamwak*, son of a whore). A.'s subsequent bride-price unaffected.

Bari. Very rare, owing to tribal morals. Marriage almost always follows. If C. refused marriage in old days he would have been speared; now his action is condemned and he is fined. The child belongs to B.: if A.'s subsequent husband takes the child he pays normal bride-price, otherwise less.

Mandari. Marriage usually follows: otherwise the man is fined a cow and a bull, and is universally condemned. The child goes to B. A.'s bride-price might be reduced, especially if the husband refused to father the child.

Nyangwara. Rare owing to tribal disapproval: if C. refuses marriage he is fined, and the child goes to A.'s father or guardian, though C. can redeem it with 5 goats. A. usually commands a reduced bride-price.

Fajulu. Very common owing to changing conditions. In two specific cases quoted:

    (*a*) C. has to pay a heavy fine, 2 cows and 20 goats, which will entitle him to the child when it is big enough to leave its mother. Till then it will be in B.'s custody and known as his *wuri*.

INDIVIDUAL LIFE

(*b*) The girl refused the marriage and was subsequently married to D. (at a reduced bride-price). The child remains with B. but calls D. 'father'.

In the old days if C. refused marriage A.'s kinsfolk would have speared all his live stock, making it impossible for him to marry at all.

Children born out of marriage do not lose 'free' status, though they are called *wuri*. There seems to be no stigma on the girl, but she will not command full bride-price, not apparently because she is 'second hand' but because she has given 'life force' out.

Acholi. Frequent: if C. refuse marriage, he pays compensation and eventually is entitled to the child if a boy; but a girl belongs to B. If A. marries later her husband must pay not only the ordinary bride-price but return his fine to C. (presumably only if he also takes the child, though this is not explicitly stated).

Moru. Not common: formerly practically unknown.

The girl's parents may refuse the marriage: otherwise C. is expected to marry her, and is fined if he does not. Usually he takes the child, because it belongs to his clan and to abandon it would be disgraceful and the child would be taunted in later life as *labi aku*, brought up outside the *labi* (custom) of its proper clan.

In most cases the girl is thereafter considered a bad lot.

From the above summaries it appears:

(*a*) That there is no such thing as an illegitimate child, a child, that is, whose status is penalized by being born out of wedlock. The social system can assimilate it; but in some tribes it may be subject to some contempt.

(*b*) The payment of the compensation often entitles the physiological father to the child when old enough (sometimes only if it is a boy). One would have expected this to be invariable owing to the complication of clan relationships.

(*c*) Little stigma appears to attach to the girl.

No reply specifically mentioned the case of seduction by a married man: these are believed to be rare. It may be presumed that in many cases the pair are already betrothed.

(*b*) Birth.

Twins. As aforesaid, the dislike of twins is confined to the Bari and the Bari-speaking tribes of the west bank. It is apparently due to a belief that they will cause the death of one of the parents especially,

INDIVIDUAL LIFE

among the Bari, if they are of the same sex, and in former days one was exposed.

In some of the western tribes there is held to be a sympathetic connexion between twins. Thus among the Moru, if one twin has to be punished, the other must be lightly chastised; a man who marries a twin must pay a trifle towards the bride-price of her twin sister.

Similarly with the Avukaiya where twins must eat together and food should be given not to one but to both. Among the Baka also twins should be punished together and if girls should be married at the same time.

(c) Burial.

Burial is almost invariably just outside the hut, on the side, with the knees drawn up, in an attitude of sleep; a man on the right side facing west, a woman on the left side facing east.

All the tribes west of the Nile and also the Madi dislike the idea of the earth falling on the body, to avoid which they make a recess at the bottom of the shaft; the body is placed in this recess which is then sealed off with wooden stakes. The Bari rain-maker's tomb is in this form.

The Latuka burial with the *nametere*, a rude effigy of the body made of twigs, is unparalleled elsewhere in the province.

A peculiar feature practised by the Bari and Bari-speakers is the pushing of a small quantity of earth into the grave by the grave-diggers, backwards with their elbows.

(d) Suicide.

Suicide is uncommon, but by no means unknown and is almost invariably done by hanging.

The motives are various: after a quarrel, by a woman who has been abused, or by old people whose relatives are dying off in quick succession (Moru); by girls to avoid an unwelcome marriage; on a wife's desertion (Bari), due to impotence (but amongst the Mandari the wife would go to the man's brother and if she has a child it will be counted to her husband); any kind of disgrace or degradation; for instance, a Latuka strong man who broke his arm; a Kakwa who had accidentally killed his wife rushed straight out into the darkness and tried to kill himself.

It is mentioned that though now not uncommon among the

52   INDIVIDUAL LIFE

Topotha it was formerly very rare because a man then could and would relieve himself of the burden either by killing the person who had caused his misfortune or by going out on a raiding expedition. The same note is made about the Latuka that suicide is being substituted for the old remedy of going out on a forlorn hope.

Suicide is always done privately and ceremonial suicide is unknown.

VII. ECONOMIC LIFE

(a) Cattle and other Live Stock.

WITH the exception of the Bari and Kuku the tribes west of the Nile have to-day practically no cattle. There seems, however, to be no doubt that a hundred years ago among the Fajulu, Kaliko, Moru, Baka, Mundu cattle were as plentiful as east of the Nile. The herds were practically wiped out under the Egyptian and Dervish régimes: with the reduction of stock and population the jungle encroached on the cleared areas and tsetse became firmly established. From Juba to Maridi is to-day an unbroken fly-belt.

The cattle are all of a small, almost miniature breed, but of a good stamp.

The Nilo-Hamites are essentially pastoralists, and their devotion to their cattle amounts to a cult. Each man has his own personal bull, with which he is almost identified; he grows its horns into fantastic shapes and makes songs in its honour. The Mandari are remarkable in that bull songs are the prerogative of the chiefs alone. Cattle are regarded as the one and only measure of wealth; and the prejudice against selling them or parting with them on any account except as bride-price still persists very strongly.

Castration by tying and bruising is practised by all tribes.

Milking customs vary greatly. Among the Latuka, Lokoiya, Fajulu, and Moru it is not done by women of child-bearing age. Among the Bari, on the other hand, both men and women milk, while among the Topotha it is generally done, in the villages, by the women. Milking is generally done into a special gourd or wooden vessel: amongst some tribes, e.g. the Nyangwara, there is a prejudice against the milkman drinking the milk which he has drawn himself.

The making of clarified butter seems little known, except among the Topotha. Elsewhere milk is drunk fresh or curdled: some tribes make a kind of cheese by compression with a piston in hollow bamboos. A mixture of blood and milk is a common article of diet especially among the eastern tribes, the veins of the neck being pierced with a stopped arrow from a miniature bow.

Sheep and goats are fairly common among all tribes. For bride-price purposes they are equated and there is not nearly so strong a prejudice against selling them as is the case with cattle. The Topotha own a particularly good breed of large pot-tailed sheep.

54 ECONOMIC LIFE

Donkeys are kept by the Topotha alone; they are of a good stamp and exist in large numbers. They are said not to drink the milk and do not use them for burden.

The Topotha, and to a less extent the Latuka, keep a few tame ostriches for the sake of their feathers.

Poultry are kept by all tribes except the Topotha (though the Jiye have them), but there is an almost universal prejudice against the eating of chickens or eggs by women.

(b) Agriculture.

Except by the Topotha, whose only crop is durra, a great number of different crops are grown. There are innumerable varieties of durra, red and white; it might almost be said that each locality has its own. The keeping quality is generally very poor, hardly any varieties will last a full twelve months, and perhaps for this reason it is extensively used for making beer. The southern Bari and Fajulu in particular have a peculiar and very useful practice of sowing a late durra crop which is cut down at the beginning of the hot weather before bearing. The roots sprout with the early rains and give a very welcome early crop.

Dukhn is grown by the Latuka; maize is widespread, especially among the Bari, Fajulu, Kakwa, and Moru.

Eleusine is widespread, particularly among the Madi; ground-nuts and various kinds of beans are universal. Sesame is grown by all, especially Moru, Kakwa, and Madi; sweet potatoes and cassava have increased greatly during the locust years, though the Latuka have not yet taken to the latter.

Cotton, grown in the Torit, Opari, and Maridi areas, is a recent introduction. Most tribes grow tobacco, that of the Lango, Kuku, and Moru being particularly esteemed.

Among Topotha and Makaraka cultivation is left entirely to the women; elsewhere there is a well-marked division of labour between the sexes. The clearing and preliminary cleaning and hoeing is done by the men, the grass being removed by the women; the sowing is done by the men, the weeding and generally the reaping by the women. Each wife has her own plot and her own grain store; but as a rule she may only sell produce with her husband's consent.

The cultivation of sweet potatoes and cassava is generally men's work.

Two kinds of hoe are found, the very long, straight hoe used by

ECONOMIC LIFE

the northern Bari, Lokoiya, and Latuka; and a bent mattock, that used by the Kuku being particularly heavy and effective.

(c) Bee-keeping.

There is a curious contrast in tribal practice in the matter of bee-keeping. Broadly speaking, the tribes west of the Nile understand and make beehives, most of those on the east do not.

To expand this statement: on the west of the Nile the Moru have great numbers of hives and are the most skilful practitioners of the art. The Bari, Fajulu, Kakwa, Kuku, Kaliko all have hives, as have the Baka and the other Maridi tribes. The Nyangwara and the Mandari have only a few, and mostly take wild honey only.

East of the Nile the northern Bari and the Luluba keep hives; the southern Bari, rather unexpectedly, do not.

The Lokoiya make a very few hives; the Latuka and associated tribes do not make them with the exception of some of the Koriuk (Imeruk and Lotese) and of the Lafit (Kidongi and Lallang). The Didinga have hives, but not the Topotha.

The hive is a cigar-shaped cylinder about 4 feet long.

Contrary to general belief, natives do not invariably kill or expel the swarm when taking the honey. The Moru, for example, working at night, drive the bees with smoke first to one end of the hive and take the comb from the other; they then reverse the process, leaving a portion of the comb in the centre. The Bari similarly do not kill the bees.

(d) Arts and Crafts.

Iron Working. Originally the smelting of iron was widely practised but this has now been entirely killed by trade iron. All tribes have their smiths, those of the Bari being particularly esteemed. The main Bari centre is at Belinian. There is another well-known centre, for the Latuka country, in northern Lafit, with a strong Bari element. It is to be remembered that the Bari smiths are a special servile class. For the Moru, the Moru Kodo and Nyemusa seem to provide a great number of smiths.

The bellows are of skin, of familiar double-piston type; tools are generally merely stones, and Bari smiths who have been given hammers persist in the use of stones.

Red Ochre. This is an important industry, the Luluba hills being a particularly well-known centre. Other well-known ones are in the

ECONOMIC LIFE

Nikor section of the Topotha; at Imeruk (Koriuk) for the Latuka; in the Adalla Hills near Opari. The process is a complicated one: the rock, a biotite gneiss with an iron content of not more than 3–4 per cent., after being powdered is buried for some two months; it is then subjected to various processes and finally roasted, after which it is ready for mixing with sesame oil.

Basket-making and Pottery are practically universal. Particularly large pots are turned out by the Latuka of Chalemni.

Rope is made of local fibres, especially by the Lango of Katiri and in the Yei District.

Stools, cut from the solid wood, are made by all tribes.

The Topotha make excellent wooden spoons.

Of representational and decorative art there is practically no trace until one gets to the extreme south-west corner round Maridi. The notched grave-posts of the Moru Kodo are well executed and symmetrical, as are the wooden horns decorating the graves of hunters. The posts of bridges may be seen finished off as human heads. Huts near Maridi are decorated with pictures and patterns in bright ochres. Just over the border is the beautiful iron- and woodwork of the Zande and Mangbettu. It almost appears as if this were a central or west African impulse and that the Hamitic strain is essentially non-artistic, a view to some extent corroborated by the fact that the Madi carve their musical instruments into the likeness of human heads and that the Madi children seem to have more idea of modelling than others. Exceptions in the favour of the Nilo-Hamites are found in the beautiful bead caps made by the Topotha (though all tribes have a flair for bead work) and the Bari pipes. The earthenware bowl of these is often very elaborate: the stem may be intricately built up of sections of ornamented brass, carved wood, and polished bone and display considerable craftsmanship. The cowry ornamentation of the Bari women's aprons is often elaborately and pleasingly done.

VIII. VITAL STATISTICS AND PHYSIQUE

SO far we possess very few vital statistics and what we have are not very accurate.

The following is a summary of the records:

	Men	Women	Children
Yei District . . .	100	111	189
Opari (excluding Madi) .	100	105	180
Madi . . .	100	109	160
Maridi . . .	100	89	120

At Maridi there is probably an exceptionally high sterility rate: over the province as a whole 100, 110, 200 might be a fair average.

Inquiries by Bimb. Derwish in Yei District as to the number of living children per mother gave the following:

Kaliko	.	.	. 2·9	Madi	.	. . 1·6
Kakwa	.	.	. 2·3	Mundu	.	. . 1·4
Fajulu	.	.	. 1·6	Nyepu	.	. . 1·4
Kuku	.	.	. 1·6	Makaraka	.	. 0·6

The combined effects of these figures would appear to indicate a receding population; actually the position is not quite so bad as that. Owing to frequent changes of boundaries it is difficult to get precise comparisons from the poll-tax lists, but they seem to show that there is a slight increase, most marked in the Latuka and Yei Districts, but that it is very slight indeed.

The principal reason is certainly very heavy child mortality. There are no records for this, but competent observers estimate it at least 50 per cent. Malaria is probably mainly responsible; spleen counts among children give 100 per cent., among adults practically nil; immunity has been obtained, but at great cost.

The increase rate is also slowed down by periodic epidemics, cerebrospinal meningitis and dysentery being particularly deadly.

It is clear that such a balance of the sexes allows of no extensive polygamy. As mentioned elsewhere, Mr. Beaton finds among the Bari that of the adult males 37 per cent. are unmarried, 52 per cent. have only one wife, and only 11 per cent. have more than one. The levirate, the system by which a man's widows are inherited by his sons or brothers, accounts for much of what polygamy there is; otherwise it is mainly confined to the chiefs and even amongst them, except

VITAL STATISTICS AND PHYSIQUE

possibly in parts of Maridi, bears no relation to the fantastic figures which occur, for instance, among the Zande.

The physique of the fit tribesman is magnificent: he will carry a fifty-pound load up a steep mountain-side without distress.

Diet varies greatly. Few tribes to-day have the blood-and-milk mixture except the Didinga and Topotha. Many of the tribes have no cattle and few sheep and goats, so milk cannot enter much into their diet. The Kuku have cattle but drink little milk. Cattle are practically never eaten, sheep and goats very rarely, fowls not very often; they are vegetarians except for the game they kill. On the other hand, they have at their disposal a large number of oil-bearing products, sesame, ground-nuts, and the like, and large supplies of beans. Their diet is on the whole probably well balanced. Among the Moru meat hunger is said to become pathological. The carrion eating of the Kuku has been noticed by several observers, and few tribes find any meat, however decomposed, too high to eat. This has indeed been suggested as a possible cause of leprosy. Some tribes will not eat eggs at all, and in most tribes they are never eaten by women. All tribes eat fish except the Didinga.

Enormous quantities of marissa are made and consumed; drunkenness is common. Spirits are seldom distilled except in the neighbourhood of one or two old military stations.

Many tribes grow small patches of hashish. The Madi and the Yei District tribes seem the worst addicts, with some of the Bari. The Moru grow a lot; the Latuka do not use it. It is extremely difficult to suppress it: vigorous action merely drives it farther into the bush. The Missions, who are alive to the danger, have more hope of success than the administration. The better Yei chiefs seem to be realizing its danger.

It was once suggested that datura is also used, but no trace of it can be detected.

All tribes seem to love bathing when water is available. As long as they are naked they are personally clean, but with the adoption of clothes, which are seldom washed, scabies becomes common. The Roman Catholic Mission lay great stress on clothing; the C.M.S. in this respect practise a wise tolerance.

Housing is generally bad, the round beehive-huts being small and either ill-ventilated or not ventilated at all. Some of the chiefs have built themselves better homes, but have gone too far in the other direction to serve as a useful example to their people.

IX. IMPACT AND CHANGE

IT requires a considerable effort of the imagination to realize the full effect of the impact of Western civilization on these tribes in the middle of the nineteenth century. There is evidence in Werne's account of some slight indirect trade contact between the Bari and the outside world; but we may say in general that those primitive pastoralists and agriculturalists, in the early iron age of development, had maintained their institutions and their way of life, stereotyped and unchanged for generations if not centuries, when almost without warning there burst on them an alien civilization thousands of years ahead of them in technical development.

The impact was all the more severe because the first phase, which lasted fifty years, was characterized by an almost incredible brutality and inhumanity. Ivory and slaves were their objective, rifles the symbols of their power. As a result the population was heavily reduced and will take several generations to recover, the cattle were decimated, communities broken up, and in the less resistant tribes the whole fabric of society weakened. That there must have been a profound psychological reaction, a feeling of hopelessness, and abandonment of effort, seems certain; and it may well be that the character for laziness and apathy given by later observers to the Bari has been due to this cause.

In its second phase, which has now lasted thirty years, the new era has been marked by an increasingly humanitarian régime, and it is of interest to examine how Western civilization is affecting these African tribes.

On the purely material side certain results are obvious enough: clothes, shoes, cooking-pots, bicycles are common and in growing demand. The introduction of commercial salt into the people's diet is probably of great importance. Other factors are less obvious.

The introduction of money is a complete revolution. By working for hire or by growing money crops a man is enabled not only to share in the material benefits now offered to him but also to free himself from his background. The existence of an effective government is itself an entirely new conception. By suppressing tribal war and improving communications it is widening horizons and extending contacts.

On the purely cultural side the African has been introduced to two

60 IMPACT AND CHANGE

organized religions, Islam and Christianity. For several decades Islam was alone in the field: northern Sudanese merchants still perpetuate its influence, and from time to time it has been reinforced in the country districts by the return of disbanded battalions nominally at least Mohammedans. It has been surprisingly sterile. The Nupi of Gondokoro and Nimule (the descendants of Emin's soldiery) are, as in Uganda, self-consciously Mohammedan, but there has been no wholesale adoption of the religion, as, for instance, in the West Nile District of Uganda; it is practically confined to the river stations such as Mongalla and Rejaf, and manifests itself mainly by sporadic cases of female circumcision.

The introduction of organized Christianity dates only from 1917, the heroic but short-lived Roman Catholic attempt in the fifties having left no visible traces. The east bank has been predominantly Catholic, the right bank Protestant. Progress has been fast, and were it not for the rigid insistence on monogamy would be faster still. There has been as yet no attempt by the Negro to develop Christianity on his own lines, but on the experience of other African countries (in the Union of South Africa there are 300 registered separatist native churches) some such attempt is to be expected. It is far too early yet to tell how far the African will be able to assimilate Western education and turn it to profitable account, in the widest sense of the word.

How are these various factors reacting on the structure of native society? It would appear that in almost every case they are destructive. The suppression of tribal war, for instance, has taken away the *raison d'être* of the warrior class. Money is a powerful solvent because the young man who formerly could own no property and was dependent on his father and his relations for his marriage can now earn the bride-price for himself and render himself independent of his elders. The emphasis of Christianity is on the individual rather than the society: its tendency, if not its avowed aim, is to destroy the native religion background which permeates society. Education creates a wide gulf between the young generation and their elders; pagan chiefs and elders may encounter difficulties from the young generation of converts, while a chief's son educated in the mission is *ipso facto* debarred from exercising those 'priestly' functions on which his father's sanction rested. Our humanitarianism is accused of encouraging sexual irregularity on one hand and witchcraft on another. It is clear that on all sides native institutions are threatened; even if

IMPACT AND CHANGE

we consider them in the narrowest sense as the framework of tribal and social discipline, it is clear that we cannot regard this with indifference.

Apart from the people's own innate conservatism, the only positive preservative factor seems to be the government policy of indirect rule, of taking native institutions and strengthening them if need be to be the basis of natural evolution. This last point needs emphasis, as native administration is constantly suspected of desiring to stereotype things as they are. Such an aim, if it existed, would be foredoomed to failure, and, in fact, institutions are evolving rapidly. The position and functions of the chief are a good case in point.

The form matters little; it is the spirit which is important. A very marked feature of African society is a communal co-operative spirit, which manifests itself in the clan. It has obvious value. There are signs that it can be worked into the modern fabric, and this may be a concrete instance of something which is worth saving.

TRIBAL ANALYSIS 1932

Tribe	Eastern	Latuka	Opari & K. Kaji	Central	Yei	Moru	Total
Didinga Group:							
Didinga	1,767	..	..	..	..	..	1,767
Longarim	752	..	..	..	..	..	752
Birra	..	156	..	..	..	..	156
Nilo-Hanitic Group:							
Topotha	5,783	..	..	..	..	..	5,783
Latuka	..	3,105	..	..	..	..	3,105
Koriuk	..	3,146	802	..	..	..	3,948
Lafit	..	1,895	..	..	..	..	1,895
Lokoiya	..	497	1,010	943	..	..	2,450
Lango	..	3,549	323	..	..	..	3,872
Dongotono	..	684	..	..	..	..	684
Bari	..	..	377	6,078	..	1,057	7,512
Mandari	..	..	..	781	..	1,572	2,353
Nilotic Speakers:							
Fari (Anuak)	..	1,150	404	..	..	..	1,554
Acholi	..	..	620	..	..	..	620
Bari-speaking Western Group:							
Fajulu	..	..	..	837	2,609	..	3,446
Nyangwara	..	..	..	954	..	1,310	2,264
Kakwa	..	..	897	..	5,100	..	5,997
Kuku	..	..	3,972	..	..	..	3,972
Nyefu	..	..	546	..	..	..	546
Moru-Madi Group:							
Moru	..	..	..	..	..	6,286	6,286
Avukaiya	..	..	..	..	700	650	1,350
Kaliko	..	..	..	..	1,113	..	1,113
Lugbari	..	..	..	..	171	..	171
Madi	..	..	1,022	..	..	..	1,022
Luluba	..	..	..	766	..	..	766
Miscellaneous:							
Mundu	..	..	..	..	936	1,005	1,941
Baka	..	..	..	..	380	2,423	2,803
Makaraka	..	..	..	..	305	178	483
Zande	..	..	..	..	..	325	325
Nupi	..	..	34	..	..	..	34
Mixed	..	..	..	201	..	..	201
Totals	8,302	14,182	10,007	10,560	11,314	14,806	69,171

PART II
INDIVIDUAL TRIBES

I. NILO-HAMITIC GROUP

THE TOPOTHA. (CAPTAIN G. R. KING)[1]

History.

THE Topotha, the easternmost tribe of the province, have their centre round Kapoeta. They call themselves Nyitopotha; they are called Huma or Khumi by the Didinga, Kum or Kumi by the Beir and Epeta, Akarra, Karra, or Nakarra by the Dongotono, Lafit and Latuka, Abō by the Acholi.

Although they are now cultivating in an increasing degree the Topotha are essentially a pastoral people whose life is in their cattle. Their country, the wide plains between the Didinga and Longarim Mountains and Abyssinia, is on the edge of the arid country on the west of Lake Rudolf and has much less rainfall than the country immediately to the west; in character, with its thick belts of thorn and absence of heavy timber, it recalls immediately the neighbourhood of Kosti or Dueim. The Topotha villages are strung out along the Thingeita and Lokolyan, but owing to scarcity of water they are semi-nomadic; in the dry season only the very old are left in the villages; all the others are in the cattle camps (*nawi*) with the herds which range as far as Moru Akipi, Kombo, and the Kuron River.

Their language is practically identical with that of the Turkana and of the Karamoja tribes, the Karamojong, Dodoth, and Jiye, and they represent themselves, no doubt accurately, as of the same stock and as emigrants from Karamoja.

Originally, according to their own account, they were one of four stocks in Karamoja—the Jiye, Topotha, Karamojong, and Dodoth. The first to move were the Jiye, at present in the extreme north of the Topotha country; at some unknown interval they were followed by the Topotha who made their way to the Liyoro River (on which Lolimi is situated: there is an important river of the same name in Karamoja) and made it their centre. Here they split into three: the Nyangatom who did not stop on the Liyoro but made their way north and east to their present habitat on the Abyssinian frontier; the Akaloto, and the Akalokidei. The two latter remained centred on the Liyoro for several generations, during which they split into

---

[1] Mr. E. J. Weyland's 'Preliminary Study of the tribes of Karamoja' (*J.R.A.I.* 1932) is valuable for comparisons with the Karamojong, &c.

F

NILO-HAMITIC GROUP

the present sections, viz. (the figures are the numbers of adult male taxpayers)—

I. *Akaloto*	II. *Akalokidei*
Mothinga (1,650)	Nikor (740)
Nmachi (790)	Nangiya (660)
Karingak (800)	Magoth ⎱ (200)
Nirioto[1]	Peimong ⎰
	Paringa (620)
	Nibunio[1]

These names were given while they were on the Liyoro and commemorate topical events. Thus the Peimong were so named for their meanness in sacrificing only one bull (*epi Nyimong*) on arrival at the Liyoro; the Mothinga because they were charged by a rhinoceros (*amothing*); Nikor means 'the dancers', Magoth the proud and aloof; Nangiya signifies the grain skins which they carried, Paringa the high Liyoro cliffs by which they dwelt, Nyibunio the poisonous plant (*ebuni*) among which they camped.

From their home in Karamoja a sacred stone called Kathingotore or Kwoto was carried by four men directed by one Lokolingara or Kuleyo of the Nituremajio clan, and was set up on the Liyoro, where it still stands to-day a centre of Topotha ritual. It is about 2 feet high with a diameter of about 1 foot at the base and 8 inches at the top, and is of hard black stone. It is said to belong only to the Akalokidei sections. It is not only the scene of the initiatory bull-killing (see below, Bull Classes) but sacrifices are made there by individuals or communities to avert drought, famine, cattle disease, or other calamities.

Eventually, due possibly to pressure from the Turkana, they moved north, probably pushing in front of them the antecedent Jiye. According to their own account the country they now occupy was then inhabited by the Epeita (the Beir and Murule), who were then driven north to their present habitats. Roughly speaking, the Akaloto (Mothinga, &c.) spread along the Thingeita, the Akalokidei (Nikor, &c.) along the Lokalyan. In the course of time owing to geographical proximity the Karingak became absorbed in the latter, the Paringa in the former; the Nyibunio were practically exterminated in fighting with the Turkana.

---

[1] Nirioto and Nibunio are small sections that are being gradually absorbed, owing to geographical proximity, by the Mothinga and Karingak respectively. Nyalingaro, shown as a section in earlier lists, is probably an area name only.

THE TOPOTHA

The Magoth at first went north to Moru Akipi and Morunyang but subsequently swung round on to the north of the Lokalyan.

It is possible to date their moves with a certain degree of accuracy. Thirteen age classes exist or are remembered (the fourteenth is just being formed), and it is said that the move to the Liyoro took place during the first, that the second all died there, and that the move from the Liyoro occurred in the time of the eighth and ninth. The exact age-class interval is still uncertain, but allowing twelve years to a class that would place the move to the Liyoro 150 years ago and the northward migration about 60 years ago. This, as the move would probably be gradual, fits in reasonably well with other facts; it is still remembered that the Karingak were on the Amosin River, on the east side of the Didinga Mountains, and Lodengamoi of the Nikor remembers his people being at Woteng Hill near one of the eastern sources of the Lokalyan. This somewhat destroys Mr. Driberg's suggestion that the Topotha preceded the Didinga on the eastern slopes of the Didinga Mountains; but it is not unnatural that two hostile and adjacent tribes should have their own names for features in the debatable land between them. There is evidence that the move to the Thingeita preceded that to the Lokalyan.

In other words, we have here a migration which is still going on. Existing maps show the Topotha east and south-east of Mogilla Mountain; and around Mogilla are many traces of villages which the Turkana admit to be old Topotha villages. The Jiye to the north have hardly settled down yet: within the last fifteen years they have been on the Lokalyan; thence to the Kuron and Kathangor; then on the Boma Plateau and driven thence to their present inhospitable location. Incidentally the presence of their sacred stone on the Liyoro would explain, apart from any other consideration, the Topotha dislike of further Turkana intrusion in this direction.

Until recently the Topotha were with good reason hostile to—and rather scared of—the Turkana: relations have recently much improved with our backing of the Topotha. With Karamoja they seem to have little intercourse. With their kinsmen, the Nyangatom, there is a strong connexion, especially with the Peimong and Nikor and probably considerable intermarriage. With the Didinga they are on terms of bare tolerance; with the Longarim they are definitely hostile—due often to disputed watering-places on the Thingeita. In a raid on them led by Amut in 1926, just prior to our occupation, they are said to have killed 70 men, women, and children, and to have taken off 1,000

NILO-HAMITIC GROUP

head of cattle. They have lately, 1934, been living on the Kuron in close proximity to and apparently on good terms with Marille there. Their language is a lingua franca along the border from the Boma Plateau to Lake Rudolf. The Jiye are on good terms with the Boma Kichepo. The upper waters of the Kengen are very necessary to them for grazing and fishing, and until recently they were on good terms with their Beir and Epeita neighbours, but since 1933 a state of active hostility has arisen in which many lives have been lost on both sides.

Prior to our occupation the Abyssinians, drawn thither no doubt by the quest for ivory, frequented and influenced the Topotha country to a considerable extent; they were not disliked, they contracted many marriages in the country, and indeed the poaching raids of later years were carried out largely by Topotha or Topotha half-breeds.

Our own occupation of the country took place in 1927; there was a not very whole-hearted attack on the camp just after the occupation, since when our relations with them have been on the whole extremely friendly. To this their fear of the Turkana has no doubt contributed.

The Jiye have been little studied: in the following pages, unless specifically stated to the contrary, the reference is to the Topotha proper.

Clans (Nyitakeri).

The clans are fairly numerous: among the Nikor (200 taxpayers) there are fourteen well-known ones, among Nangeya (700) there are eight. They are not confined to the sections but partially distributed through them, thus:

Karingak	Nmachi	Peimong	Nikor	Nangeya
Nyikuren	..	..	Nyikuren	Nyikuren
Nyilepo	..	Nyilepo	Nyilepo	..
..	..	Nyiloto	Nyiloto	..
Nyikateok	Nyikateok	Nyikateok	Nyikateok	Nyikateok
Nyangeya	..	Nyangeya	Nyangeya	..
..	Nyidodotho	..	..	Nyidodotho
Nyigobali	..	Nyigobali	..	..
..	Nyiboya	..	..	..
Nyidocha	..	..	..	..
..	..	Nyipacholo	..	..
..	..	..	Nyithigari	..
..	..	..	..	Nyilete

It is said that sometimes marriages will take place between distant members of one clan, but these are always opposed.

THE TOPOTHA

The ears of the cattle are cut with the clan mark (*nyiponei*); individual owners will also put their individual brand (*nyomachari*) on the flanks.

Particularly interesting is Nyikuren, the fire-making clan.

Sacred Fire-making.

Sacred fire-making plays an important part in Topotha ritual: its practitioners are restricted to one clan, the Nyikuren. This clan is found in several sections but not in all; *vide* the table in the preceding section.

There are grounds for thinking that not only have the Nyikuren their own chief in each section but that they have one senior fire-maker for the whole tribe, possibly Loleng.

The fire-makers are in possession of sacred fire-sticks (*nyidomei*) which are handed down from father to son: but the virtue lies in the man not in the sticks and should he lose them he can borrow or cut others. The power is hereditary and passes directly from father to son however young the latter may be.

Their functions are numerous. One or two fire-makers accompany a fighting expedition. When the party arrived near its objective—generally on the evening before the attack, which usually takes place at dawn after a night march—the warriors were halted and the fire-makers made a fire on the path leading to the attack. The column tramped through the fire till it was extinguished, and once he had passed it on no account was a warrior allowed to look over his shoulder. The same ceremony was observed on a big hunting expedition.

The fire-makers, as described below, play a big part in the creation of the new bull classes. In times of emergency, drought, sickness, cattle plague, they attend the councils of the elders. They make the fire in which the sacrificed animal is burned. The ashes of the fire are collected on the following day after it has burned out and carried by the elders to the various villages when the plague or drought will be stayed.

Should an animal be stolen from a fire-maker he can bring sickness on the thief by kindling the sacred fire. But he can only do this in respect of his own property, and cannot affect the thief of some one else's stock.

Age Grades and Age Classes.

The whole subject of age classes is extremely complicated and confusing. Only the outlines are known and there are many gaps to be

NILO-HAMITIC GROUP

filled in. But thanks to Captain King certain main facts have now been elucidated.

Age Grades. These are as follows:

Nyede: young boys: their heads are shaved except for a circle on the crown of the head.

Nyikapanak: youths approaching puberty.

Nyath: young men, beginning to grow the warrior's head-dress.

Netherok: warrior's head-dress grown.

Nyikurunok: elders.

Omogongit: old men.

The most important are the *Netherok* and *Nyikurunok*.

Age Classes (anaget). Age classes are of two kinds, the age classes proper and the 'bull classes' which in due course absorb them. The age classes are divided into (probably) three sub-classes, filled when there are sufficient candidates for admission. The point at which a lad enters an age class and the manner of his admission is still uncertain. The extraction of the two lower incisors (customary but not universal) is performed by itinerant 'dentists' who tour the country and is done soon after the second teeth have appeared, that is, in early childhood. There is a hint that age-class candidates are potential poll-tax payers, perhaps 16–17 years old, so we may guess that it is on passage from the *Nyikapanak* to the *Nyath* grade that the age class is entered.

The following is a list of the age classes existing or remembered:

1. *Nyithiokop.* Led the migration from Karamoja.
2. *Nyikiror.* All died at the Liyoro.
3. *Nyigirin.*
4. *Nyipuwath.*
5. *Nyikorinyang.*
6. *Nyibero.*
7. *Nyipei.*
8. *Nyigio.*
9. *Nyibukoi.* Started the movement from Liyoro.
10. *Nyimor* (a stone). Only two or three alive in 1934.
11. *Uwurna* (horns of a bull growing naturally). Now old men.
12. *Idongo* (bull's penis). Elderly men.
13. *Nyikaletho* (ostrich). Subdivided into:
    (*a*) *Merikopiri.* Existing in 1922 (Mr. Driberg's reports).
    (*b*) *Nyikurunya.*
    (*c*) *Ngoroko.* Not yet admitted to bull class.

THE TOPOTHA

14. *Nyimor*:
  (*a*) *Nyitapatulia*. Not yet admitted to bull class.
  (*b*) *Nyikwakeleng*.   „   „   „   „
  (*c*) Not yet formed.

Age classes are apparently formed on the demand of the young men 'to be given a name' or on the decision of the elders after the matter has been discussed. What ritual is observed has not yet been recorded, nor do we know at what intervals the classes are formed, though on the analogy of other tribes we may not be far wrong in guessing that the sub-classes are formed every four to five years. The new class is sponsored not by the class immediately above it but by the next but one: thus the *Idongo* were sponsored by the *Nyimor*; the *Uwurna* are the sponsors of *Nyikaletho*. There is an obscure story of the *Idongo* refusing to 'absorb' the *Emorru* (apparently the *Nyikaletho*) due to the latter's practice of slaughtering animals by cutting the throat and leaving the tongue and windpipe—which are believed to contain the spirit—in the carcass. The traditional method is to slit the body lengthwise and remove tongue and windpipe, and the *Emorru* practice was held responsible for bringing sickness to people and stock. A possible explanation of this story is given in the following section.

There seems no doubt that, like the bull classes, the age classes are tribal and not sectional, i.e. the same classes occur in each section.

It is recorded that the *Idongo* were the left wing in war and hunting, the *Nyikaletho* the right, but the point requires further elucidation.

From time to time the warrior class is expected to give a dance for the senior class. At one observed in 1932 the participants wore full war-dress and the dance was of the mimic warfare nature. At the close of the dance a prominent elder made a long speech on topical affairs, particularly a recent friendship pact with the Turkana, the keeping of which he strictly enjoined.

It is probably at the time of his admission to his class that a man is presented with his personal bull. This is the centre and focus of his being, almost identified with him. He will tend and groom it, train its horns in some particular shape and compose a song in its honour, sung with his arms extended in the shape of the bull's horns. Although when a man dies no dance is held, if a man's personal bull dies a dance is held; the bull is eaten by the women only, another being provided for the men.

NILO-HAMITIC GROUP

Bull Classes. The age classes are periodically 'raised' to 'bull classes', entry into which gives the members warrior status. The term *nyithapana* is used for the bull class (or possibly for the ceremony of forming it). The exact relation between the age and bull classes is not accurately established, but if we correlate Captain King's lists of the two we get the following:

Age Classes	Sub-classes	Bull Classes[1]
UWURNA	1. ?	*Nyichuma nyang* (*a*)
	2. ?	,, *bong* (*b*)
	3. ?	,, *baling* (*c*)
IDONGO	1. ?	,, *bok* (*d*)
	2. ?	,, *ngor* (*e*)
	3. ?	,, *puth* (*f*)
NYIKALETHO	1. *Merikopiri*	,, *meri* (*g*)
	2. *Nyikurunya*	*Nyiwelangor* (*h*)
	3. *Ngoroko* (not yet bulls)	
NYIMOR	1. *Nyitapatulia* (not yet bulls)	
	2. *Nyikwakeleng* ,, ,, ,,	
	3. Not yet formed	

It is specifically stated that (*b*) is an *Uwurna* class; that (*f*) is *Idongo*; that (*g*) and (*h*) are *Nyikaletho*, and that the last bull class was formed in 1930 (when it was much overdue).

Thus, though verification is required, there are grounds for saying that the bull classes correspond exactly to the age sub-classes; that the entrants to the lowest classes are very young (probably 16–17) and have to wait till they have attained full manhood before their class is raised to 'bull' (warrior) status.

As in the case of the age classes, sponsors are required from the class next but one in seniority. It is said that the *Uwurna* who are now the senior age class had refused for a very long time to initiate a new bull class and that as a consequence men of 40 and over were initiated in 1930, the last initiation—of the *Nyikurunya-Nyiwelangor* presumably —and that as a result many younger men who in the natural course of events would have been initiated were denied.

The bull classes are tribal, not sectional. The following account of the raising of a new class has been collected by Captain King:

When, after talking the matter over, the elders of the senior age class —to-day the *Uwurna*—decide that the time has come to initiate the

---

[1] *Nyichuma* means 'the people who stab' the white bull, the dappled bull, &c.

THE TOPOTHA

junior class the word is passed round from section to section that a meeting must be held at the Liyoro. In many cases the very senior elders are too infirm to make the journey and deputies are elected. The numbers attending vary, but each section is represented by several elders. In 1930 the Jiye did not attend; probably as a separate branch they have their own separate class organization. Large numbers of people are also present with their flocks and herds. After a three days' feast the elders with the people by their sections in the background assemble at Kwoto, the sacred rock, and a bull of some special type is sacrificed, the type of bull and who shall produce it having been previously foretold by the witch-doctors by shaking stones in a gourd. The name of the new bull class, corresponding to the bull sacrificed, is thus conferred, e.g. *Nyichumangole*, the bull with the white blaze. Certain rites are then performed; it is possible that the bull is burned in a fire kindled by the senior fire-maker. The bull must be thrown looking towards the stone and with the head pointing to Zulia Mountain.

The elders then disperse to their various sections and the class to be initiated is called up, in all sections, on the same day. They are lined up by the elders according to physique and character, those of poor physique and bad character being placed at the end. A bull conforming in character to the clan name is brought and a spear—known ever after as the spear of the clan name—is given to the candidate at the head of the line, who steps forward and stabs the bull lightly without looking at it. Withdrawing the spear he passes it, looking over his right shoulder, to the candidate next behind him who does likewise, and so on.

The bull usually dies beween the tenth and fifteenth stab, and those who have been lucky enough to stab it while it was still alive are recognized as the elders of the class. The remaining neophytes stab the carcass in turn. The candidates then have to 'run the gauntlet' down a lane of the elder class, e.g. in 1930 the *Uwurna*, who beat them with switches. The sacrificed bull is then cut up and the new class have to throw the limbs into a fire, probably kindled by a sacred fire-maker.

It will be seen from the above that each class in each section as it is admitted is furnished with its own leaders who are the potential elders of the section. To-day the *Uwurna*, the present-day elder class, have one elder left in the Peimong, one in Nmachi, three in Paringa, and four in the Nikor. The *Idongo*, the next senior class, lost

NILO-HAMITIC GROUP

most of its elders in fights against the Turkana, but there are three left in Mothinga and two in the Nmachi. *Nyikaletho*, the present warrior class in which there are some quite elderly men, have seven well-known elders in the Nikor, five in the Peimong, three in the Mogoth, and four in the Nangiya.

Chiefship.

There seems no doubt that prior to the advent of the Abyssinians even the idea of 'the Chief' was entirely unknown to the Topotha; the affairs of section and nation were regulated by the elders of the ruling class, next but one above the warrior class, whose creation has already been described. Gifted individuals such as Tuliabong or Lotukol, himself an elder, might by their force of character or prowess come to exercise unusual sway; but this was purely personal and there was no conception of it passing on his death to his son. Mr. Driberg writing in 1925 says:

'The Topotha recognize no chief but are governed by councils of elders who have considerable authority. They are responsible for internal discipline; no raid can be conducted without their authority and blessing, all disputes are brought to them for settlement. When the Abyssinians came on the scene they found it convenient to appoint a chief but respected the tribal council to the extent of nominating the leading elder to the Chieftainship. This was logical and he was respected by the people not in his capacity as "Chief" but as elder.'

He points out that the appointment of chief and the consequent slighting of the elders is unfair to the 'chief' who will be expected to exercise a non-existent authority and will at the same time be exposed to the very effective jealousy of the elders.

The difficulty is that the elders who are mostly exceedingly old (and often too infirm to get about) and naturally excessively conservative with no love for any new régime are exceedingly hard to win over. Little can be hoped from them during the present generation; but we can reasonably hope that future age-classes which have known us as young men will be more ready to co-operate.

Crime and Punishment.

Cases of murder, wounding, and adultery, unless summarily avenged, were brought for arbitration to the elders. A murderer, especially if a man of bad character, would generally be killed by the relations

THE TOPOTHA

unless he managed to escape: if he got away and took shelter in another section he was not followed up and was safe (though one would have expected the dead man's clan brothers to be hostile); but unless the matter was settled by arbitration he could not return and so was effectively banished. If the matter came to arbitration the blood-money varied with the circumstances of the parties, but 40 head of cattle was apparently a maximum. Wounding was fined proportionately, sheep being often paid; thus a broken arm might be assessed at 2 head of cattle, a leg at 5 with 30 sheep, an eye at 6 with 20 sheep.

A cattle thief if caught was generally killed out of hand.

Adultery was—and still is—most seriously regarded. Formerly both parties were liable to be killed; now 10 head of cattle and 30 sheep is a typical fine.

Rain Chiefs.

The Topotha have no rain chief of their own of any importance. Minor rain-makers seem to exist, functioning locally in a very small way. On important occasions the Topotha have recourse to Alukileng, the famous rain-maker who lives in the Longarim Hills.

Rain may be 'stolen'. (Other tribes share the belief.) Thus in 1933 the Magoth believed that some Tirma had stolen their rain and a party was sent to bring it back. To do so they had to take, unobserved, some water from a Tirma watering-place and bring it back in a gourd to their people.

No trace of the *monyekak* has been observed.

Spirit Doctors.

The spirit doctor, *nyimarun*, is a doctor, caster out of spells, a minor rain-maker, and a forecaster of the future, for which purpose like the Bari *bunit* he throws strips of leather (*akala malamamuk*) like sandals upon the ground and takes the auguries from the patterns they assume. But one individual does not combine all these functions. Women, even young girls, may be *nyimarun*. The pretended extraction by suction of foreign bodies from the patient is a common form of 'cure'.

The evil eye is strongly believed in and it is the doctor's business to detect it; certain acts are also believed to cause sickness or death, such as a woman, naked, bringing food to her husband, or to enter a hut with an unsheathed spear.

NILO-HAMITIC GROUP

Birth, Marriage, and Death.

Twins are not killed or disliked. The very mention of twins caused intense merriment. One is usually put to a wet nurse.

A man will eventually have at least three names, his birth name, his father's name, and his bull name.

Premarital intercourse is not uncommon and providing there is no child is not regarded very seriously, though the girl's father may lie in wait for them and give the pair a sound thrashing if he catches them. Should there be a child and the seducer marry the girl there is no stigma. Should he refuse, or should the father refuse to allow the marriage because the man cannot provide the bride-wealth, he has to pay compensation, commonly a cow and 20 sheep, though the amount varies with his family's circumstances. The child then remains in the father's house until the girl marries—her bride-price is not thereby reduced—when the husband takes the child also.

Child betrothal is common: the bride-price is arranged and paid, the girl remaining with her people until she is old enough to go to her husband.

Polygyny is the ideal, though many men from poverty have only one wife. Six wives is the most known to be possessed by one man.

Bride-price varies according to the circumstances of the families, 3 to 10 head of cattle appear to be the limits, with sheep in addition. The bride-price is divided amongst the family, the girl's mother taking the largest share, followed by her father. Her paternal and maternal uncles also share, the former preceding; something also goes to her eldest brother. The husband also has to produce a bull to be eaten by the women of the bride's village, otherwise she will be sterile.

If a woman is childless by her husband he will sometimes call in another man. Should a daughter then be born, one head of her bride-price when she marries will be paid to her physiological father.

If a wife dies childless, the husband has no claim on his father-in-law for another wife, though if they are on good terms another may be given at reduced bride-price.

As already described, adultery is regarded as an heinous crime. If a girl runs away to another man her father must repay the bride-price to the husband.

Burial is not always practised, the body often being merely left out in the bush. If burial takes place the head of the dead man is shaved by the women and a skin placed at the bottom of the grave on which the body is laid, on the right side, with knees drawn up and the hands under the right cheek. A cairn of stones is made over the grave. A bull is sometimes killed and for a varying period offerings of twigs or stones are placed over the grave by the relations. No dance is held, though oddly enough a dance is held at the death of a man's personal bull. The near relatives smear mud on their heads and faces for three days: the widows shave their heads, take off all their ornaments and wear their kilt tied tightly between the thighs. The mourning period varies from one to five months.

Dress, Ornaments, and Weapons.

The men go completely naked: a skin 'spine pad' covering the small of the back and tightly tied in front by narrow thongs round the waist is often seen. Beards are occasionally worn (also by the Longarim and Turkana), probably in imitation of the Abyssinians.

The warrior's head-dress is the same as the Karamoja *emedot*, a felted 'bun' on the back of the head. The more elaborate Karamoja *etimat*, a heavy pad falling between the shoulders, is not used.

Important men wear a large skull cap entirely covered with red beads arranged in circular patterns on human hair, extremely fine pieces of work.

Very treasured are large opalline beads: these are worn on the breast strung in a rectangular pattern thus:

They are said to be very old and to be a valued part of the inheritance. How they come into the country is not known. There are modern imitations which have little value.

On festival occasions strings of bells are worn in a spiral round the leg from ankle to thigh.

Unmarried girls have their heads shaved except for a central ridge of hair: this is shaved off on marriage and the hair allowed to grow in rats' tails. Married and unmarried wear an apron in front and a skin skirt covering the buttocks. The married women, and sometimes the girls as well, have a skin cape. They wear masses of beads, red seeming very popular.

They have shields of the 'pointed rectangle' Acholi type. The use of bows and arrows is unknown. Besides the usual throwing and

78 NILO-HAMITIC GROUP

stabbing spears they have a peculiar spear with a heavy broad head about 2 feet long and a small haft much shorter than the head. It looks like a short broad sword and is said to be so used. Small game is knocked over with sticks: wrist and finger knives are common. Not only the wrist knives but the spears as well are guarded by a narrow leather rim, very cunningly fitted to the edge. I have noticed this amongst the Acholi but not elsewhere in the province.

The shoulders of the warriors are tattooed with patterns of small dots to show they have killed an enemy, on the right shoulder for a man, on the left for a woman.

Before going to war the warriors are painted with clay prepared by the girls.

Cattle and other Live Stock.

Their cattle are extremely numerous and in their eyes transcend any other form of wealth. They are bound up in them; they talk, think, and dream cattle and in consequence detest the idea of parting with them. They are a family possession and, as described, a man's cattle are 'entailed' on his sons.

They practise castration by tying and bruising.

In the villages the milking is done by women: a wooden vessel is always used and may not be used for any other purpose. In the grazing camps the milking is done by the young men and a gourd may be used. Blood and milk is the common diet in the *nawis*, and milk is also curdled. Small boys will often suck direct from the udder.

If a cow produces two calves at a time the calves and the cow are killed.

They also keep sheep, goats, donkeys, and a few ostriches. Chickens are not kept except by the Jiye and a very few with the Mothinga and Magoth. Eggs are not eaten.

Their sheep are a big fine fat-tailed breed far superior to any others in the province. They are not very unwilling to part with them and trade considerable numbers to other tribes.

If a ewe goat produces two kids at her first delivery it is a bad sign; but good if she produces two at birth subsequently.

Their donkeys are of a good stamp, easily broken to work. Their attitude to them is curious. They do not customarily use them for carriage or burden, do not drink the milk, very rarely eat them, and yet are not very willing to part with them. They are unique in the province in possessing donkeys.

THE TOPOTHA

Land Tenure and Cultivation.

There are probably section boundaries and possibly clan boundaries, inside which the land is free to any one who chooses to clear it. Unlike most tribes the individuals do not cultivate scattered plots here and there but adjacent to each other, farming one very large cultivation area which is often fenced. The individual boundaries are settled by the men in the dry weather. Perhaps because they are essentially pastoralists and may have probably only taken to agriculture fairly recently, cultivation is essentially women's work. The man seldom does more than one day's work at the beginning of the season—there is generally no heavy clearing to be done—and the hoeing is done by the wives, each of whom has her own individual plot, the unmarried daughters, and sometimes the young sons if they are not out with the herds. At harvest the grain is cut by the men but carried by the women.

If a man abandons his plot any one else taking it up is supposed to ask his permission. This is generally given, but the land seems to be regarded as still belonging to the original owner. Quarrels seldom occur, but there are occasional disputes about boundaries.

It is said that on a man's death each widow retains her plot which when she dies goes to her eldest daughter and her husband. This would imply that the plots of a man's different wives might be widely scattered and requires confirmation.

If a woman leaves her husband she is entitled to half her crop. The young unmarried men are landless and live off their relations.

Agriculture is practically confined to durra. Ground-nuts and sweet potatoes are not grown.

The Topotha themselves have a memory of the time when they grew no grain, as is shown by the following legend. A long time ago, in a time of famine when the stock were dying and there was famine in the land, a young Topotha set off to see if he could find food. After travelling a long way he came to a people who grew grain. They treated him hospitably and fed him but would not let him take any grain away with him to his own country. At length he stole some grain and hid it by tying it under his testicles and so took his departure without his hosts being aware that he had grain with him. When he reached his own country the corn was planted out and came up quickly in amazing quantities and so he was able to feed the Topotha.

80 NILO-HAMITIC GROUP

Property and Inheritance.

When a man marries he allots to each of his wives a certain number of his cattle not as her property but in trust for her sons. If he dies while his sons are still young his brother, who has probably married the widow, becomes the guardian of the young son and the cattle until the son is grown up and takes them over. This leads to endless disputes regarding the disposal of the offspring of the cattle during the son's minority.

The following are typical cases:

(1) A. marries three wives, B., C., D., and allots them cattle and has issue as follows:

$$
\begin{array}{ccc}
\text{A.} = \text{B. (6 h/c)} & = \text{C. (5 h/c)} & = \text{D. (3 h/c)} \\
| & | & | \\
\text{E. (a son)} & \text{F. (a son)} & \text{childless.}
\end{array}
$$

At his death E. and F., assuming they are of age, take the cattle allotted to their mothers. D.'s cattle go to E., the son of the senior wife.

(2) On a man dying unmarried the 10 head of cattle he owned were divided by his mother and brother as follows: 1 to his full sister, 2 to his half brother, 7 between his mother and full brother.

Their inheritance rules are most complicated; but mothers and sisters seem frequently to obtain a share.

Building, Arts and Crafts, Industries.

The Topotha houses are of the beehive type, poorly constructed owing to the lack of suitable grass. When grass is used they employ ridged thatching, but along the Thingeita and Lokalyan doleib palm leaves are generally used. As in Karamoja a second story is often made in the roof for storing grain, hides, or other property; but this is not done by the Jiye or Mothinga.

Pottery of the Karamoja type is universally made by the women, and is bartered for sheep, &c.

They make excellent spoons of the same shape as European spoons, from horn and also from wood, in which they appear to be good workers, their stools (single leg, curved seat) and head-rests being excellent. Ivory bracelets are also made and are sold.

There are a number of smithies, especially at Lotelepei and Nagiye (Mothinga). The iron comes from outside their country:

THE TOPOTHA

they say that they prefer local hoes to trade hoes, as the former wear better.

They are conspicuous in not having drums, and no musical instruments except the whistle have been observed.

Their principal industries are:

(1) The manufacture of red ochre. The best comes from beyond the Lokalyan, from the Nikor who do a big trade in it.
(2) Salt is brought from Mogilla or Moru Akipi. Apart from cooking it is mixed with tobacco for chewing. So-called 'salt' is also obtained by burning certain grasses and straining water through the ash.
(3) Clarified butter is universally made and is used as an article of trade.
(4) Ostrich feathers, used for head-dresses, are bought and sold.

Religious Belief.

The name for God is *Nakwuge* who is apparently believed to live in the sky, vide the legend recounted below. He decides how long a man is to live, but is apparently regarded as taking little interest in the affairs of mankind.

They probably have an ancestor cult but this has not yet been studied.

The sacred rock *Kwoto* has already been mentioned. There is a hill called Moru Nakwuge, 'the Hill of God', a day's journey beyond Lomonichek, and other sacred rocks and trees are believed to exist.

Dancing is forbidden during the cultivation season, as it is believed to bring drought or too much rain or heavy winds that spoil the crops. The dance on the death of a man's personal bull is postponed for this reason.

They share with many other tribes the following 'creation' legend, though the finale is typically Topotha. Long ago all the people lived up above with *Nakwuge*. One day a bird flew up from earth to heaven, carrying in its beak a long rope. The rope was seized by the people who started sliding down it till they reached the earth and found grass and trees, cattle and sheep (N.B. No mention of grain); they milked the cattle and liked the taste of the milk. A lot of people came down the rope but some still remained above. Presently a woman who was near her time with twins tried to slide down, but the rope broke and some people were left above and some on earth.

82 NILO-HAMITIC GROUP

THE LATUKA GROUP. (COL. LILLEY; MR. ARBER)

OMITTING for the moment reference to the Didinga and Longarim, the next big group of the Nilo-Hamites west of the Topotha consists of the Latuka-speaking tribes.

This is a complex group consisting of :

A. In the central plains the Latuka proper (chief centres Tarangole, Muragatika, Iliu and Chalemni, Laronyo Losito and, in the southern Lafit, Idali); in the hills to the south and south-west the Koriuk (Longairo, Imaruk, Ifoto, and Lukwe; Iro, Aiyirri, and Alia in Opari District). The Koriuk resemble the Latuka in language, dress, social organization, and practically all their customs, and are spoken of by the Latuka as identical with themselves except for being hill dwellers. But that in itself is a suggestive difference which together with the similarity in name (which means 'black') to 'Oghoriok', the proper name of the Lokoiya, and the absence of fire-making in the initiation ceremonies of the Imatong (Lukwe) group, raises a suspicion that some at any rate of them may be pre-existing stock driven into the hills by the incoming Latuka, but to date there is no confirmatory evidence of this and the Latuka definitely consider them as one with themselves.

B. (1) To the south the Lango comprising the sub-tribes of Logir (northern Dongotono Mts.), Dongotono (central D. Mts.), who are probably of quite different stock, and Logiri (southern D. Mts., the Imatong Mts. east and west of Mt. Kinetti and Tereteinia). Of these the Logiri resemble the Latuka very closely. The term 'Lango' though convenient is unfortunate as implying a completely non-existent connexion with the Lango tribe of Uganda. It is said to derive from the Acholi word for 'foreigner'.

(2) To the north-west the Lafit inhabiting the northern end of the hills of that name (Ngaboli, Dorik, Mura, Mekajik, and Lokotok).

(3) To the west, the Lokoiya or Oghoriok (Liria, Lueh, and around Magwe in the Opari District).

According to Dr. Tucker the three units of *B* above form a single dialect group, while the Latuka speak the same language in a considerably more developed and difficult form.

Since the above was written, the following note has been made by Mr. Arber:

The term Koriuk is of course only an anglicized version of 'Oghoriok'. Its application cannot have been entirely haphazard and it is a reason-

THE LATUKA GROUP

able supposition that the plains Latuka hearing the Lokoya so call themselves, applied the term to all people who had preceded them and whom they found in possession of the country west of the Kineti towards Liria. It is not really correct to refer to the people straddling the Imatong from Lomo and Lopulong and Molongori to Lukwi as Koriuk; they are called Imatong both by the Lokuko and by themselves.

I am more inclined than before to group all the people from Lomo across the hills to Lukwi, Ifoto, Loferika, Imeruk, Edo, Lobuli, Kataluro, Langairo as representing the pre-Latuka wave; and to go farther and include the Lowudo of Losito. I have always been at a loss to explain the difference of Lowudo from the rest of Latuka; their short stature, square face, and slightly different speech made them resemble rather the Imatong. Now it seems likely that there is direct connexion. The legend of Nyangeri's first migration may be read to fit this theory, if it be assumed that it may have been considerably more than ten generations ago and that he represented the wave in front of the pure Latuka who followed in due course under Imukunyi. It is suggestive that he came from the tip of the Imatong. The Labama clan of Imatong who hold the rain claim affinity with the Lowudo. Following the attack by Imukunyi the Lowudo were either dispersed or absorbed by the Long Latuka. The influence of the latter was, however, predominant and affected everything about the so-called Koriuk, even to the extent of pushing in an Igago chief at Ifoto (Abilli's family).

The following are odd pieces of confirmatory evidence:

1. Stature and facial resemblance already mentioned.

2. Direct evidence from Kataloro that the original Lowudo dispersal concentrated on a place near the present Kataloro, whence they afterwards colonized Loferika, Imeruk, Lobuli, &c.

3. Edo on the Opari road was an original Lowudo settlement and there is a Lowudo rain-maker there to-day. Lowudo are friendly with Edo and Imeruk to-day to a much greater extent than they are with Latuka. Lowudo have always been a thorn in the Latuka side, Lokidi in recent times having made efforts to subdue them.

4. Clan distribution; Lowori runs from Lomo (S/C Lobugu) to Imeruk and Kataloro; so does Ilaregi, which corresponds to Lowudo, and Aburi's assertion that Ilaregi were the Xobu clan may thus have some substance.[1]

---

[1] Aburi, the Chief at Obbo in the Opari District.

NILO-HAMITIC GROUP

5. The whole group including Lowudo differ linguistically from the Long Latuka.

Kataloro and most of the original dispersal from Lowudo have acquired a certain amount of Lokoya idiom in their speech due to proximity with Lueh. The Lueh–Lokoya migration from the northern Lafit by way of the old Lomini settlements at Kula Hill must have followed much the same course, being finally cut off from their source by the Long Latuka's intrusion at Lowudo when the latter probably obtained their hold on the Lomini. The through route to Liria and the river always lay through Lokila until very recent times and made the Lowudo area a strategic point.

Lowudo viewed in this light is of interest administratively because it opens up the possibility of amalgamation to the west of Kineti under Lowudo hegemony.

I find on subsequent inquiry that old Issara, the present Lowudo rain-maker and father of Lakaranya, is actually a relative of Aburi's from Obbo and is therefore better described as a reintroduction. It throws some light on the connexion between Ilaregi and Lowudo.

LATUKA (*with whom are included the Koriuk*).

The Latuka have a number of characteristics which differentiate them very strongly from the rest of the tribes of the province. Their clans are remarkably few, only six in number apparently, the biggest being subdivided into three. Unlike all other tribes except the Moru the clans are not only totemistic (the Bari have faint traces of totemism), but the souls of the deceased are believed to pass into the associated clan animals after death. Their funeral customs, especially the subsequent exhuming of the bones, are peculiar to themselves. Fire-making plays an essential part in their initiation ceremonies. Most remarkable of all, they live in real villages, as contrasted with the scattered hamlets of the other tribes, of considerable size and with a highly complex village organization. They have evidently been affected by some influence which has left the rest of their neighbours untouched, but whence it came is quite unknown.

History.

To-day they appear to have no memory of immigration from another region, but they told Emin that the place whence they come to people Latuka was Jebel Kyelamir, pointing to the north-east.

THE LATUKA GROUP

At the present day their traditions give Chalemni and Iliu in the extreme east of their country as their centres of dispersion (pointing perhaps to an arrival through the Iliu gap) and there is evidence for their gradual extension from east to west.

Lasang, the mythical ancestor of the Igago clan, appeared first by the Ibong stream, near Isoke and not far from the sacred Itaraba pool, living near or in the river. He was befriended by the goatherds until the people became aware of his presence, and he became their first rain chief (*xobu*, pl. *xobok*).

The first dispersion from the east was that of Nyangeri, the ancestor of the Lowudo clan who ten generations ago led a migration from Iliu to Ngarama, at the extreme tip of the Imatong, and Kileu. Having quarrelled with and cursed the Kileu people for killing a bull of his he moved north to Longolo Hill, a small party going farther on to Lafon. These subsequently incited an attack on Longolo by the Anuak of Lafon who penned the Latuka on the hill, demanding the surrender of Nyangeri. Several men gave themselves up in his place and were killed, but without avail, and at last Nyangeri, when thirst threatened all his people, gave himself up. He was killed, cut into small pieces, and his flesh cooked in a great pot in which bull's meat had also been placed. The Latuka were then compelled to eat and those who ate the chief's flesh died.

The Anuak then returned to Lafon, taking with them Nyangeri's wife who was big with child. She was delivered the first day on the road; and the infant was stolen by a Latuka named Irifai who had followed up the Anuak and contrived to put in its place the fruit of a sausage tree wrapped in a leopard skin. He took refuge for about a year in a cave near Ngaboli till the Lafit discovered and befriended them. The child was taken back to Longolo and eventually became chief. His name was Lonoka.

His son Nolong succeeded at his death. Another son who had colonized Segelli killed Nolong by sending him poisoned tobacco. Enraged, his people joined with the Imatari Latuka, attacked the Segelli villages, killed the criminal, and the people were dispersed, to Lueh, Liria, Lokila, Langairo, Nguleri, and Belinian.

Nolong's son Manyimarik became chief, and moved to Laudo, where this branch has been ever since. He married an Acholi wife from Obbo named Ikang.

Another dispersal was led from Iliu eight generations ago by Imukunyi, an early Igago hero, who having quarrelled with his brother

86 NILO-HAMITIC GROUP

Pachar, chief of Chalemni, founded Imatari, close to Logurren Hill. From here he joined in the attack on Segelli mentioned above. In his old age his son Lokorak usurped his father's authority and drove him out accompanied only by his dog. Imukunyi journeyed to the Akarra (Topotha) country and led them against Imatari which they sacked and burned, the people being dispersed to the hills, Lofi, Chalemni, Lobira, Isoke, and Loronyo. Lokorak was killed, but a baby son of his, Loyalala, was carried off by the Topotha.

Imukunyi remained at Imatari as chief, but when it was again sacked a few years later by the Topotha, the survivors abandoned it and built on the top of Loggurren Rock. Imukunyi's son Lokomo apparently moved to Tarangole, of which he became chief. His 'son' Kujang or Amoya was the Tarangole chief mentioned by Baker. Loyalala in due course fled from Topotha country to Iboni, where he was recognized as Lokorak's son and made chief of Loronyo. With his son Maya we come to comparatively recent years.

The Clans (xang).

The Latuka clans are remarkably few, only five so far having been identified. This must, one would think, make their marriage arrangements extremely difficult. By far the biggest and most important, as containing the most influential rain-makers, is Igago, which is sub-divided into three, Kidonge, Ijukho, and Narafat. As already related Lasang, the first *xobu*, is regarded as their progenitor and Imukunyi is their famous hero.

The next in merit, it is said, is Lomini. When an Igago rain-maker dies the grave must be dug by Lomini. In old days a Lomini was buried in the grave; and Seligman mentions that the Lomini act as assistants to the Igago rain-maker. A considerable amount of mystery surrounds this clan. It has no rain-maker, rain area, or high place in Latuka country and was formerly thought not to be a *xobu* clan. But we find that Ikang, the present 'Queen' of Tarangole, is, and admits to being, Lomini. But she is a Lokoiya from Liria and her clan there, the Oxoiyu, is the big Lokoiya rain family, the origins of which they refer to northern Lafit. So doubt arises whether Lomini is really a Latuka clan at all. Laudo is a *xobu* clan whose ancestor Nyangeri has already received mention.

Lomia is also a *xobu* clan, the rain family to-day being at Iboni in the Lafit. Its origin is obscure. The first recorded *xobu* was Latabat, who was brought to Iboni as an infant in arms by his mother, the

THE LATUKA GROUP

chief wife of a Lomia *xobu* who had driven her out, possibly from Lobule or Langairo.

In the Iboni area there is a clan called Lesoba, originally, according to the story, one with the Lomia, until a Lesoba man seduced a Lomia girl when the Lomia, incensed, separated the clans and decreed that they might intermarry. The Lesoba bury the Lomia *xobu* in the same way that Lomini do the Igago.

There is also at Iboni a minor clan called Acoxi.

Labalwa and Ajogok are two very small non-*xobu* Latuka clans.

A puzzling feature is the co-ordination of differently named clans among the Koriuk, Lango, and Lafit with the Latuka clans. Thus the Itibok and Moxoi of the Koriuk are said to be 'the same as' Lomini and Lomia; Lowang (Lafit), Labama (east Koriuk), Ilareji (west Koriuk) correspond to Lowudo; Imoru (Lafit) is the same as Lomia, while as we have seen the Lomini are the Lokhoiya Oxoiyu. The reason given is that the founders of these clans came from the Latuka, but this does not account for the change of name.

A tentative table of these 'equations' is given below:

Latuka	*Koriuk East*	*Koriuk West*	*Lango*	*Lafit*	*Lokoiya*
IGAGO	Igago	Igago	Igago	Igago	..
Subdivisions:					
Kidonge	..	..	..	..	..
Ijuxo	..	..	..	..	..
Narafat	..	..	..	..	..
LOMINI	Lowori	Itibok	Itibok Lowori	Lomini Atabok	Oxoiyu
LOWUDO	Labama	Ilareji	..	Lowang	..
LOMIA	..	Moxoi	..	Imoru Sub. Lesoba Acoxi	..
LABALWA	Ifiloxi (Itilbai at Ifoto)	Itilbai	Ifiloxi	..	..
	Lataxaji	..	Lataxaji	..	..
	Many others	Loteri Liboji	Very many others	Twari Lueh	Very many others

The Latuka clans are not only totemic, each clan having an animal associated with it, but unlike all other tribes of the province except

NILO-HAMITIC GROUP

the Moru, the Latuka believe that at death the soul passes into the clan animal. Details will be found in Professor Dr. Seligman's *Pagan Tribes*.

Tribal Functionaries.

The important tribal functionaries are four, the rain-maker (*Xobu*), the *Labaloni* or *Lamonyemiji* (father of village), the *lamonyefau* (father of the land), and *Lamonyedupa* (father of the drums), and reflect the social organization of the tribe. The rain-maker's authority extends over a definite, territorial, rain area which is subdivided into villages, each under its *Labaloni* or *Lamonyemiji*. Each village is subdivided into 'quarters', *namangat*, each with its own name, and each centering in the drum house, *nadupa*, which is the focus of its social life.

The Rain-maker. The functions of the rain-maker have been fully described by Dr. Seligman and need not be elaborated here. They comprise the annual rain and fertility ceremonies, the annual new year ceremonial hunt (*nalam*) when the auspices for the coming year are taken from the entrails of the slain animals, and, at about sixteen-year intervals, the initiation by fire-making of the new age-grade. His importance and prestige are immense; his people till his lands, build his house, often tend his herds, escort him on ceremonial occasions, and for these duties will generally wear full dance-dress of helmet, plume, and beads.

It seems certain that the rain-maker's significance is territorial, from the place rather than from the clan. The Latuka country is divided among a number of territorial rain areas, and though it might be tempting to regard the rain-maker as a clan functionary, it seems certain that this is not so, and that particularly at the initiation ceremony in which the aspirants are members of all the different clans, the emphasis is definitely on the place. A diagram of the rain areas is given.

The Lamonyemiji. Mr. Arber writes as follows:

This name is correctly translated as the 'father of the village'. Dr. Seligman defines this functionary (*Pagan Tribes*, p. 323) as the first builder of a settlement or his officiating descendant, male or female, who bears the hereditary title and magics the crops and village for good, which is an accurate description: but some confusion has occurred by the translation elsewhere of the name as the 'father of the land'. Raglan's account, quoted on p. 4, *S.N.R.* viii, should be read to differentiate between the hereditary headman and the owner of the

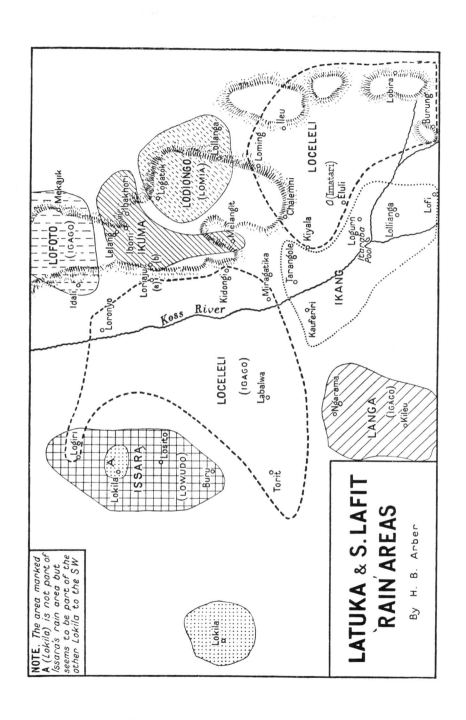

NILO-HAMITIC GROUP

land. The former is the *Lamonyemiji*, also referred to as the *Laboloni* (big man), and the latter the *Lamonyefau*. One man may, however, combine both functions in himself.

The *Laboloni* is essentially the representative of the people and is often referred to as the *Monye wati*, 'father of the people'. Among the Latuka his position is hereditary but not necessarily in the line of direct descent, for some latitude of choice appears to be given to the people within the limits of the family. For instance, when the last *Laboloni* of Torit died, the *Monyemiji* chose as successor one Lodongi who was not actually his son: this man was, however, a policeman and refused and their next choice was Nyong, the present *Laboloni*. He may be male or female, as is shown by the instance of Nassara at Losito. He is not necessarily of Khobu clan; Nyong of Torit is Igago, Nassara is Lowudo, Lobugu of Chalemni is Igago, Lokyoro of Loronyo is Kidongi, Boye of Kiyala, who is also the sub-chief, is Lomia, Kide of Iliu is Lomini. As descendants of an original colonist the *Abolok* may also be *Lamonyefok* in their original village; Nyong, for instance, is *Lamonyemiji* for Torit, Labalwa, and Muragatika, but *Lamonyefau* only in Muragatika; there are other *Lamonyefok* in Torit which is a subsequent colony.

The *Laboloni* holds an important position in the magico-religious sphere and stands next in importance to the rain-maker, whom he assists in rain-making ceremonies; (*vide* Seligman wherever he mentions *Lamonyemiji* in connexion with rain rites and p. 309 where *abalok* is the plural of *Laboloni*). He appears to act as the rain-maker's local representative and will transmit his orders to the *Monyemiji*. His function is to *ihuhumio Naijok* or propitiate God for the villages of his area: as Jok is looked upon in regard to the community as a vague impersonal power who may bring prosperity or misfortune on the village in many ways, the *Laboloni* will be called upon for sacrifices to avert disease from the people or the herds; or to keep locusts away: for a general sacrifice at the beginning of the cultivation season; to bless new village sites; he will oil and spit upon the spears of hunting parties to bring them luck; finally, he is particularly concerned with the initiation of the *Monyemiji* in his area, both individually and communally when he will perform the actual fire-making. His position relative to that of the rain-maker is clearly shown from the fact that while the *Monyemiji* cultivate a field for the rain-maker in every village in his area, the *Laboloni* is only entitled to the services of the Laduri Khorwong, though occasionally the *Monyemiji* will assist if he

THE LATUKA GROUP

is popular. There are not many *Labolok*, as they tend to combine villages which have sprung from their original place.

Lamonyefau. This is the correct term for the father of the land who is the descendant, usually direct, of the original cultivator of certain areas. He is concerned with the land and crops of his inheritance and has no power in religious matters to compare with that of the *Lamonyemiji*. There may be several in one village; they may be male or female, and of any clan. They take dues from those who cultivate on 'their' land, but of course tenure of land by ordinary people holds for year after year, and the *Lamonyefau* is the arbiter when disputes over plots of land occur. They perform the ceremonial sowing in their land; the rain-maker will perform an initial ceremony in the village where he lives to signify the start of the cultivation. The *Lamonyemiji* will sacrifice locally and take the auspices for a good year; but the *Lamonyefok* perform the particular ceremonies in the cultivations. This they do by sacrificing a goat, usually black, and sprinkling the entrails on the ground to be sown; the flesh is eaten by the cultivating party. Often seed will have been carried to the rain-maker for him to spit upon. They have no claim upon the services of the *Monyemiji*, but the *Laduri* will be sent to them. There are three *Lamonyefok* in Torit; Loliha of Lomini, a woman Aguta of Lowudo, and Lochiha of Igago.

Lamonyekhari. This title is of small importance; there is in fact only one recorded case of this functionary in the whole of Latuka; Loliha of Kang Igago in Torit who owns a crocodile pool above the Mission.

Latuka Age Grades and Initiation.

The following note by Mr. Arber amplifies the accounts of these initiations given by Professor Seligman (*S.N.R.* viii. 14–17 and *Pagan Tribes*, pp. 323 and 324). As a preliminary simplification, it is to be understood that each individual is initiated three times. First, on attaining manhood he is initiated as a member of his village; initiation is yearly and each yearly class has its own name. After four years approximately the resulting four classes are initiated as one class by the *Lamonyemiji* and are given a collective name by him: they also assume drum-house names corresponding to the different *namangat* (quarters) into which the village is divided, each *namangat* having its own drum-house (*nadupa*). Meanwhile the *Lamonyemiji* of other communities are doing the same, and when four of these village classes

NILO-HAMITIC GROUP

are complete, i.e. after about sixteen years, all those in the rain area are initiated as a grade, generally by the rain-maker, and take over the country from predecessors.

General. Latuka age grades and age classes have been particularly prominent during 1933 owing to the coincidence of the new-fire ceremony of initiation (*nongopira*) in the three main Latuka groups, and it has become increasingly clear that they continue to play a large part in the social organization. The absence of their original stimulus war, far from weakening their influence, appears rather to have led to their increased activity in many communal matters; and this perpetuation of the communal spirit is for the Latuka their main protection against detribalizing forces to which their mode of life and their situation might lay them open. By making the most of their age-class duties they allay some of the repression which enforced peace imposes on a fighting tribe. The age classes in their regimentation under the rain-maker are the motive power of the community.

There are only three age grades: the *Monyemiji* (protectors of the village), who are the grade in power; the *Lamaurwak* (would presumably be about 48 when they quit office) (old men), who are the retired grade; the *Laduri Khorwong* (boys behind: i.e. supporting rank in war), who are the coming grade. These grades may be taken as sixteen-year periods. They prevail throughout Latuka, but there is no single area system as among other tribes (the Didinga and Lango for instance); there are indeed different grades and classes from village to village and other complications; the Latuka have become divided into territorial groups under their rain-makers and there is an age-grade system for each group. The initiation ceremonies in these groups coincide so closely, however, that the *Monyemiji* are of approximately the same age throughout Latuka and would constitute a single grade and class if they could be brought to unite. As it is, they have become localized.

Age-class Divisions. The Latuka owe four allegiances in their social life: to the clan, to the rain in the person of the rain-maker, to the place in the person of the *Lamonyemiji* (*Laboloni*), the father of the village, and to the drum-house in the village. The age grades and classes stand in direct relation to all of these except the clan to which they, as the chief integrating forces in the tribe, may be said to be opposed (cf. Driberg, *At Home with the Savage*, p. 129), and to which in fact they have no relation whatever beyond the distant one of allegiance to a clan rain-maker. (In relation to this point it will be

THE LATUKA GROUP

shown subsequently that at the Lowudo initiation the clan rain-maker took no part.) The sixteen-year age class under the rain-maker is the aggregation of *all* the *Monyemiji* in his rain area, comprising the territories of several *Lamonyemiji*, and will have a single name given to it by him; the age class under the *Lamonyemiji* consists of all the *Monyemiji* claiming descent from an ancestral place, will have a separate collective name for each village in his area (if more than one); will also have its special drum-house sub-names; and will be divided into four-yearly classes each again with its own name. The following examples illustrate this:

A. Rain-maker . . . . . Loceleli.
  R.'s name for grade . . . *Naboro* = Sand.

This name will apply to the whole of his area, and is extensive from Logire and Loronyo and Torit in the west to Lobira and Burung in the east. There will be a number of *Lamonyemiji* (*Labolok*) in such an area; to take one therefore, the *Lamonyemiji* of Torit, Labalwa, and Muragatika:

B. *Lamonyemiji* . . . *Nyong*.
  L.'s class-names:
   at Torit . . . . *Khima* = Grain.
   at Labalwa . . . *Nyong* = L.'s own name.
   at Muragatika . . *Ibwoy* = Lazy.

The name of the ancestral place which is celebrated in the ceremony is called *Latara Lamonyu*, outside Muragatika.

C. Drum-house.

Each *nadupa* (drum-house) stands in a *namangat* (quarter); there are three such in Muragatika in which Ibwoy will call itself as follows:

  in Torok . . . . . *Ikholo* = Heron.
  in Pwara . . . . . *Lemye* = Lion.
  in Tomugu . . . *Ibirokwan* = Overthrowing.

D. These divisions of the class do not exhaust the list, for the class in each place is divided into four yearly sections, e.g. the class *Ibwoy* at Muragatika has these four subsections:

Oldest: *Apotir* = Wart-hog.
    Amoka = Overdrinking.
    Ikarak = (a woman's name).
Youngest: *Logobe* = Grinding Stone.

NILO-HAMITIC GROUP

Duties of the Age Classes. The *Monyemiji*, as their name implies, are the fighting force of the village, and their primary duty is that of protection. Nowadays this is reduced largely to the protection of flocks, tracking of thieves, and similar duties.

Taking their allegiances one by one: they owe most to the rain-maker and may be said to be at his beck and call for almost any duty which he cares to put upon them. They go out to the *nalam* (oracle hunt) at his command and bring the spoils to him. They cultivate fields for him in every village in his area; first the ceremonial cultivation when he first makes rain, and afterwards upkeep during the year until they harvest it for him. They always escort the rain-maker to and from the place where he makes rain (e.g. Tarangole carry Ikang home in state from Kiyala when she goes to Logurn for any rain-making duty). The rain-maker is always entitled to a haunch of any game which they kill. They will also build his house for him, dig his ground-nut crop, and often tend his flocks. For most of the above duties they will wear full dance-dress of helmet, plume, and beads.

Their duties to the *Lamonyemiji*, except in so far as they are identical with their duties to the village, are relatively slight: they can be said to be under his command in all communal activities of the village, death dances, village hunts, leopard tracking, and similar matters fall within his sphere. He is responsible to the rain-maker to collect them for his functions and lead them to their rain duties. The *Monyemiji*, however, do little for him personally; sometimes a small body cultivate his fields, but this is usually left to the *Laduri Khorwong*. Nor do they as a class do anything for the *Lamonyefau*.

In any communal duty of the *Monyemiji* all of the class who are in the village are expected to turn out; if one of the number fails to do so, the rest will go in a body and raid (*ibyala*) his house, taking a goat or two, ground-nuts, or beer for their own consumption.

The *Laduri Khorwong* have the hardest time; the *Monyemiji* remembering their own apprenticeship, train the boys by laying a variety of tasks and demands on them. They are, too, entitled to knock them about at dances; they eat any game that they kill; about once a month the *Laduri* have to produce beer for all the *Monyemiji* of their *namangat*, either from grain of their own growing or from their fathers. The *Laduri* will be sent to work in the *Lamonyemiji*'s fields and are usually loaned in small gangs to the *Lamonyefau* and other village notables for their cultivation. They can expect of course some reward of beer for this. Generally they have to fag for the class

THE LATUKA GROUP

above them: in war they would carry provisions and look after the animals. Among themselves they ape the *Monyemiji* and raid one of their number in the same way for absence from duty, but they must avoid giving offence to the *Monyemiji*, who are quick to exact penalties.

This organized work-party spirit is of particular use for Government purposes and it is a general rule, for instance, that the *Monyemiji* (helped by the younger and older members of the classes above and below them) are responsible for all heavy roadwork, while the *Laduri* with the *Lamaurwak* do weeding and care of the rest-houses.

Privileges of the Age Classes. Of their various allegiances the drum-house has the strongest hold on the *Monyemiji*; it stands for the privileges which mark a man's entry to full manhood. The *nadupa* is the club-house of the *Monyemiji*: they share it with the class before them, but they have their own place in the *namangat*, e.g. their own platforms; if there is a dance or beer party, the *Monyemiji* will drink in the central place and the *Laduri* to the sides. The privileges consist of the right of entry to the *nadupa*, to beat the drums, to sit on the tall (*nolobele*) or small (*nobele*) sitting platforms, to eat and drink with the other *Monyemiji* any game or beer brought by the boys, to lead in the dances, and to be able to fag the boys. But most of the privilege is the mere fact of being a full member of the *namangat*; for each *namangat* is a focus of considerable team-spirit and each one has its own especial dance step, drum beat, trumpet rhythm, and dance décor. The rivalry between them in big villages is tremendous in these days when the Latuka finds no outlet for his spirit in war, and many recent village fights are traceable to ancient enmities inflamed by some trivial cause: as for instance recently by the misappropriation by a *namangat* of Torit of a particular method of wearing an ostrich feather pom-pom: and in Tarangole of a particular quick beat on the long bamboo trumpet which is normally the property of only one *namangat* in a big village.

Initiation. Each *Monyemiji* has to be initiated individually into the class, and the class as a whole has to be initiated in each of its three connexions (Rain, Place, Drum-house). This is done as follows: the class is initiated as a whole at the rain-maker's fire ceremony (*nongopira*) held every sixteen to twenty years, and it then proceeds to take over all the duties of the outgoing class who become the *Lamaurwak*. After this the *Laduri* class who are coming on are admitted singly to a share in the *namangat*; they are grouped in the four-yearly sections shown above; each individual is admitted to the *nadupa* when he takes a

NILO-HAMITIC GROUP

woman. He must take a goat to the *nadupa* which the *Lamonyemiji* will kill; the latter will then first sprinkle the initiate's body with the blood and afterwards the roof of the *nadupa* four times with the entrails. The initiate then enters the *nadupa* with the *Lamonyemiji* who then covers his body with ashes from the central fire; they skin the sacrifice and the *Lamonyemiji* binds strips of the skin round the wrists and knees of the initiate. The *Monyemiji* eat the flesh. There is no beating ceremony as among the Lango. The initiate is thus a full *Monyemiji* as far as the *namangat* is concerned, but no more; for it is only when the next *nongopira* arrives that these four four-yearly sections are gathered up and initiated as a whole class to take over the village.

The above account applies to the *Lamonyemiji*'s own village. In a 'colony village', e.g. Labalwa or Torit, this primary initiation is presumably done by the *Monyedupa*.

The actual ritual of initiation for the class is symbolized by fire-making, and this is used for all three class initiations, with the Rain-maker, the *Lamonyemiji*, and in the Drum-house. The sticks used are sacred and carefully preserved; the rain-maker keeps his which he also uses in rain ceremonies; the *Lamonyemiji*'s are kept in the *Nadupa* of the *pwara* (central) *namangat* in his village; and there are firesticks in every *nadupa* kept with the *Monyedupa*. The first initiation of a class is apparently in the place under the *Lamonyemiji*, and it will then adopt its place-name; at Tarangole an initial ceremony was held for building *nolobele* for the outgoing class and giving the new class its place-name, but without fire-making. Torit, Muragatika, and Labalwa, however, held a place initiation with full fire-making by the *Lamonye-miji* in preparation for Localele's area initiation this spring. Next the main class initiation is held with full fire-making by the rain-maker, as at Logurn by Ikang. The rain-maker chooses his name for the class and bestows it at this ceremony. Finally, a modified fire ceremony may be held in each *namangat*. The main feature of the collective initiation is the carrying of brands from the fire then kindled to each of the *namangat* where a fire is lit from wood already prepared; this constitutes the initiation of the *namangat*, but it appears that fire-making is used at a later stage in each *namangat* when the necessity of rebuilding or reparing the *nadupa* arises. Generally the choosing of the names for the classes appears to be settled in advance by the old men; the exception is the choosing of his name for them by the rain-maker; Locelele has not yet bestowed his name, but every one knows

THE LATUKA GROUP

in advance that it will be *Naboro* = sand; the name is given on account of their numbers; Ikang kept her class name secret until the ceremony; it was *Ama* = locusts. The names usually commemorate hunts or happenings.

The Platform Towers (nolobele) and Initiation.

A peculiar feature of the Latuka villages are the high platform towers which may occur in ones and twos or in great numbers. There are not primarily look-out towers but are intimately connected with the age classes and initiation.

Mr. Arber writes (1933) as follows:

Preparation for the *nongopira* of the Tarangole group has already started; the actual ceremony is due to take place at Logurn in October, but the *laduri*, the incoming class, who are called *Ngokhe* (Dogs), have recently taken at Tarangole a preliminary step towards initiation. This consisted of the erection of *nolobele* in all the five sections of the village, *namangat* Fagile, Tangul, Ifarang, Iripoi, and Logorunyu; and they celebrated this with a dance.

It is not clear why the previous class should have had no towers; there is no question of their having been burnt by the Government; it is said to be because the rain-maker did not grant them. The distribution of these towers varies considerably as between villages; the majority of the villages in Loceleli's group have them, but some, e.g. Muragatika, have none, while others have an excessive number for their size, e.g. Chalemni. This apparent duplication of towers in each *namangat* in a village is partly explained by the procedure at Tarangole; the towers now erected are not for the new class; they may use them now on sufferance, but at the conclusion of their initiation at Logurn will hand them over to the *lamaurwak* and build themselves new ones at a different place in the *namangat*. The *lamaurwak* naturally continue to exercise their rights as members of the *namangat* and presumably in villages, where they have had them, their towers continue to stand; but if they fall, they are not rebuilt. Excessive duplication as at Chalemni, where one section contains over half a dozen towers, was explained to me that although they were now of only one *namangat*, the *Monyemiji* kept up *nolobele* as memorials of the sections of the large village long ago on the hill-side.

The *nolobele* of Tarangole are all of six stages, except that of Tangul which has eight.

The people are very definite that an even number of stages is lucky

NILO-HAMITIC GROUP

and an odd number unlucky (*odwa*). Dr. Seligman mentions five or seven but probably overlooked the ground-level stage which is counted. Any one of the *Monyemiji* may sit on any stage as he pleases.

It was interesting to note in the dancing at Tarangole in one section about three youths dancing rather sheepishly in the rear and not wearing any of the general finery except little round hats of parchment-like wood. They were evidently the final initiates to the class and had not yet been accepted; but they will probably be developed sufficiently for full admission by the time the class is closed in October.

Particular Ceremonies.

The following details of class initiation ceremonies in different areas are given by Mr. Arber:

Logurn. A preparatory dance was held in Tarangole in March 1933 to celebrate the erection of *nolobele* there. The right to erect these towers is awarded to a class by the rain-maker; the reason that there were none in Tarangole was that the class before had not received them and not because they were burnt by Government. On this occasion the incoming class were erecting towers for handing over to the outgoing class and would build their own after the main *nongopira*.

The main *nongopira* was held early in the new moon of the Latuka month *Lolong*. The *Monyemiji* gathered at Logurn from Tarangole, Kapurire, Logurn, and Lofi in the *pwara* on the evening before the appointed day and sat through the night fasting. At the first glimmer of dawn Ikang took the firesticks of the rain-maker and setting them by the *nalore* (drum-poles) of the *pwara* twirled them four times; she was followed by the *Lamonyemiji* of Logurn, Lotoro: then the representatives of the various *namangat*, chosen for their speed in running, came forward and worked the sticks in turn until fire was made and the wood kindled. Each then lighted an ebony brand and set out to run to his *namangat* to kindle the central fire there. The remainder ranged around and were addressed by Ikang and other venerable people in turn on their duties as a class. No animal was sacrificed, nor were the initiates sprinkled in any way. They then proceeded to dance to a four-beat on the drums and trumpets and danced four times round the base of Logurn Hill. Each man had a cornstalk (*nabakhala*), and no spears were allowed. No one set foot on the hill. When the dance was completed they all left for their various villages. The ceremony was then continued for eight days in the villages. Goats were sacrificed in the *nadupa* and the initiates sprinkled with the blood. The fittings

THE LATUKA GROUP

of the *namangat* were renewed; the building of *nolobele* and rethatching of the *nadupa* were, however, left for the dry weather. A general dance was held in their old place, Khusialari, just outside the village of Tarangole towards the Kos River, where drum-poles are left standing. Finally a hunt took place and the proceeds were given to Ikang.

Names

Rain-maker's Name	*Ama*	= Locusts.
Tarangole Place-name . .	*Ngokhe*	= Dogs.
Subdivisions	(1) *Kheret*	= Intestines.
	(2) *Ngoboli*	= (place-name in Lafit).
	(3) *Perek*	= Wanderers.
	(4) *Naburu*	= Cheetah.
Drum-house Names: Tangul . .	*Logwachir* =
Ifarang and Iripay . . .	*Loyama*	= Marriage.
Logurunyang	*Akara*	= Tapothans.
Fagila	*Manis*	= Muhandiz, which is their name for the Agricultural Inspector.

Torit and Muragatika (N.B. This is a village initiation of a four-year class.)

The new *Monyemiji* of Torit left Torit one afternoon of late November (Lolong) and slept that night at Labalwa, where they danced that night and the next morning. In the afternoon they collected the initiates of Labalwa and went on in a body to Muragatika, where they spent the night fasting in the *pwara*. At the first sign of dawn the *Lamonyemiji* Nyong made fire with his firesticks. The chosen representatives ran to their *namangat* (it is about seventeen miles from Muragatika to Torit). The remainder sat down and were addressed by different people on their duties. Then they took a bull and strangled it, no spears being allowed except for slitting its stomach afterwards. All the new *Monyemiji* gathered in relays in the *nadupa*, while the *Lamonyemiji* sprinkled the roof four times with the animal's entrails. Then they emerged and sprinkled themselves with the blood. They started to dance to a four-beat on the drums and trumpets, and later went outside the village to their old site called Latara Lamonyu, where they continued the dance. They slept a further night in Muragatika and continued the rejoicing; proceeded to Labalwa and stayed there and intended to complete eight days' celebration in Torit. The new *Monyemiji* built no new *nolobele* in Torit, but took over the old one of eight stories and renovated its bindings; this *nolobele* which stands in the *pwara* is for some reason the only tall one in the village although

NILO-HAMITIC GROUP

there are three *namangat*, Langauru, Brohotole, and Lodikieh; Brohotole contains the *pwara*, the *nolobele*, and a very large drum-house. The other *namangat*, however, all have their *nadupa* and drums; the *Monyemiji* of Langauru, for instance, recently held a minor ceremony for erecting new drum-poles; they went in a body into the bush to cut the ebony always used, and subsequently erected them to the accompaniment of a general dance; the *Monyedupa* was in charge of the ceremony.

Lowudo. This account was obtained from a more reliable participant than in the case of the other ceremonies.

The *nongopira* for all the Lowudo Latuka under the rain area of Issara was held in November 1932 at the conclusion of a successful harvest. The moon was five days old and the month was the Latuka month of *Lolong*. The Lowudo people, while of course intermingling with the rest of Latuka, have contrived to remain a separate territorial entity under the rain-makers of the Lowudo clan since their original colonization of Longolo Hill. Their class initiation therefore had about it more completeness than those of the larger areas.

On the evening appointed all the members of the in-coming class, called *Ituko* = blind, gathered standing round the house of the *Lamonyemiji*, Nassara, daughter of Lokori, who traced his descent from the original colonist of Longolo Hill. They were dressed in full dance décor, brass helmet and plume, ostrich feathers and beads, but instead of spears were carrying only cornstalks. A leader called to ask if they were all present, and they then sat down in a great ring round the house and remained so all night without eating or drinking. The outgoing class, also in full dress, sat at a distance away from the circle. The night was spent in talk; the older men would come forward one by one and instruct the initiates in their duties to the village; in the protection of flocks and crops; in the art of hunting; or some would tell stories glorifying their class. At the first sign of dawn the *Lamonyemiji* made the new fire; she set the hollowed stick on the ground, and placing the upright in it, twirled it four times and let it fall. Then the chosen representative of each *namangat* came forward and worked the stick until fire was made. When the fire was burning from the shavings that had been prepared, ebony brands were thrust in and each initiate took one and ran to his *namangat*—to Mutarram, to Bur, to Bari, and so on—and kindled the *nadupa* fire there. They then returned to the gathering and reported their task accomplished. Every one then left the house of the *Lamonyemiji* and went to the

THE LATUKA GROUP

pwara of Losito Hill. There *Ituko*, the new class, ranged themselves in four ranks according to the subdivisions of their class; first rank *Mudda Katir*, so called because some years ago one of their number was given a life sentence; second rank *Dotiti*, 'manÿ people stretching a long way'; third rank *Etarokhomiji*, 'ruining the village'; fourth rank *Achwada*, the name of a dance introduced from Acholi. A goat was sacrificed by some of the old men and its entrails sprinkled over the initiates generally; its flesh was subsequently given to the old men to eat. *Ituko* now began a circular dance keeping their rank, while the outgoing class gathered and danced opposite them. They continued dancing for some time, until at a signal both classes mingled and danced. Then the various *namangat* of both classes separated out and started off to run to their several villages; as they ran the distance began to tell on the older men and Dukaro fell behind; the old men bewailed their damaged legs and backs, while the more energetic presumably did not over exert themselves, with the result that the new *Monyemiji* arrived first in their *namangat* and so took possession of it. Apparently this form of race takes the place of the sham fight in which the new class drove out the old, and which some of the Latuka say was discouraged by Government.

The second day was devoted to celebration in the different *namangat*, where one of the first duty of the *Monyemiji* was to go and cut new wood for the fittings of the *namangat*. Later a goat was sacrificed by the *Monyedupa* and its entrails sprinkled over the new *Monyemiji*, and all people of the *namangat* joined in a general dance. At the conclusion of the dance all the *Monyemiji* took their hunting-spears to the house of Nassara the *Lamonyemiji*, who with her helpers oiled and sharpened them.

At dawn of the third day all the *Monyemiji* gathered once more at Nassara's house and received their spears; they went into the bush west of Losito to hunt. All the spoils of their hunting they carried back to the house of Nassara as her reward and that of her helpers, and the ceremony of their initiation was completed.

Conclusion.

The above accounts cover the three main Latuka groups, but the same form of initiation is also in the Lomia group at Iboni and in many small groups. Fire-making is the symbol of initiation from the rain group of Lodiongo in south Lafit to the Koriuk group of Abilli (clan Igago) in Ifoto and Khidi (clan Lowori) in Imeruk. It is, however,

NILO-HAMITIC GROUP

not found in the people of Imatong, who are also referred to as Koriuk, nor among the people of north Lafit, nor among the Loggir or Logire of the Odongotono Mountains.

There is obviously no fixed form for the ceremonies, and various discrepancies are evident in the accounts. The main fact stands out that the *Monyemiji* are initiated in their various connexions by fire-making, and it is also clear that they are primarily the Guardians of the Village; the local celebrations are really of more importance than those under the rain-maker. This may be the explanation of the fact that the Lowudo ceremony was held not by the Lowudo rain-maker but by the *Lamonyemiji*—a woman.

A point in the various ceremonies which at once catches the eye is the magical importance attached to the numeral 4 or its multiple 8; the firesticks are twirled 4 times; at Logurn they danced 4 times round the base of the Hill; at Mura the *Lamonyemiji* sprinkled the *nadupa* 4 times; at Losito they were ranged in 4 ranks; the 4-beat is used in connexion with the dance which accompanies fire-making; the correct number of the stages for a *nolobele* is 4 or 8, though 6 is common. They can give no reason for this beyond that it is a tradition handed down by their forefathers.

Drum Customs.

The following account is given by Mr. Arber:

Among the Latuka, and to a lesser extent the Koriuk, the use of drums is regulated by the rain-maker. The latter holds two main ceremonies during the year:

(1) The initial rain-making at the beginning of the cultivation season (May) on which occasion all the *Monyemiji* turns out to till his fields and a goat is sacrificed to bless the cultivation. Following this no drums may be used at all in ordinary dances and music is provided by the *natur* or long trumpet only. The only occasion on which the drums may be used is for the death of one of the *Monyemiji*; but for the death of any one else their use is considered *odwa*, unlucky.

(2) The *nalam* or new year hunt at which the omens for the year are taken by the rain-maker from the entrails of the slaughtered game. This is usually held in October or November at the conclusion of the harvest, and thereafter the *natur* is put away and drums may be used in all dances. In the interval between the harvest and the *nalam* the drums may be beaten singly four times as an invocation to the *Naijok*; I heard this happen in the evening on Losito Hill, and it was followed

THE LATUKA GROUP

by a general cry and lulu-ing. In this year also an important exception was made for the *nongopira*; the *Monyemiji* would naturally have to be initiated before the *nalam* (in the case of Locoleli's general initiation they will be initiated before the other ceremony of his cultivation). Following on the fire-making the drums were produced from the *nadupa* (drum-house) and used only for the four rounds of the *Monyemiji*'s dance; they were then put away until the *nalam*.

This abstention from drumming probably holds good for the Koriuk and Logire and south Lafit, but not for the Logire section of the Lango. No special reason for the abstention is given.

Spirit Doctors and Witch Doctors.

Colonel Lilley has analysed in detail the different classes of practitioners, of whom there are four:

1. The *Leboni*. Regarded as beneficent. His particular functions are the detection of malefactors generally by handing a small stick to each of the assembled suspects, then walking round and smelling each stick; the recovery of lost property; healing the sick (this function is generally exercised by women (*lamuroni*); they have a knowledge of medicinal herbs, which they may give orally, and healing ointments. They profess to extract foreign bodies from the patient. Their powers of suggestion are not to be ignored: fortune telling, by clearing a small space in sand or dust and throwing their stones on it like dice. They were consulted before a raid; the *xobu* also consults them as to the likeliness of rain; some are said to be poisoners, in this form they are definitely injurious.

The office of *leboni* is hereditary.

2. *Adiemani*. Those who put a spell on those they dislike, corresponding to the 'evil eye' and no doubt to the Bari *demanit*. There are large numbers of these, and the quality or defect is not a matter of teaching but of heredity. They are known to every one and consequently are apt to be blamed for anything untoward which happens.

3. *Lamomolani*. Definitely evil and anti-social. Not found among the Latuka proper but practised by the Lango and Koriuk. Causes death by putting a spell on small pieces of his enemy's hair, nails, &c.; or by wailing outside his hut at night; by acts of bestiality will cause cattle to sicken and die, or by spitting inside the *zeriba* at night: always practises his craft at night. Generally known to the people and

NILO-HAMITIC GROUP

formerly driven out of the village for the first offence and killed for the second: hence he was more afraid of the people than the people were of him. Nowadays the position is rather reversed owing to Goverment's prohibition of killing.

4. *Ladofani.* The most anti-social of all: they are few in number, work secretly, and practise not against their own enemies but for others for a fee. There are several in the Lafit Hills. They work through the medium of a *nakhetu*, a gourd or pot with magic properties. It can move itself from place to place, or become invisible at its master's wish. It is kept in a cave or hidden in the forest, and to touch it is fatal; his power resides in it; if he breaks it he can be killed with impunity.

Marriage and Divorce.

The following note is by Mr. Arber:

When a son comes to marriageable age, he is usually guided by his father in the choice of a suitable girl to woo; the father makes searching inquiry into the girl's parentage to make certain of her clan descent and to find any taint of wizardry in her stock or reputation for childlessness or idleness among the women. The girl at this time is a *nodwoti* (maiden) and still wears the chain fringe which is the Latuka symbol of that state; she is probably 11–13 years old. The young man is 15–18 and will not yet have been initiated to the drum-house. If the girl accepts his suit they meet in the evenings for flirtation away from the parents' house; this wooing (*nasanga*) may include limited sexual intercourse, but as with other primitive peoples, childbirth therefrom is exceptional. A girl may have a number of lovers before she accepts one. The parents of the girl will hear of the wooing, and provided that the young man is an eligible party, take no action. At length when the girl has accepted him, the young man carries her off to his house (*itadiraro*) for one night and she sleeps with him there. She may come willingly; if she is coy or uncertain, he may bring her by force by sending some of his friends (*lelekoxa*) and so make up her mind for her. On this occasion the girl takes off her *nodwoti* chain fringe (*naririk*) and the young man gives her the apron, skirt, and beads which he has prepared for her: she wears them thereafter in the manner of an engagement ring. The next morning before sunrise the young man sends his *lelekoxa* to the parents to tell them not to look for their daughter as he has taken her. The mother of the girl then curses the young man long and loudly and finally accompanies the *lelekoxa* and brings her daughter home. The parents have, however, made up their

THE LATUKA GROUP

minds to accept the young man on trial and thereafter he works in their house and cultivation for perhaps a year; he sleeps in his own house and may only steal the girl away occasionally for flirtation.

When the parents are satisfied that the young man is a good worker and of good character, they call upon him to produce his marriage goods. The young man brings these goods (*neyemiti*) in the dance floor (*pwara*) for all to see. The father inspects them and accepts them if they are good and total at least 40 to 60 goats; he will stipulate a further number to be paid to make the total 80. If the suitor is discovered to be poor and has insufficient goats to satisfy the father, he must pay the girl's parents compensation for their daughter (*nengasa*) of 11 goats; this includes one goat for sacrifice to purify the girl. She then returns to the *nodwoti* status, resuming her *naririk*, and the young man takes back his skirts.

When the father has agreed to the *neyemiti*, the young man's *lelekoxa* take them to the father, and when they are accepted, he sends one *lelekoi* with a female goat (*nemojit* = token of receipt) to bring the girl to his house. If the father accepts the *nemojit*, the *lelekoi* returns to fetch the prospective husband; together they ask the mother for her daughter; if she agrees, she calls the girl and after giving her good advice hands her to the *lelekoi*, who takes her to the husband's house.

There the girl remains for four days; her mother meanwhile prepares the marriage feast of beer and food. On the fourth morning, before sunrise, the mother goes to the husband's house and knocks: her daughter answers her and is told to tell the husband that all is prepared. She tells him and he then instructs his *lelekoi*, who is sleeping with them, to go and tell the senior woman of his clan (an aunt perhaps) whom he has already asked to help in the ceremony. She comes to the house and they all four go while it is still dark to the mother's house; she hands them a new gourd of beer and they take it in turns, the best woman first, the husband, the wife, the *lelekoi*; they must each drink and spit out (*ijaxa*) the beer four times. Then two gourds of grain are brought and the husband and bride stand side by side in the entrance of the house and the mother pours grain on the head of each. They enter and lie down for a while perhaps to sleep. Meanwhile the mother heats a big pot of water behind the house; when it is warm she calls them; they go behind the house, wash, shave each other's heads, and anoint their bodies with oil and red ochre. The mother works very quickly to get food ready and calls them; they go in and eat with her while a friend of hers is hastily preparing the

106 NILO-HAMITIC GROUP

beer from the fermented grain (*nengwok*) which she has already brewed. It is now dawn and the father-in-law (*xomonye*) brings a goat and kills it for food. When the sun is up, the members of both clans gather round the house and eat and drink all day from the fare provided by the mother-in-law. The bride and bridegroom join in. As it gets towards evening, the husband brings tobacco which he distributes to them all, and they sit round discussing the marriage and wishing the pair luck. The bride and bridegroom sleep that night in the mother-in-law's hut and she sleeps elsewhere. Next day the bridegroom brings a goat for food and the mother provides more beer and a repetition of the feast is held. The marriage is then complete.

Thereafter the husband continues to live with his wife in her mother's hut and to work for his parents-in-law. This lasts until their child is born, when he may take his wife to his own house. The mother-in-law quite often takes over the care of the first child.

The husband will have completed the payment of his *neyemiti* up to 80 goats by this time. A further payment, however, remains to be made to the parents-in-law (*nengasa*); this is 30 goats and is payable on the marriage of the daughter of the bride and bridegroom: *nengasa* may be paid for two daughters' marriages but seldom more. *Nengasa* as a term is used for most remaining payments. It is an obligation which becomes obscured by the passing of years, as there are many cases of *nengasa* brought in the courts to-day. The Latuka dowry is thus reckoned at a total of 110 goats.

In the marriage ceremonial the forcible abducting of a girl from her parents' house (*itadiraro*) may be a simulation of old-time capture; it often amounts to little less, as the parents are not consulted and the girl is not let off if she has previously shown any sign of accepting the suitor. This practice leads to many cases for seduction in the courts.

The Lango Ceremony. The Lango ceremonial differs from the Latuka. Following the usual flirtation the young man takes the girl to his house, but the process of *itadiraro* is much less rough than among the Latuka and girls are less forced into marriage whether by their parents or lovers. The *nodwa* do not wear *naririk* as the Latuka, and it is doubtful whether the suitor gives his girl any engagement token, although the brass wrist rings may play the part. When the mother comes to look for her daughter, the man refuses to give her up until a female goat is given in ransom. Then the young man summons his *kang* (clan) and announces his intention of marrying the girl. A meet-

THE LATUKA GROUP

ing between his *kang* and that of the girl is arranged. The young man and his father offer some 50 goats; the *xomonye* demands 30 more to complete 80, and these are usually subscribed by the members of the *kang*. There is a more liberal spirit of sharing among the Lango than the Latuka. The usual dowry is 80, and 35 are left as *nengara*.

The *xomonye* distributes tobacco all round and the matter is finally settled. (It should be remembered that in a Lango village the *kang* are comparatively small.) Then at a subsequent meeting both the father of the young man and the *xomonye* bring goats for killing and eating (*lengotit*) and they make sacrifice. The *xomonye* sends his *lelekoxa* to fetch the *neyemiti*. After this the girl sleeps five days in the young man's house. Then the father of the young man produces a goat, and in the evening two girls and two young men of the *kang* take this to the mother of the girl. The next morning the girl is returned to her parents' house; they provide her with a small hut where the husband may sleep. Her father gives her a skin for them to sleep on. Thereafter the husband lives with and works for the parents-in-law until a child is born.

When *nengasa* is payable on the subsequent marriage of a daughter by this marriage, the in-laws are entitled to 35 goats. When the 35 are handed over, 10 are at once exchanged for a bull by the *xomonye*, and once again a feast is held at which the bull is eaten and shared by the members of the two *kang*s.

As regards the distribution of the *neyemiti*, both among the Latuka and the Lango this is done by the *xomonye*. He will take the bulk of the payment, probably 60 goats or 6 head of cattle. He will give the paternal uncle (*imanye*) 10 goats or 1 bull, and distribute goats singly to his other brothers. The maternal and paternal aunts (*iyani*) receive 1 female goat and a kid each. The married brothers of the bride are also entitled to small payments. The maternal uncle is of course concerned with the *nengasa* when it falls due.

In general there appears to be little dispute about original *neyemiti* payments, and cases only occur when the girl or her parents change their mind after payment has been made. Divorce for incompatibility before a child is born is countenanced. As already mentioned, it is the payment of *nengasa* which is a source of litigation. About *neyemiti* there must remain an air of respect which discountenances disputes, except in cases which go beyond tribal sanction (e.g. seduction and removal of girls by Government employees), but about *nengasa* there is much less feeling of good form.

108 NILO-HAMITIC GROUP

Marriage by Arrangement. Two other forms of marriage remain to be mentioned: the Latuka loveless marriage and the Koriuk child marriage. The former is not very common nowadays; if a man of some wealth makes repeated attempts to love a girl but is always refused, he eventually chooses an eligible girl and sends a *lelekoi* to her father with an offer of marriage expressing his willingness to pay what *neyemiti* the father wants. The father with full knowledge of the suitor's wealth is attracted by the proposal and informs his daughter that he has arranged this union for her: she of necessity bows to his will. The *neyemiti* are handed over, the suitor sends his *lelekoi* with the *nemojit* goat to fetch the girl, and after that the ceremony follows the usual form. This method often entailed great brutality, for the girl ran away from her rich and generally old husband and was thereupon beaten by her father until she consented to go back; for he had no wish to see a good *neyemiti* payment returned. Now, however, that brutality to women is discountenanced, such marriages are less common or are marked by greater willingness to allow a girl to leave a distasteful husband. The Lango by contrast have never been fond of this method, and no blame is attached to girls if they refuse to their father's face. Both the Latuka and the Lango allow considerable mutual selection. This is directly opposed to the Koriuk (not Imatong), who from Ifoto via Imeruk to the semi-Lokoya of Lueh practise child betrothal. Marriages are arranged when daughters are mere infants, and the suitor puts his iron ring on the child's finger. He agrees to pay the father so much *neyemiti* and to work in his fields every year until he can marry the child. This leads to endless complications, for the girls are no different from their Latuka sisters and refusals are common; they are stoically capable of withstanding their fathers' methods of discipline. The rejected suitor then claims back not only advance of *neyemiti* he may have paid, but also payment for all the time and labour he has spent on the father's fields; as the latter may amount to several *gugus* of grain, such a suit too often results in the complete impoverishment of the father. For many reasons, therefore, the custom is being discouraged and cases relating to it in the courts of those areas are quashed. This form of marriage is called *ocoro* (*otyoro*).

Seduction. The payment of *nengasa* in cases where the girl has been taken by the *itadiraro* method has already been mentioned. The limit set by Government in the case of seduction of maidens is 5 goats with a fine of 1 to Government. This is half the traditional *nengasa* of 10, and it is probable that in ordinary village life the

THE LATUKA GROUP

full *nengasa* is paid without the case ever being brought to court. It would be illogical if it were, as the process of *itadiraro* following flirtation is the normal preliminary to marriage. The majority of these cases in court are definite instances where a girl is seduced by a man with little or no intention of marriage, a habit that increases *pari passu* with detribalization. Where, however, this seduction is productive, marriage usually follows. It is very common in these days to find girls seduced by soldiers, police, &c., who subsequently run away repeatedly from their parents to join their lovers until the parents are forced to accept the marriage. Girls are often beaten unmercifully by their fathers or brothers for this reason, and indeed in any case where their lover is unacceptable.

In cases where a girl gives up her seducer but the seduction is productive, the man has a right to a son for clan reasons, and because the father must find son's dowry provided full *nengasa* is paid; the parents of the girl take a daughter. The full *nengasa* for productive seduction (and productive adultery) is fixed at 20 goats and a fine of 5 to Government in the courts (*itayedo* = putting with child).

The Latuka are always alive to the possibilities of litigation, and on several occasions seduction cases have been found in the courts and quashed in which fathers were suing for *nengasa* in respect of erotic play among little children.

Divorce. In the old days divorce was extremely rare: husband and wife had to live with each other for better or worse. Naturally a woman's parents considered that the husband must bear the onus of his choice after marriage, except that a girl may always leave her husband in the period before she bears him a child. Nowadays, however, divorce between fully wed couples is said to be increasing; the grounds are usually incompatibility of temperament. The woman returns to her family and they pay back the dowry less full *nengasa*: he may take sons by the marriage and the parents the daughters. The increase of divorce must be ascribed to the decisions of either British officials who have influenced the courts or possibly of Mamurs who have had wives returned in the Mohammedan fashion and accepted the third flight as final. There is no doubt that formerly these women would have been beaten not only by their husbands but also by their families.

Adultery. The matter of incompatibility, however, is usually solved to-day by the woman finding a lover who will marry her and pay the husband the amount of his *neyemiti*. This is a modern solution, as adulterers were liable to be killed in the old days. There is now much

NILO-HAMITIC GROUP

adultery among the Latuka with married women. The penalty in the courts has long (1924) been set at 10 goats (called *nebuto* = rape, in a general sense) and a fine of 5 goats to Government. Cases occur where the aggrieved husband attacks the adulterer though he has not been caught *flagrante delicto*, but generally he overcomes his rancour and accepts the *nebuto*. In cases where the husband and wife are on bad terms the adulterer will marry the woman, particularly if the adultery is productive. But in many cases the husband appears to bear little ill feeling towards his wife and overlooks her lapse. It is not beyond possibility that some plains-Latuka husbands turn a very complacent eye to their wives' affairs in the knowledge that *nebuto* may accrue! In all cases of seduction no blame or responsibility is ever held to attach to the woman; rape is unknown, and a woman's consent is regarded as inevitable once pressure is put upon her. The exception is when a woman is very promiscuous in her affairs and is dubbed *osom* (prostitute). In the courts a man may only claim *nebuto* three times for a wife; after that she is classed as *osom*. For productive adultery (*itayedo*) the compensation is 20 goats and 5 fine to Government. If the woman dies in child-birth following an adulterous union, the adulterer must compensate the husband and her family the full death compensation in addition to the *nebuto* of 20.

Higher compensations' limits are set for the seduction of chiefs' wives or adultery by chiefs themselves; 20 goats in both cases instead of 10. It will be appreciated that this helps to deter the chiefs from bloody revenge or promiscuous appropriation of other people's wives.

The Calendar.

Mr. Arber has the following observations on the calendar, in which the lunar months are adjusted to fit the agricultural or solar year:

The Latuka year is primarily based on the crop cycle and the ceremonies connected with it, and is therefore solar. The people celebrate under the direction of the rain-makers three main festivals in the year:

(1) *Nekanga* (Trumpet) is held at the conclusion of the harvesting; it is celebrated with sacrifices and much beer drinking. Drumming is not allowed during the cultivation season, only the big trumpet (*natur*); the approach of the *nekanga* is signalized by the blasts of the *natur* in the evening. The *nekanga* marks the resumption of drumming for the dance and the *natur* is laid aside.

(2) This is followed at usually two moons' interval by the *Nalam*

THE LATUKA GROUP

or new year's Oracle Hunt. This is carried out at the direction of the rain-maker, who gives earth to the *Monyemiji* to sprinkle in the cultivation lands and draws omens from the entrails of the game they kill, for the ensuing year. This marks the opening of the hunting season and also bears on the ceremonial for the preparation of rain during the dry weather.

(3) After the fall of the first rain the rain-makers celebrate the *Netalixi fau* or cooling-earth festival. A final hunt is held, at its conclusion the rain-maker spits on the seeds for the new sowing and sends the *Monyemiji* to till his land in the different areas. The *Lamonyefok* also perform sacrifices in their hereditary land at this time.

The moons are adjusted by the wise men to fit these festivals. They may be expected to fall in the western months of October, December, and March/April respectively; the moons are given names which connect them specifically with the solar or harvest year.

	Latuka Moon		Festival	Approx. months
	Lolong	= Sun	*Nekanga*	October
	Ilefyu	= Cleaned up	..	November
	Isyar' imanyi xari	= Thirst	*Nalam*	December
Nameyu	(lit. give your uncle water)			
=	*Camidok*	= Ophthalmia	..	January
Winter	*Xiromo*	= Let them dig	..	February
	Nanyim	= Simsim }	*Netalixi fau*	March
	Nataxas	= Summer }		April
	Owas	= Grain in the ear	..	May
Nataxas	*Longorony*	= Dirty mouth	..	June
=	*Owete*	= Drying grass	..	July
Summer	*Ofilima*	= Sweet grain	..	August
	Lomomo	= Sausage tree	..	September

The moon names represent an adequate picture of the year. October ushers in the hot sun and thereafter burning starts everywhere and the land is thus cleaned up; by December all the bush water-holes have dried and the carrying of water starts. January sees the hot and dust-laden winds blowing. In February it is time to start cutting the trees for new cultivation. Some people plant simsim in March. April is the start of summer with abundant rainfall. In May the grain begins to form its ear. In June the grain stalks are pulpy enough for the children to have dirty mouths through chewing them. In July the bottom leaves of the grain and grass begin to dry off. In August

NILO-HAMITIC GROUP

the grain is red and ready for harvesting. In September the sausage-tree blossoms into fruit.

Although the pure-Latuka festivals are not found among the Lango and other tribes, the names of the moons appear to be quite universal.

Miscellaneous.

Their burial customs, fully described by Dr. Seligman (*Pagan Tribes*), are unique. A rude effigy is made round which the funeral dance is held. The actual body is buried: the effigy is taken into the bush and burned by four old men. After a period the bones are dis-interred by members of the wife's clan and preserved in an earthen pot near the village. This appears to be regarded as conducive to fertility and to prevent disease; but in view of the passage of the soul into the clan animal the process of thought underlying this custom is obscure.

No spirit shrines are made for the dead.

The brass helmets of the Latuka, with their lengthy stiff plumes of red durra bird feathers are also unique, as are their narrow body-length shields with a slit at the top for vision. Instead of brass the helmets may be of red earthenware. It is of some interest that their helmets have been much evolved since Baker's time, when the warriors wore their own hair in a piled up mass, with a brass plate in front. Broad belts of blue beads are characteristic.

There is little doubt that they were formerly pastoralists, but they have lost most of their cattle. Women may not milk and a man will not drink from a vessel into which he has milked himself.

Chickens are kept and eggs are eaten by all except women of child-bearing age.

In agriculture, the heavy work of stumping, tree-cutting is done by the men, turning the soil and weeding by the women.

Fair quantities of dukhn (bulrush millet) are grown in addition to the usual durra.

Ground-nuts are grown extensively, but sweet potatoes and cassava have so far not become popular. Cotton is a recent introduction.

As regards land tenure the emphasis seems to be on the individual rather than the group. The most important, the dry-weather cultiva-tion (*natorit*), moisture-holding land on which a dry-weather grain crop can be raised, is handed down from father to eldest son for many generations. It is said that land can be bought and sold between individuals.

Wild fruits may be gathered by any one anywhere except in the

THE LATUKA GROUP

Lafit, where there are a few *lulu* trees which mostly belong to the village and permission would have to be obtained before an outsider could pick them. A few of the larger trees are owned individually.

Water-holes have owners, generally the descendants of those who originally dug them.

They indulge in organized wrestling, the women as well as the men.

THE LANGO

Of the three components of the Lango, the Logiri and Dongotono are confined to the Dongotono Mountains. The Logir are found on the western side of the same range and all the eastern slopes of the Imatong Mountains across the valley, and extend over the crest of the mountains to Issure and Lomarite on the Opari side.

The Logir are practically indistinguishable from the Latuka proper: they are recognizable by a particular method of scarification, two heavy lines radiating backwards from the eye at a wide angle. Of the Dongotono we know practically nothing: they probably belong to a separate language group and are possibly allied with the Didinga, whose style of hairdressing they also used to use. Formerly they had a very large and heavy bow, some 7 feet long, but this seems to have disappeared.

The Logiri in many respects resemble the Latuka. They practise exhumation, but only very rarely, to give relief in difficult cases of child-birth.

Their clans have animals associated with them, which may, however, be killed and eaten by their clansmen. They have an age-class system which is, however, tribal and not local. It seems to follow the sixteen-year pattern. Entry into the warrior class is signalized by a 'running the gauntlet' ceremony. The class names show definite correspondence with those of the Didinga. They do not use the characteristic Latuka helmet.

Their chiefs have no rain-making function, and to-day they have no rain-makers in the tribe, former practitioners in old days having been killed for failure.

Unlike the Latuka, they make spirit houses for the spirits of their ancestors. These are dolmen-shaped, made of flat stones and placed just outside the door of the hut. In these are placed small offerings of beer and food. If the house is moved and rebuilt elsewhere one of the stones is removed and incorporated in the new spirit-house.

A dead branch set up and decorated with hunting trophies is also

NILO-HAMITIC GROUP

a common feature of their villages. On the mountains they have shrines at which ceremonies are held to ensure good hunting.

The Lango have not lost their cattle to the same extent as the neighbouring tribes, and a few years ago a rough census revealed 20,000 head of cattle.

Their mountains abound with running streams, and they practise irrigation, drawing the water off the streams by long and cleverly contoured irrigation channels.

The Lango women are very liable to hysteria.

LOKOIYA. (MR. BEATON)

The name Lokoiya used by the Bari and the other surrounding tribes is a 'foreign' name, their own name for themselves being Oxoriuk. This suggests a connexion with the Latuka Koriuk, but we have been able to find no evidence or belief that such a connexion exists. Their dialect is said by Dr. Tucker to be the same as that of the Lango and Lafit.

They inhabit the Ngangala–Liria Pass and the Luluba foot-hills in four villages, Liria, Langabu, Ilangari, and Ngulire, and Lueh Mountain to the east. There is also an outlying settlement round Magwe in Opari District.

They regard the northern Lafit Hills as their original home; but whether they were driven out by the Lafit, or were themselves Lafit driven out by some one else, e.g. the Anuak, is never clear. Xurla Hill between Lafon and Liria was certainly a stage in their migration. The ornaments and 'get-up' of their youths are very similar to those of Lafon. Their oldest remembered ancestor is Luruböt, who at least ten generations ago purchased Pirisak Hill from Okali of the Luluba by giving him his daughter Aito in marriage, since when the two tribes have lived in amity. Luruböt talked with God, who sent him down two rain-stones from heaven (now held by Lupiti of Ngulire). They seem to have been a warlike and truculent tribe, a menace to their other neighbours. In Baker's day they had practically driven the Bari off the east bank on to the islands; and in the early days of our occupation they came more than once into conflict with the administration.

Clan System.

Unlike the Latuka their clans are very numerous; at Ilangari, for instance, there are twenty-four. Generally each clan is confined to its own village, but a few of the more prolific ones have thrown out

LOKOIYA

colonies to other villages. The reckoning of relationship appears to be very strict. It is said that if, for instance, an Ukurcuk man marries an Ototo girl further intermarriage between their families is forbidden (but this may be another way of saying that marriage into the mother's clan is forbidden). Related clans may not apparently eat meat of another's killing. Thus if an Onyati man is marrying an Olineri girl each family gives the other a sheep, as a gift which the recipients kill and eat apart.

The clan is a territorial land-owning unit. Their land system is very similar to that of the Luluba (q.v.), except that the allocation of land is done by the rain chief and not by the *Monyekak*.

The most important are the two rain-making clans, Onyati at Ngulire and Oxoiyu at Liria. It is interesting that the Oxoiyu is equated with the Latuka Lomini clan. Both are said to be one stock from Lafit and marriage between them is forbidden.

In spite of careful inquiry no evidence can be found that the Lokoiya clans are totemic.

The Rain Chief.

The rain chief is a person of paramount importance, though how much 'executive' power he had over the clans in the old days may be doubted. The rain power is transmitted in the male line, to son, brother, or nephew. It is said that if the only possible successor is a small boy some female relative, preferably a sister, will act for him until he grows up. The new rain-maker is ceremonially installed. A dance is organized, much beer is brewed, and bulls are slain for the feast. During this celebration the spittle of the *Monyemiji*, *Oxobolo*, and *Omarwok* (warriors, elders, and old men) is collected in a gourd and smeared on the new chief's body. Rain-stones are used.[1]

Disputes are usually heard by the rain chief and the elders, but any one present has the right of speech. Blood-money is a maximum of 50 goats, but payment can be commuted by the surrender of a sister or daughter to the aggrieved clan. Destruction of a limb is assessed at proportionately lower rates. Ordeal oaths of the usual type are in vogue: if the accused after a prescribed period has escaped the consequences of his oath he can claim compensation.

---

[1] A rain-maker's skull (possibly of the grandfather of the present chief) was long ago dug up and taken to a hill called Nyemetua. Here it has been placed in a small pond formed by a spring. The place is called a 'place of God' and a goat is periodically sacrificed there.

NILO-HAMITIC GROUP

Age Grades and Age Classes.

The grades are: boys (*Okelipinok*), who tend the goats; warriors (*Monyemiji*), who hoe, build, and fight; elders (*Oxobolo*), who talk; dotards (*Omarwok*), who merely sit. Each grade has its own appropriate portion of a beast; if a boy insults his elders, his father must provide a feast of corn and beer to the offended grade. As the elder grade is thinned, new members are co-opted to it, the new entrant providing a beer party or killing a goat.

The age-class organization is highly developed. Classes seem to be formed every four or five years and the sixteen-year cycle of the Latuka has not been traced. Initiation by tooth extraction is ceremonial, each village doing its own. The extraction is done by an expert: boys and girls are done together, generally alternatively, and for boys at any rate it is a definite test of courage. Class brotherhood is an exceptionally strong tie; it is on his age fellows that a man relies in the major affairs of life. The grade will hunt as a unit. Each age grade has its own dancing kit, the higher grades wearing leopard skins and enormous head-dresses of black and white ostrich plumes. Strings of bells wound in a circle from ankle to thigh are a frequent feature and one class wears a cow bell slung on the breast.

The unmarried men sleep in special houses (*balia*) with the drums.

The Monyekak.

The chief of the land (*Oxobumiji*) performs two annual ceremonies. When the rain breaks he hoes a small patch, pours in simsim oil, and sprinkles over the ground the stomach content of a sacrificed goat, of which the old men then eat the meat. At harvest time a goat is sacrificed, and until this is done it is not lawful to reap, unless the owner cuts the corn level with the ground, instead of just below the ear as usual, so that it may not appear that reaping has been done.

Mr. Richardson mentions that the *monyekak* blesses hunting parties and gives further details of one of the fertility ceremonies. In this the *monyekak* takes the goat to a steep place about half-way up the hill and sacrifices it for the fertility of the land and the women: with the blood he smears the rock Upöni and leaves the carcass for a time in a crevice near by where lives a snake. Then the entrails and fat are left under a lower rock Ikoiyich, where also there is a snake. Descending, the *monyekak* finds all the people waiting under the tree Atoromong and smears them with the blood and stomach content. This tree is a sanctuary under which property may be left unharmed.

LOKOIYA 117

He adds that the Lueh people used to live at Liria and are still the *Komonyekak* for that place.

Birth, Marriage, and Burial.

Twins are not regarded as unlucky in themselves, but the father will kill two sheep to avert his wife's death.

The bridegroom works for the bride's family, hoeing and thatching, till the birth of the first child. Barrenness is no ground for divorce of an obedient wife; if a wife dies childless the husband cannot claim a sister in her stead, though the father-in-law might provide one instead of paying back all or part of the bride-price. Widows pass to the sons or brothers in the usual way.

Illegitimate children of unmarried girls are few because of a healthy fear of tribal disapproval, though it does not prevent young people sleeping together without full sexual intercourse. A male child so born is called *Lomiang*, a girl, *Ipuxe*, and if the parents do not marry it is referred to as 'born in the grass': and will be scorned as 'son of a whore'.

Burial is just outside the house, men on the right side, women on the left. The relatives shave their heads and cover their bodies with ashes for a month. When the corn is in the ground the mourners only weep very softly lest wind beat it down. At this period all drumming is forbidden; and even if the rain chief die only a small drum is tapped and that only three times.

Live Stock and Agriculture, Housing and Weapons.

They still have a certain number of cattle: sheep, goats, and chickens are all kept. Eggs are rarely eaten. Women do not milk: this is generally done by the boys who may drink from the udder but not from the gourd.

Clearing and hoeing out the grass, and the sowing is done by the men, cleaning and reaping by the women. Each wife has her own patch and her own grain store. Their huts are round with low eaves: each compound is enclosed by a high fence of plaited bamboo, near which urinals are made with a small channel leading under it.

They have both bows, spears, and shields; the Acholi pattern wrist knives are sometimes seen. They also have 'quarterstaves', stout staffs about 6 feet long with a hand-guard in the middle, used for defence.

NILO-HAMITIC GROUP

Religious Beliefs.

These are apparently very vague; God is the author of thunder and lightning; he made men and when he pleases kills them; but is not the object of worship. Ancestor spirits are venerated, but chiefly in time of need.

In every enclosure in Ilangari, and presumably in the other villages, are found peg shrines (*luto*, pl. *lutojin*), thin stumps projecting 2 or 3 inches above the ground, usually but not invariably arranged in groups of three. They are set at convenient distances apart so that spears and arrows may be laid on them; this is done before a hunt when the weapons are sprinkled with boiled grain to give them virtue. After the hunt the heads of animals killed are set near the pegs and cooked the next day. Groups of three sacrificial fire-stones, recalling those of the Bari, are also found dedicated to the ancestors where at harvest, grass burning, and village hunts a goat is killed and cooked.

One peg shrine seen was made—

but no explanation of the middle peg was given. In another enclosure the peg shrines were found in conjunction with the fire-stone shrine, and whereas the three fire-stones dedicated to the father were accompanied by three pegs, the mother's three stones were associated with four. These were used for sacrifices in case of sickness, for a clan sacrifice before sowing the grain, while at harvest time four heads of grain for the dead mother and three for the father were hung on the grave stakes.

The shrine illustrated by Dr. Seligman (*P.T.*, p. 344) is said not to be dedicated to any ancestor of Ilangari, but to be a place of general sacrifice at seed-time, when a goat is killed and each man takes a handful of seed which has been mixed with the dust from the shrine.

THE BARI. (MR. BEATON)

THE Bari are the largest tribe in the province, occupying both banks of the Nile Valley for 100 miles. They are additionally important because their language, and to a large extent their culture, are those not only of the Mandari to the north, who are probably cognate with them, but of a large block of tribes to the west and south-west—

THE BARI

Fajulu, Kakwa, Kuku, &c., probably of originally different stock. The Bari language or dialect is actually spoken by 37 per cent. of the total population of the province.

History.

They call themselves Bari, said to mean 'strangers', and are called Bari by all their neighbours. While there is no reasonable doubt that they were originally immigrants from the east—Dr. Seligman quotes a tradition collected by Dr. Tucker to this effect (*P.T.*, p. 239)—it is safe to say there is no general memory of this. To them Shindiru, the home of their rain-makers, is the cradle of their race.

Local histories of their sections are being published shortly by Mr. Beaton. It suffices to mention that Yoyok, the first-remembered rain-maker, is the fourteenth of his line from the present day, even if there are no gaps in the table. It may safely be said that they have been in their present position for at least 300 years and probably much longer. Yoyok received his powers of invoking rain from God in heaven (*Ngun lo ki*), who declared he was to be the lord of all rain chiefs.

There are circumstantial traditions that some generations ago the Luluba, Fajulu, and Nyangwara dwelt around Shindiru and out-numbered the Bari, who by stratagem drove them out to the hills and across the river. Thereafter attacks by the Luluba and their friends and allies the Lokoiya were frequent. Baker found the Bari practically driven off the east bank.

Father Spagnolo (*Grammar*, p. 278) records a tradition of an invasion in Pintong's time (fifth from Yoyok) of a people from the east who he thinks may have been Galla invaders. The Bari call them *Lomukudit*, 'very numerous'. Passing Ngangala, i.e. coming through the Liria Pass, they dispersed the Bari far and wide until at last Pintong rallied the Bari, defeated them and drove them back whence they came.

Sectional warfare seems to have been always common, and there is no trace of the Bari ever acting as a coherent whole.

The first Europeans who made contact with them were those of the Khedive Muhammad Ali's expedition in 1841, which Werne accompanied. To them they were extremely friendly; Werne gives a very good account of them and describes them as having a big population in numerous villages with widespread cultivation. They were in touch with the Berri or Föri of Lafon with whom friendly relations and considerable intermarriage continue to-day. It is surprising to

NILO-HAMITIC GROUP

read that Logono, the rain chief of Belinian, was dressed in a blue shirt, perhaps a sign of indirect trade contact with Abyssinia or the Zanzibar Arabs. Glass beads were also common.

The next fifty years were disastrous. The efforts of the missionaries, led by Knoblecher, were shortlived; and the slave-traders, of whom the notorious Abu Saud is still well remembered, soon followed. Their unhappy relations with Baker are well known. Under the slave-traders, the Egyptian Government, and the Dervishes they suffered not only heavy losses in cattle but radical depopulation. It is small wonder that they almost gave up the struggle with an impossible world and gained a reputation for idleness and general uselessness. In the last few years there are welcome signs that they are beginning to pick up and regain their self-respect.

The Clans.

The basis of Bari society is the clan. These were no doubt originally territorial units of which the present-day territorial sections are the relics. The clans are now dispersed; that is to say, several clans will be found in any one village. But in the village they maintain their corporate existence; and definite foci of their original distribution are still traceable.

A detailed study has been made by Mr. Beaton which can only be very cursorily summarized here. They are exceedingly numerous; he found 143 clans varying in numerical strength from 792 adult males to 1. Ninety-eight clans consist of less than twenty men. They fall into two classes, divided and undivided. Of the undivided the biggest is the Gala (386). Subdivisions are often very numerous. To take the Bekat as an example, these are divided into the Bekat, the B. Limat (the great rain clan), B. Leparan, B. Lobur, B. Lokwe, B. Malasuk, B. Manabur, B. Nyayenki, B. Romo. Rongat, Dung, Mingi (178 males in 14 sub-clans), Nyori are other examples of divided clans.

The divided clans fall into two classes; in a few—Biajin, Sera, Le, Pelenyang, and Sura, are the recorded instances—intermarriage is forbidden between the subdivisions; in the others all or most of the subdivisions may intermarry.

The causes of splitting the clan seem to be three. It might be due to mere increase of numbers at the dictate of the clan head. 'Where the father of the Clan saw their cattle growing numerous he would call all his "sons" together. To one he would say "cut the ears of your cows thus", and to another, "cut thus", until all were divided. Then

THE BARI

his sons and his sons' sons would cut their cattle thus and thus until the young men grew up who had forgotten the ancestor who thus commanded: and they would intermarry.' On such occasions topical names might be given by the clan head from incidents of the moment; such are the '*Rongat* of the snapped bow-string'; *Rongat*, 'smoothers of the bow-string'; *Rongat*, 'cutters of calves ears'; '*Rongat* at the grain store legs'.

Quarrels or hostility were another cause of division, as when Manabur in wrath at the sacrifice of his sister Juan broke away from the Bekat Limat and founded the Bekat Manabur. So a quarrel divided the Biajin. Or splitting might be due to a desire to marry relatives, or to cover such marriages as amongst the Lokwiya'ba clan. In such cases there is a 'dividing ritual', which is used not only for the deliberate splitting of the clan but for individual marriage where ignorance of clan connexions or excessive affection have led to violation of clan exogamy and an illegal and incestuous marriage which will bring sterility, disease, and death not only on the guilty couple but on the whole group. The bride's father cuts a forked stick and stands in front of his house with the husband's clan brother on his left holding a stick, and the wife's clan brother on his right holding a spear. At a signal they three times make a circuit of the house, returning to their places besides the father when they thrust their stick or spear into the thatch. After the first circuit the father says 'Peace, my sons-in-law'; and after the second 'Peace, my sons-in-law and' (to the husband) 'thou rich in cattle'. After the third circuit a female goat is placed parallel to the door with its back to it; the husband sits on its shoulder, the wife on its quarter; the wife's sister's son holds its legs, while the husband's sister's son holds its nostrils and mouth till it is suffocated. They then cut it in two, lengthwise; the husband's brothers take the left side, which they cook and eat on the spot; the wife's brothers take the right side which they take away. Each then takes his spear or stick from the thatch and they disperse to their homes.

A few of the clans have animals associated with them, usually as having befriended ancestors and so deserving special honour. Birds and trees are also similarly respected. Thus the Lot do not eat jackal flesh (though not forbidden to kill it); the Ludara have a special reverence for the dog; the Lumbari do not kill their brothers the leopards, nor do leopards kill them; should one do so accidentally it will not eat the corpse; the Moje abstain from the heart of all animals; the Moru will not kill or eat the *moru* (rat). The Kanam will not kill

122 NILO-HAMITIC GROUP

the ground hornbill which they regard as their brother; the Kariak do not kill the wagtail, and if they see another kill it demand compensation as for a brother. This in old days was paid in cattle, but now in 'white stones', as all the cattle in the area are dead. The *Kalogo* (oriole) is not killed by the Keken. The Konyum will not burn the wood of the *lukokönyumi* tree; the Dung Kaliri will not cut the *liri* tree; the Lukananok whose ancestress Kunguli is said to have descended from heaven amongst the Kuku avoid drinking water from rain-pools while it is fresh. Dr. Seligman gives other examples.

No trace whatever has been found of any belief that after death the soul passes into the animal or bird.

The Bari draw a sharp distinction between *lui*, freemen, and *dupi*, serfs, in which latter fall not only serfs proper, but blacksmiths (*tomonok ti yukit*), fishermen (*tomonok ti kare*), and hunters (*yari*). Mr. Beaton mentions ten *dupi* clans (the largest with only sixteen members), such as Gunya, a smith's clan at Belinian and Tokiman, and Bongkolong, a fisherman's clan at Uma. There are also fourteen very small clans of immigrant foreigners such as Onyati, a Lokoiya clan at Ngangala, and Ponyili, a Mandari clan at Uma.

Apart from its marriage significance the clan still remains the main feature of Bari social life. It is the owner of the land; it is with the clan mark that the ears of the cattle are cut. It retains sufficient corporate existence and sense of corporate responsibility to be made the basis of poll-tax. It is an enlarged family, affording its members comfort in trouble and help in distress. If a man is fined, his clan fellows will, if need be, subscribe to assist him in payment. They will help him in collecting the bride-price, and when he is married will turn out in a body to help in hoeing his field.

Chiefship.

The Bari draw a sharp distinction between those who have rain powers (*kör*, sing. *köntio*) and commoners who have no such powers (*bömön*, sing. *bömöntio*), and in the original Bari conception possession of rain power was essential to the chief. In one sense the great Rain Chief of Shindiru—and to a lesser degree their collaterals at Belinian and Mögiri—might be considered as paramount chiefs, not only of the Bari but of the adjacent tribes, the Mandari, Fajulu, Kakwa, by whom they are greatly reverenced. But they were not paramount in our sense; they owed their influence to, and functioned in, the spiritual sphere of magic and religion; and though they influenced temporal

THE BARI

affairs they did so from afar. To quote Mr. Beaton: 'The idea of an administrative chief is foreign to the Bari; to him the Chief is not one who bustles about collecting taxes, inciting men to more strenuous cultivation or awarding punishment for crime but a remote being approached only by the wealthy as spokesmen of the village, whose mere existence emanates fertility, who has in times of stress the rare power of combating dearth; and who might be seen at council but rarely speaking; whose rare speech is greatly to be feared; who in time of great crisis might intervene with his Iron Rod.'

In purely secular matters the clan heads had no doubt considerable local influence, and even before the coming of foreigners there appears, from the local histories, to have been a tendency for the growth of territorial groups—aided perhaps by clan dispersal—whose rulers' ancestors, though usually possessing rain powers, might have owed their influence to mere wealth or force of character. The ancestors of the Gondokoro chiefs seem to have been only commoners; while Soka of Tokiman, though he wielded an iron rod, owed his power solely to wealth of cattle. The coming of the foreigners accentuated this tendency, and with the appointment of the secular, executive chief, the Foreigners' Chief (*matat lo gela*), a new idea began to overlay the original Bari conception.

Bari chiefship was never autocratic; the ordinary affairs of life were dealt with by the council (*putet*) of old men whose experience qualified them to direct the affairs of the group or deal with individual complaints, and whose decisions were taken to the chief for corroboration. The Bari court procedure, where the litigants address the headmen, reflects this custom. A feature of the council is the 'talking stick', a special rod whose holder 'has the floor' and lays it down to be picked up by another, when he has finished his discourse. The Kakwa have the same practice.

Various oaths and ordeals are in vogue if the truth cannot otherwise be ascertained. These include swearing by the door-posts of the cattle kraal, by the roof of the house, or the head of a daughter; by jumping over a spear (the idea of only licking it is very modern); by drinking powdered ivory, scraped from a bracelet, mixed with water; to rebut a charge of murder, by drinking some of the grave dust mixed with water. This is common amongst other tribes. In a case of suspected poison, the rain chief may dip his iron bar into a mixture of flour and water and give it to the suspects to taste; or, if medicines are found with them, they may be made to drink them.

124 NILO-HAMITIC GROUP

In general the Bari seem to pride themselves on being law-abiding and respecters of the goods of others, 'unlike such pilferers as the Lokoiya.'

The Rain Chief.

The rain chief has been described in detail by Dr. Seligman (*P.T.*, pp. 248, 280, &c.); it is sufficient to say here that he operates by the manipulation and the washing of the sacred rain-stones after sacrifice. The stones are regarded as male and female; and in some cases seem to be old stone implements. He is assisted in the ceremonies by his serfs, *dupi*; between him and them there seems to be a strong mystical connexion. He does not claim to make rain of himself; his ancestors were given their power, and their rain-stones, by God, and by the virtue of his ancestors he intercedes with God to send down the blessing of rain upon his people. Evil influences may bring the sun, scorching the crops; these it is his duty to combat. In the old days as a last resort he might decree the sacrifice of a girl by burial alive; an instance has already been mentioned. In the history of the Dung Kaliri clan a double sacrifice is recorded; of a *dupiet* boy of the Logura and a free daughter of the Bekat Limat. He is rewarded by rich tribute for his ministrations but should these fail was liable to be killed. Unlike the rest of the people his hair is worn long and his teeth are not extracted. Werne specifically mentions this point in his description of Logono, the Belinian rain chief, in 1841.

Sacred spears are also used for rain making. According to Mr. Richardson's account, at Belinian they are used in the first instance; if the rain still fails the applicants return and the stone ritual is then observed. The ritual consists of the production of the spears, which are barbed, from the rain-chief's house; a sheep is sacrificed and the deputation smeared with the stomach content. The spears are very sacred; the Belinian spears were twice taken by Arabi Dafa'allah, the Dervish Emir, and twice returned owing to the misfortune they appeared to bring.

There are many minor local rain-makers, but none can compare with the rain chiefs of Shindiru of the Bekat Limat clan and to a lesser extent their cousins at Belinian and Mögiri. The ministrations of Fitia Lugör of Shindiru are in request by the Mandari and Fajulu, and probably other tribes also.

The power descends in the male line but not apparently necessarily from father to son; possession of the rain-stones is essential; but it is

THE BARI

apparently not necessary, as amongst the Latuka and Acholi, for the transmission of the powers that the mother should be of a rain-making family also.

The Earth Chief.

The 'earth chief' or *monyekak* (also known as *monyekurök*) is the functionary whose duty it is to allocate the clan land and ensure its fertility. They are essentially associated with the clan and are therefore numerous. We may suppose that there is at least one in each village. As a result they are not as a rule of any great importance outside their own community; and the *monyekak* is not the clan 'head' in such matters as rendering labour to chief or government or the collection of tax. It is probable that the *monyekak*'s clan will indicate the original clan of the locality, but owing to the possibility among the Bari of 'sales' of land by one community to another, this does not necessarily follow.

As mentioned above, the *monyekak* has the duty of allocating the clan land to the different families and individuals. Any changes in occupation are made under his auspices; he would presumably be the arbiter in any disputes which arose, and it is to him that a stranger would apply for land to cultivate.

Secondly, he performs ceremonies to ensure the fertility of the land and to bring success in hunting. At seed-time a black ram is sacrificed and eaten by the whole community, and oil is smeared on each man's breast. Similarly at harvest, where the rain chief exists, a black ram is killed, its stomach content sprinkled on all houses, trees, fields, and the men's foreheads and chests. The rain chief dips his iron bar in sesame, oil, and milk, and touches each man on the breast. Another goat is killed and eaten by the *langet* of the *monyekak*, a third is given him as a present.

At the hunting which takes place when the grass is burned the rain chief also assists, smearing the spears with ochre (from observation the Latuka have the same practice) and stroking them with the hook-like *ködipi* thorn so that they may bite home while the *monyekak* kills a red goat which is eaten by the men.

Interesting light on the *monyekak* is given in Richardson's account of Juba (*S.N.R.* xvi. 185). Originally belonging to the Nyori clan, it was sold by them to the Bekat Monabur from across the river. The Monabur finding themselves in difficulties from disease persuaded the Nyori *monyekak* to return and his sons are still with them. A rock called *Pita* is called 'grandmother' by the headman: and to another

NILO-HAMITIC GROUP

rock, *Berumi*, the *monyekak* would in times of trouble summon the people and sacrifice a bull. A darker sacrifice is still commemorated by the ebony post which marks the grave of a girl buried alive to avert disaster, no doubt by the *monyekak*'s orders.

Judging by the text given by Father Spagnolo (*Grammar*, p. 322), translated for me by Mr. Beaton, human sacrifice was also a feature of the installation of a new *monyekak*.

'When the Bari wish to choose a new *monyekak*, he should take his daughter and the daughter of his *dupiet* (serf) and a girl who is better than all her grade. Diggers are summoned: a large hole is dug in the middle of the enclosure and the earth opened wide. All the village collects and the girl is dressed in all her finery and laid in the hole which is then closed. Then a crowd collects to dance over her and they praise their chief with sweet songs.

'When they have finished he takes two bulls and kills them for the dancers. They eat them and afterwards wash their hands and assemble in one place. They then collect their spittle in a gourd and give it to one of the elders who anoints the chief's head with it and smears it over his breast and all his body down to the feet. When this unction is over they say, "This is the spittle of our village, so that you may rule over us, the followers of your father". Then they inform all the village, saying, "You know him, he is the chief, who is the Iron Bar of the village. If you see anything amiss, or death coming on our country, do you assemble by him that he may touch you with his iron bar so that death may not come on our land. If, however, you do not listen to his commands he will call down death upon us."'

The practice of such sacrifices by the rain chiefs has already been mentioned.

Age Grades and Age Classes.

The age grades amongst the Bari are:

1. *Kalipinök*, small children.
2. *Lupudyet*, youths, who tend the live stock.
3. *Teton*, the warriors, who hoe, build, hunt.
4. *Temejik*, the elders, who speak.

The grades are not distinguished by any special dress or ornaments, but when a ceremonial animal is killed each grade has its own appropriate portions.

The age classes are an important feature of Bari life. The Bari youth has two main loyalties, to his clan and to his class, and the two words most frequently on his lips are *lungaser*, my brother and *ber kwe*, my age fellows.

THE BARI

There is no regular period for initiation. As the youths grow up the matter is talked over by the elders and finally the decision is taken that the time has come for a new class to be filled. In a big well-populated village this will occur about every four years; in a small one the interval will be longer.

The class is a village concern, not a sectional or tribal one: some larger villages are in two parts, each with its own classes.

Initiation is marked by the extraction of the four lower incisors and is followed by a two months' fast. Extraction is done by the *kasayanit*, the dentist, who may be male or female and receives a fee for his services. Boys and girls have their teeth extracted together; the affianced husband pays the fee for his betrothed. On the day of extraction the Big Man of the village—or his son if he is a neophyte—names the grade unless it has already been decided in advance. It is the duty of the *matat lo ber*, the chief of the class, to feast his comrades once a year on the anniversary of the ceremony.

For two months after the ceremony the initiated youths and girls live in the household of the headman or a notable, where they dance and are feasted by their mothers who bring them corn and beer. The owner of the drum receives a fee, while the extractor is paid a further reward when the gums have healed. If there are few initiates they sleep in one house; if many, the girls sleep in one house, the boys in another. Sexual intercourse between the initiates is supposed to bring an evil influence on the class and is conventionally discouraged, though in actual fact it may take place to a certain extent, especially as many of the girls are already affianced and are merely waiting the end of the feasts before they join their husbands.

Class names may be war names, such as *Amunga*, those who hedge in their foes; cattle names, *Lomuriye*, red and white like a cow; sex-attraction names, *Dirago*, compelling the girls' glances; character names, *Losiwa*, like bees; topical names, *Ngongkure*, those who endured thirst, in a year of drought and famine.

Marriage to-day is in no way tied up with entry into the grades and there is no indication that it ever did. There are no drum-houses or sleeping barracks for the unmarried men. In the old days they slept in the sheep or cattle house; nowadays they build themselves an ordinary hut (though in a household described by Mr. Richardson there is a big hut (*balia*, cp. Lokoiya) used normally as a sleeping-place for the boys and girls below the age of puberty and at festival times as a rest-house for the guests).

128 NILO-HAMITIC GROUP

Although the old decorations and ornaments are still remembered, the old distinctive dress of the grades, so prominent a feature farther east, have entirely died out except at Belinian, Mogiri, and Ngangala, where except for a distinctive brass collar they strongly resemble those of the Lokoiya. In Mr. Beaton's words: 'The grades form an important part of Bari social life. Age fellows afford each other mutual hospitality and gather yearly to enjoy the feast given by their Grade Chief: they readily lend money, goats, weapons, or tools and in return for a brew of beer assist one another in cultivation. They help an age fellow who has been fined, give advice to a friend who is thinking of marriage and give him moral support at the *nyerja* ceremony when he goes to his father-in-law with the final instalment of the brideprice, to which, if he is a relative he will have subscribed. Finally, at feasts and festivals the village sits by age-grades and each receives its appointed share, while at the dance which follows the grade forms together and as they dance they sing their own grade songs extolling the strength of the Namuja, the bravery of the Wanyang or the fearlessness of the Despisers of death.'

The *langet* is not a class organization but a voluntary association around a chief or a rich and influential man whose war-band they would have been in the old days. At present the village or hamlet headmen look upon their village as their *langet*, while the chief regards his headmen and their people in the same way. The *langet* also exists among the Kuku.

The Servile Classes.

Mention has already been made of division of the Bari into *lui*, freemen, and *dupi*, serfs, regarded as on a lower plane and with whom the *lui* do not intermarry. The *dupiet* proper is remarkable not only for his menial position but for his mystical relation to the rain chief. He is his assistant at the rain ceremonies and helps him to manipulate the stones; he is sent out by him to perform rain ceremonies in other villages and, vide Mr. Beaton's description in *S.N.R.* xv. 84, plays an important part in the rain-maker's funeral. It is the *dupi* who dig the recessed grave; a small son of a *dupiet* is put to watch the grave for four days and nights; a *dupiet* descends sometimes into the grave to watch the body till it bursts (a relic perhaps of the time when he was buried alive with his master); as the last step in the ceremonies the *dupi* visit the grain stores and throw out of each a small portion of corn, after which and not till then the sons may take the grain for food.

THE BARI

They have an influence on fertility; there is a custom by which, if many of her children have died, a pregnant mother is put in the care of a *dupiet* until she bears a child, which, if it is a boy receives a special name, *Wari*. At Belinian a freeman whose wife or wives have died will marry a woman of the smith class so that his next free wife shall not die. Smiths (*tomonok ti yukit*), fishermen (*tomonok ti kare*), and hunters (*yari*) are also considered 'servile' and do not intermarry with freewomen.

There are 'servile' clans, but in his detailed analysis of the Bari clans Mr. Beaton only finds ten very small ones, comprising fifty-nine males; and of the ten only one, Ludiri, is a *dupi* clan proper, the others being smiths, fishermen, or hunters. The majority are presumably regarded as attached to the clan among which they live.

On the other hand, they can apparently become emancipated by absorption. Mr. Beaton quotes the case of a Makaraka *dupiet* of Fitia Lugör, the present Shindiru rain chief, who married a free-woman and whose sons are now classed as of the Bekat Limat clan. Incidentally, although foreign captives or clients occupying a sub-ordinate position are not unknown, it is interesting to find from the case above that they can be the *dupi* of a rain chief. Another case of apparent emancipation is afforded by the Lunyölu clan, who at Belinian are smiths but at Fagar certainly and at Tokiman probably are free, having presumably become emancipated by emigration.

Mr. Whitehead, who gives much information about them (*S.N.R.* xii. 1), has suggested that the *dupi* may be the representatives of an earlier stock absorbed by the Bari. Two points mentioned by Mr. Beaton bear on this. Of the small Nyongit clan, their sole representa-tive at Mögiri is the *monyekak*, who would presumably represent the oldest local clan, while at Tokiman they are all smiths. On the other hand, Dogala Gore of Mononyik tells of an ancestor of his who found a wild race, the Biajin, living in the bush and living on the milk of wild buffaloes, whom he brought back to Mononyik and civilized. But the Biajin to-day are all *lui*.

The *dupi* are confined to the Bari and the western Bari-speaking group. It is certain that nothing of the kind exists among the Latuka; they are found among the Kuku and, with their edges somewhat blurred, so to speak, amongst the Kakwa and Fajulu.

A quite different subordinate class amongst the Bari are the *pena*. These are foreigners (and probably war captives and free Bari as well) who from poverty or other misfortune have been obliged to attach

130 NILO-HAMITIC GROUP

themselves as clients to rich men, who in return for their services feed them and provide the bride-price to enable them to marry (and receive the bride-price of every daughter). They are apparently equivalent to the *Dupi Wuri* among the Fajulu and Kakwa, recorded by Mr. Giff.

Were it not for their mystical connexion with the rain-maker the Bari explanation (given by Mr. Whitehead, loc. cit.) that the *dupi* fell into their present serfdom through poverty, which obliged them to rely on their patrons for marriage cattle, that they are in fact the same as the *pena*, would appear adequate. But the Bari distinguish between the two and moreover, as Mr. Whitehead mentions, realize a physical difference between themselves and the *dupi* who are shorter and hairier; the mystic connexion is strong and needs explanation, which the *pena* theory does not afford. But there are some indications elsewhere (Kuku, Luluba) that the incoming rain-divining stock feel the need for the 'earth-powers' of the tribes whose country they over-ran and that the *monyekak* may be the representative of these latter. If that be so the association of the *dupiet* with the rain-maker may be the same phenomenon which would strengthen Mr. Whitehead's theory of an aboriginal origin. But Fitia Lugör's Makaraka *dupiet* who assists in the same ceremonies, although a comparatively recent acquisition, presents a difficulty unless the continual emancipation of the real *dupi* to which Mr. Whitehead calls attention is obliging the rain-makers to adopt *pena* in their place.

Religious Beliefs.

We owe the first coherent study of religious beliefs to Dr. Seligman's article, 'The Religion of the Pagan Tribes of the White Nile', which appeared in *Africa*, vol. iv. 1, since elaborated in his *Pagan Tribes*. *Ngun*, God, has a double aspect, *Ngun lo ki*, God in the sky, associated with the rain, and *Ngun lo kak*, God below the earth, associated with cultivation and so sometimes called *Mulökötyo lo kinyo*, the spirit of food. The conception of *Ngun* is extremely vague: he is armed with power and like the moon he comes and goes; as *Lo-ki* he created men and keeps them alive, creating a hundred every month; as *Lo-kak*, he destroys them and they die, killing a hundred every month. *Ngun lo ki* lives in the sky; the story of the rope which connected the dwell-ings of *Ngun lo ki* and *Ngun lo kak* is told by the Bari but not apparently universally.

More definite is the belief in the spirits of the dead. These are

THE BARI
131

called impartially *Mulökö, Kadudwe*, or *Nyörinyikö ti Ngun* (nephews of God), and dwell below the earth. They powerfully affect human destinies; their anger has to be appeased with sacrifices and their favour courted with gifts. Twice a year a cow or a goat is killed in the morning, and if sickness comes on the family a sacrifice is made in the morning and in the evening. If sickness is on the land or the crops, then the rain chief must appeal to his ancestral spirits to avert the doom. Twice a year in the afternoon the spirit of the grandmother, which is identified with the wagtail and a snake (*jogitat*), is honoured with a cooking of beans because she is the Mother of Food (*Ngote Kinyo*); the wagtail is never harmed and the snake is sprinkled with milk when it appears in the house.

There are no spirit-houses, but each enclosure has a set of special fire-stones (*salesi*) for the grandfather and grandmother, where the yearly sacrifices are made and cooked.

Certain trees, rocks, and streams are sacred. Mr. Richardson has described the sacred trees at Belinian, each with its own special name and its guardian, and in some cases its snake. Mr. Beaton adds that in one case the guardian is also the local *monyekak*, but that this is accidental only; *Ngun* goes from tree to tree; when he enters a particular tree the guardian is aware of it and a sacrifice must be made. The guardian prays: 'O *Ngun* of our village, forgive us our sins (of omitting sacrifice) and keep death, illness, and blight from our village.' The trees belong to the Panyigilo and Lumbari clans, and there seems to be here a suggestion of a local clan deity. The same suggestion appears in Mr. Richardson's description of the sacred rocks at Juba (*S.N.R.* xvi. 11). The rock Pita is addressed as 'Grandmother'. Close by is a small rock Kaka, said to be the daughter of Pita, the father being the big hill Kuruk which dominates Juba. Close by is another rock, Berumi, at which sacrifices were made in time of need.

The rain chief Fitia Lugör has a holy stream called Kwe, to cross which is death, and there is another called Ngungwi, north of Fajer, which holds the same taboo.

Blood-purification ceremonies vary according to whether the death was caused by accident or intentionally. In the first case the bark of the *pepe* tree (a *Bauhinia*: Spagnolo) is tied to the weapon, a spear is driven into a mahogany (*kir*) tree, and the man cleans his body with the *pepe* bark. In the latter case a red sheep is taken to a mahogany tree and killed and eaten by the old men and women of the clan, the tree is speared and the blade licked; three days later

NILO-HAMITIC GROUP

the man's head is shaved. For death in battle the same ceremony is performed.

Blood-money for a member of a rain clan originally was paid to the rain chief up to a maximum of 40 cows for death and 8 cows for wounds according to the dead man's importance. The ordinary amount for commoners is about 5 cows.

If a man's body is lost, a stone is half buried in the place his body would have occupied; while if a man revives after apparent death a sausage-tree fruit is buried in the already opened grave because a relative would die if the grave were filled in again without an occupant.

Considerably mystery attaches to the grotesque effigies figured by Junker (i. 253). He describes them (p. 496) as 'carved human figures, only met with among the Bari and tribes related to them . . . very small, barely twelve to sixteen inches high and . . . undoubtedly representations of deceased persons, "Penates" hung under the roof in memory of those who have passed away'. To-day the practice seems to have entirely disappeared and no such figures can be traced, but Werne mentions that Chief Logono and his wife brought on board a 'wooden female doll' and were apparently amused when asked if it were God.

Responsibility for death is extremely wide. If a man breaks his neck collecting honey for another, the latter must pay compensation. Not only so but if A. performs some quite trifling service for B. and dies shortly afterwards, B. may be considered responsible for his death.

From the time that the grain sprouts until harvest there is no drumming except for the funeral dance should a chief die.

Magic and Witchcraft.

Practitioners take the usual forms.

1. The *bunit* or spirit doctor, who heals bodily and spiritual ills and misfortune by treatment or suggestion and detects, by throwing the skin 'sandals' (*kamaka*) who or what is exerting an evil influence, and prescribes how it may be averted. He will apparently extract foreign bodies from the patient: in a number of instances observed he prescribed a communal meal or ceremony. Illness or misfortune may be due to the sufferer's own behaviour, to the spirits, or to malign human influence consciously or unconsciously exercised by the evil eye, the bogy, or the poisoner.

2. The *demanit* (evil eye) casts evil on man and cattle. Traditionally he should be flogged and have boiling porridge forced down his throat

THE BARI 133

and smeared over his body: the victim after his cure smeared the *demanit*'s body with his spittle to induce a better spirit. In one case the man was possessed by a wind (*wuri*) which, if he did not allow it to kill, or periodically kill a goat himself, would kill him. Possession is often susceptible to cure by modern drugs, strong purges, or other more humane methods.

3. The *rube* (bogy, for want of a better word) has a snake in his entrails, goes by night to dance or spit blood outside the house to bring death on the occupants. He may faint while doing so because his snake has gone out of him; and if so found an arrow should be thrust into his anus.

4. The poisoner (*kasumanit*) decocts poison from snakes' heads and puts it in his victims' food. Among the Kuku he (or she) is terribly feared; but among the Bari to-day little is heard of him.

Birth, Marriage, and Death.

If the birth of twins is a family trait both are preserved. Otherwise, if they are both of one sex, the elders at the father's request meet, eat a goat provided by the father, and 'will' that one of the children shall go to another place. It is left to God to choose which shall die. The reason given is that the children, after they can walk, may meet after walking round the house and argue about their parents. Naturally son favours father and daughter mother, so unless one or the other die twin males will spell the mother's death and vice versa. If the twins are one male and one female, there is no danger.

Monorchids are regarded as evil spirits who bring death to their brothers. Nowadays they are sent to the missions, formerly they were exposed. Children born with teeth are not suckled and die.

The Bari have a peculiar system of nomenclature, fully described by Mr. Beaton, by which the individual's name depends on his position in the family. Thus Kutang is a first-born son, Lado a second, Wani a third; Kinyong is a second-born whose elder brother has died. Lensuk has an elder sister, Könyi is the first son after many girls, Lukulö is posthumous; Wulang is a twin whose twin sister is called Ile. There are many variations and the same system is applied to girls.

There is also a system of 'insult names' used between friends, terms of opprobrium which if used to a stranger would provoke immediate retaliation.

When the time comes for a man to marry his age fellows assist both in choosing a suitable girl and in contributing towards the bride-price.

NILO-HAMITIC GROUP

Youth, slimness and cleanness of limb, skill in cookery and brewing beer, seem to be the chief desiderata in the girl. The parents of both sides meet to discuss and fix the bride-price, which naturally varies with the circumstances of the families: 10 cows, 60 goats, and 2 bulls seems a typical payment for a chief, 2 cows and 50 goats for a commoner. A rinderpest epidemic disorganizes marriage arrangements for years. The bride-price does not go exclusively to the father but is divided between the girl's relatives (for details *vide Pagan Tribes*). Infant betrothal is common, the bride-price being paid by instalments. Should a girl refuse a distasteful marriage—and it is becoming well known that the courts will uphold her if she does—the bride-price must be repaid: and as it has generally been used for the marriage of a son or of the father himself this leads to great difficulties. When the bridegroom-to-be takes the final instalment to his father-in-law, dancing takes place, the *nyerja* ceremony (unless the corn is sprouting when drumming is forbidden). The young wooer, unless he is very rich, is expected to work for his bride's family, hoeing, building, and thatching, so that her mother may be well disposed, and in this his age fellows will help him. Also it frequently happens that the girl will weed her fiancé's crops for some time before marriage.

The newly married will never refer to their spouse, even directly, by name, but will call them 'child of so and so'.

Avoidance of the mother-in-law is practised.

Polygyny is the ideal, but is not very common. On a detailed investigation of the whole tax-paying population, Mr. Beaton finds that 37 per cent. are unmarried, 52 per cent. have one wife, and only 11 per cent. have more than one, and of this small proportion a very large proportion must be due to the levirate.

Premarital intercourse, if there is a child, is greatly frowned on unless the couple are affianced. The seducer is expected to marry the girl, otherwise, in the old days, he would have been speared. Now he is fined. As already described, adultery is regarded as a heinous crime.

Within limits a woman can get divorce, but the bride-price must be repaid. If owing to ill treatment she has gone back to her father, repayment must await her second marriage; if she has gone to another man he must repay. But if she has borne children to her original husband in both cases the bride-price is halved.

If a wife dies childless the husband may ask, but cannot claim, another from his father-in-law at reduced bride-price, but if a young fiancée dies before marriage, a sister can be claimed instead.

THE BARI 135

When a man dies the widows are inherited by the brothers and sons. If there be only one she will go to the brother (clansman), but if they be married the 'brothers' take the elderly ones, while the younger wives go naturally to the sons and nephews and can usually exercise their choice in the matter. (For details *vide Pagan Tribes*.)

The mother's brother is a man of great importance, and the grandmother is an object of great respect in life and of veneration if not worship after death.

The burial of a rain chief has been described in detail by Mr. Beaton (*S.N.R.* xv). The part played by the *dupi* has already been mentioned. The use of a recessed grave is of some interest. Graves of this type are universal west of the Nile; to the east, as far as is at present known, the grave of the Bari rain-maker furnishes the only example of its use.

For commoners the shape of the grave nowadays varies, formerly it was round: the body is on its side with the knees bent up.

In sign of mourning all shave their heads; women and girls put ropes of palm-leaves round their arms and smear their body with ashes; the men and boys tie a rope of palm leaves round the neck. Mourning lasts for three months, when outsiders bring goats which are sacrificed (but at harvest time this is omitted); the grave is smoothed over with new earth and the signs of mourning removed (except that the tuft of hair on the widow's head is left for a year). The wives are now divided between their various inheritors.

The following is a summary of Father Spagnolo's text describing the funeral ceremonies (*Grammar*, pp. 108–11) translated by Mr. Beaton.

The dead man's head is shaved and his body anointed by an old woman; it is carried to the graveside, where the children come to have their breasts anointed with oil; the eldest son plucks a blade of grass, cuts it and throws it on the graveside crying out, 'If you have found death from another's curse, this is his blade of grass.' After the body has been placed in the grave the gravediggers kneel, three on each side, facing outwards, and push a little earth into the grave backwards with their elbows. The grave is then filled in and the earth beaten down, and a gourd of water is set on the grave in which the gravediggers wash their hands. Then they are given a goat which they kill and eat, apart, behind a tree so that the contamination of the dead may be lost in the bush. The stomach content is sprinkled over the village. The old woman is given a goat. The wife goes to a stream outside the village where another old woman shaves her head leaving only a tuft

NILO-HAMITIC GROUP

on the top. She must not touch grass. The place under a grainstore is swept clean and ashes poured on it, and for three days until the 'eating of the oil' she sits there with the small children.

After three days a mat is spread on the grave on which the children's heads are shaved by the old woman. Then the wives and children enter the house to drive out the contamination; they are bathed and anointed; sesame is ground and the oil mixed with saltless flour; they eat it with the door shut. Then the old woman enters; the eldest son holds her heel and they crawl out of the house, led by the old woman, each holding on to the one in front, the eldest son first, the last wife last. They stand up, seize corn stalks, and run three times round the house brandishing them; they then face the west and throw the stalks away. Then there is a feast and dance, and funeral songs are sung and all disperse.

After a year beer is brewed, the gravediggers assemble and scrape away the mound from the grave which is smoothed over with earth from a black ant-hill. The old woman again shaves the children's heads over the grave; the tuft of hair is shaved from the wife's head. The children drink beer kneeling on the grave and more beer is drunk by all. The elders of the family hold a council and divide up the widows and property of the dead man.

No mention is made in the above account of the notched grave stakes (*feiti*) which are erected over graves and which, according to Mr. Whitehead, are specially connected with *Ngun lo kak* (*P.T.*, p. 274). At the rain-maker's funeral, described by Mr. Beaton, there were two which were brought from the father's grave and will in due course be transferred to the son's. The small one was called the sentry, the larger was pronged, one prong being called the male and the other the female. Other examples are illustrated in *Pagan Tribes*.

Dress, Ornaments, and Weapons.

Clothes—for the men—are now becoming almost universal, but until quite recently the men went entirely naked. The distinctive ornaments of the different age classes have most unfortunately died out except at Belinian.

Young girls wear an apron of narrow iron slats or of thin chain and often a long thong hanging down behind almost to the heels. Older women wear a small fringe of cotton strings in front and, covering the buttocks, a skin apron which hangs almost to the knees; the edges are decorated with patterns of beads, most skilfully and artistically

THE BARI 137

worked. A bunch of strings made of bark is sometimes substituted for this apron. Bracelets and anklets of iron, bracelets of ivory and bead necklaces and other ornaments innumerable are worn.

Both sexes commonly have the head shaved.

'Shin-guards', narrow iron rods down the front of the shin, are often seen, apparently worn as a precaution against illness.

Red ochre is much esteemed, and bright-red girls may often be seen covered with it from head to foot.

Unlike the other Nilo-Hamites the Bari are bowmen, and their reliance on this weapon is said to have placed them at a considerable disadvantage in their encounters with the Lokoiya spearmen. They have spears of the usual types, but no shields, though Werne noticed a few small painted shields among them.

Live Stock and Agriculture.

The enormous herds of Bari cattle are described by Baker. Casati tells us that when Aloron was executed the Bari were fined 3,000 head of cattle, and even allowing for some exaggeration on the part of the early explorers the Bari herds 100 years ago must have been immense. The successive depredation of the 'Turkiya' and the Dervishes greatly depleted them; rinderpest of later years has played considerable havoc. But although south of the River Kit fly has come in and cattle can no longer be kept, the herds elsewhere are recovering fast and are now considerable.

As with all Nilo-Hamites cattle were the be-all and end-all of their existence, the sole form of wealth, never parted with, except for marriage purposes or as offerings to the rain-maker; never slaughtered except on ceremonial occasions. The refusal of the Bari to part with their cattle was one of the chief reasons for their bad relations with Baker. Times are changing and the Juba merchants no longer have to import cattle for the necessary meat supply; but the feeling remains: the boy still has his personal bull, bull songs are still composed and sung, and the custom of training the bulls' horns into fantastic shapes still lingers on.

The cattle are of a small and compact stamp.

Milking is done by both men and women, always into a gourd. In the old days it was not generally drunk fresh but stood till it soured, was made into butter, or mixed with blood. It is also pressed into soft cheese with a piston in a hollow bamboo. Cows' urine is used for scouring the vessels but is never mixed with the milk.

NILO-HAMITIC GROUP

Sheep and goats are not in the same category of value as cattle, but again are seldom slaughtered except on ceremonial occasions. Some women will not drink sheep's milk because they say it makes them sick.

Chickens and eggs are kept and eaten by the men but not by the women.

It is possible that it was only with the loss of their cattle that the Bari took seriously to agriculture; and they do not give the impression to-day of being very convinced agriculturists. The best cultivators are those on the east bank in the extreme south and there is a curious difference in the implement, for whereas those, like the Kuku, use the bent mattock (*goma*), the rest of the Bari employ the long straight hoe (*kole*), much less effective for tillage.

Cultivation is done by the men, assisted by the women. Clearing is done individually, not communally, though for help in this and other work a man looks to his age class and clan, in return for which he is expected to regale them with beer. In grain cultivation the man sows and hoes; collecting the grass, weeding, and reaping is done by the women. Each wife has her own plot and her own grainstore; a surplus may be sold, but the proceeds are not hers but her husband's.

For ground-nut cultivation the women and boys prepare the holes for the seed which the women sow. For manioc and sweet potatoes the labour is exclusively male.

Land Tenure.

All rights in the land are vested in the clan, the members of which are assigned their portion by the local *monyekak*s. The clan lands have definite and well-known limits.

If a clan has to expand it may purchase more land from a neighbouring clan. The price is usually a bull and the vendors forfeit all rights. In a case among the Mandari, whose customs are similar, the complainants were definite in their refusal to accept a bull from people who had poached on their land, in order to retain their rights. A specific case is recorded by Mr. Richardson (*S.N.R.* xvi. 2), the sale of what is now the site of Juba Town. Originally the property of the Nyori clan, it was sold by them to Logono of the Bekat Monabur from across the river. It is interesting that the Monabur, having had trouble from disease in their new site, persuaded the Nyori *monyekak* to return. His young sons were brought up in the Monabur headman's house.

Temporary cultivation rights may be acquired by payment of a

THE BARI 139

sheep, but the 'tenant' may be ousted at any time after gathering his crops. A man who elects to live in his wife's village may be allotted a plot to cultivate but can never 'own' it.

The eldest son, if his father is dead, inherits his land when he grows up—or possibly only that portion cultivated by his mother. If the clan becomes extinct in the male line the inheritance will pass to the senior *nyoringi*, sister's son, whose mother is of course married into another clan.

Grazing and watering rights inside the clan land are free to all its members; but they must not poach on the land of a neighbouring clan. Thus a river along its length will be divided between the clans on its banks. Islands are included in clan lands and fishing also must be done in home waters. For felling a tree on strangers' land, e.g. for a canoe, permission must be had. Permission must be asked before a clan may hunt over another's land, and they must give the owners a share of the meat.

There is individual ownership of ant-hills, the flying ants being considered a great delicacy, by men and women, and even after her marriage a woman keeps her ownership. It is a crime to rifle another's ant-hill; in their folk-lore the crafty *Lotole* (hare) is represented as doing so after raising a false alarm that enemies have driven off his cattle. His friends rush out to recover them and he seizes his opportunity.

THE MANDARI. (MR. BEATON)

ACCORDING to their own account the Mandari originated on the eastern bank, between the Bari and the Dinka, and subsequently crossed to the west bank, where they now spread as far as Tali. The name Shir is applicable to the northern Mandari.

The western (Tali) Mandari are sometimes said to have been reduced by the Aliab to a condition of virtual servitude until relieved of them by the new province boundary.

They claim to be indigenous and to have no relationship with the Bari, with whom they have nevertheless a strong superficial resemblance.

Their language is predominantly Bari, but has a strong admixture of non-Bari words.

Clans unlike the Bari are few and large and concentrated, not dispersed.

The elders play a prominent part in the settlement of disputes and

NILO-HAMITIC GROUP

can cause the chief to revise his judgement. The chief cannot sit in judgement without them.

The chieftainship is hereditary in the male line. He is not a rain-maker, and the Mandari 'have not got rain', resorting if necessary to the famous Bari rain-makers. There is, however, a sacred tree at Kursamba, their head-quarters, at which a rain sacrifice may be made by the elders. This tree, according to Mr. Richardson, is called Serika, is inhabited by a snake which is the *Ngun* of the Gula clan, is a sanctuary for property and the place of village councils. At it their leading chief, Lokolong Leggi, as *monyekak* holds a ceremony: standing almost in the tree-trunk he exhorts the assembled people to remember their fathers and to thank their *Ngun* for his favours. A black ram is slaughtered and left by the tree—it is not eaten—and the people plaster the trunk with simsim oil. It may not be climbed, nor its twigs broken. Lokolong Leggi, who is a twin, seems to have little or no rain power, though his ancestor, Lukaji, three generations back had the power.

The *monyekak* exists, but his functions do not appear to be very strictly defined. He conducts a special ceremony when a village is moved, smearing the fat of a sacrifice on the breasts of the men.

Age classes exist, are ceremoniously initiated by tooth extraction, the girls being done at the same time. There is no special dancing kit; and the class loyalty does not seem to be so intense as among the Bari.

The Mandari are strongly pastoral, and those of the east bank have retained their cattle more than most tribes. They still have the blood-and-milk diet. They are peculiar in that women as well as men eat eggs freely.

The west bank Mandari have lost nearly all their cattle from disease in recent years, and there are said to be numerous cases of girls remaining unmarried because no one can produce the cattle for the bride-price. On the other hand, their girls seem to be highly esteemed by the Aliab who have ample cattle and so can draw off the best of them, which may be having an adverse effect on the tribe.

In spite of their cattle, bride-price is low (but rising). The number of polygamists is very low—5 per cent. Early betrothal is exceptional and a girl may refuse a distasteful marriage. A man whose wife dies childless may require another wife—or the bride-price—from his father-in-law. The birth of a child reduces the amount of bride-price repayable (e.g. in compensation), and if two children have been born it is considered cancelled.

THE MANDARI

Adultery is regarded as shameful, as is pre-marital intercourse.

Both sexes are buried in a long grave. Grave stakes are erected and some of a man's possessions hung thereon.

Each householder makes a thanksgiving sacrifice at harvest, also on the anniversary of a man's death; otherwise there is little veneration of spirits and spirit shrines are not built.

There are but few spirit doctors and those that exist have little reputation. In old days the poisoner was speared, the Evil Eye beaten to death.

Men, women, and children eat apart. Their cultivation usages follow those of the Bari and they use the straight Bari hoe.

II. OTHER TRIBES OF EASTERN MONGALLA

THE Madi of the Opari District and the Luluba of the Central District are related to the Moru-Madi group and will be considered thereunder.

In addition there are certain exceptions to the statement that all the tribes of eastern Mongalla belong to the Nilo-Hamitic group.

These exceptions are:

1. The Didinga-Longarim of the eastern district, belonging apparently to a separate language group.
2. (*a*) The Anuak, known locally as Fari or Berri, at Lafon Hill in Latuka District, and also in Opari.
   (*b*) The Acholi of the Opari District.

Both the latter belong linguistically to the Nilotic group, i.e. are related to the Anuak, Shilluk, &c., to the north and to the Nilotic Kavirondo of Lake Victoria. The Acholi language is said (Tucker) to be much closer to Anuak than to Shilluk.

THE DIDINGA-LONGARIM[1]

THESE inhabit the hills which bear their name, and form as it were a wedge between the Toposa and the Latuka.

They speak virtually the same language as the Beir (Ajiba) of the Upper Nile Province and the Murule (Kapeta) of the Boma Plateau. From a Tirma vocabulary, compiled by Captain Whalley, it seems likely that Driberg is in error in including the Nyikoroma in the same group.

The affinities of the group have not been studied. A vocabulary and elementary grammar has been published by Driberg (*M.S.O.S.* xxxiv. 1, Berlin, 1931). A considerable number of resemblances to Bari in vocabulary are noticed by Mr. Beaton, but the structure seems generally quite different.

Driberg regards the Didinga as immigrants from the south-east, perhaps 300 years ago. They drove the Topotha off the eastern slopes of the Didinga Mountains, which they then occupied.

The Didinga and Longarim are so alike that for practical purposes they may be regarded as one tribe.

In spite of their membership of a different language group they have very numerous resemblances with the Nilo-Hamites. For instance,

[1] Taken almost entirely from Driberg, *S.N.R.* v. 4 and viii. 2

THE DIDINGA-LONGARIM 143

they are intensely devoted to their cattle—it amounts to a cattle cult—they have their favourite bulls, and use the blood-and-milk diet, using the miniature arrow to open the vein as do the Lango. The men work their hair into a 'tam o' shanter' which is decorated with feathers and beads, but go naked, while the women wear aprons and skin mantles. They do not use bows; they have the 'Acholi' type of rectangular shield. They have the age-class system, but apparently at approximately four-year intervals—not the sixteen-year cycle. In their names, the age classes show marked resemblances to those of the Logiri, and, rather similar to them, initiation is said to consist of thrashing the youths.

Their political organization is very weak: it seems certain that until recently they had no chiefs as such, though individuals might attain to temporary eminence, but that tribal guidance was in the hands of the elders.

They have exogamous clans, dispersed throughout the tribe: there are certain diet prohibitions, especially against the eating of the head and feet of animals, but there is no trace of totemism. They appear to include Topotha and Latuka elements, possibly because until recently their hills were an 'Alsatia' for outlaws from all parts.

They have only one rain-maker Alukileng, who lives in the Longarim Hills and to whom the Topotha also resort; but local ceremonies are performed by the elders in certain localities.

Infant betrothal is not practised, and the girl has considerable freedom of choice. The bridegroom-to-be must cultivate for his mother-in-law. Divorce is extremely rare, and barrenness is not a valid reason for it: if a wife dies childless, her father is expected to provide a sister in her place or return the bride-money.

Burial is performed by four men of a different clan.

They have no drums: a set which they used to have brought ill fortune and was buried in some place that has never been disclosed.

By our standards they seem to be much more musical than most other tribes, their bull songs and marching choruses being very attractive.

In the past they had a considerable reputation as truculent raiders. In consequence of their misdeeds there were two patrols against them, 1911 and 1921, the last of which led to their permanent occupation.

Lilley records a tradition that at one time the Longarim lived in the Topotha country, the Topotha living along the foot of the Lafit Hills. The Topotha, having quarrelled with the Lafit who lived on the

OTHER TRIBES OF EASTERN MONGALLA

hill-tops, attacked the Longarim and broke them up, driving them into their present hills, while one section made their way to Irenge in north-east Lafit (Irenge being the Latuka name for the Longarim). This happened some eight generations ago.

THE ANUAK

THE Berri or Fari of Lafon Hill are quite definitely Anuak from the north who came down many years ago in a series of migrations of which at least five are still remembered. The leader of the largest was Lubula, ten generations ago. They have epic memories of their fighting with the Latuka.

Northern Lafit is indicated as having possibly been an early settlement. In outward appearances their young men are so strikingly like the Lokoiya lads, with their massive brass wire armlets on the upper arm, as to suggest there might be some connexion.

The tribal structure of the Lafon people has not yet been studied. They live closely concentrated round the hill, and their chiefs and bigger men build themselves very fine huts.

They have the age-class organization, each age class being common to the whole community, apparently of the four-year and not the sixteen-year type, and many of their age-grade names are the same as these of the Lokoiya.

They say that until fairly recently they maintained communication with their kinsfolk in the north, when communications were cut by the intrusion of the Beir.

Other large colonies of the same people exist in Opari District, namely, the people of the chief Ollaiya at Panikwara, whose pedigree goes back seven generations to a leader called Mac; and those of Chief Paito, who is thirteenth in descent from Ocak and claims that they also came from the Anuak in the north via Lafon. It is perhaps legitimate to wonder if there is any connexion between the tribal name Fari and Opari the place-name.

THE ACHOLI. (*Based on* MAJOR GROVES'S *article in S.N.R.* No. ii. 3, *supplemented by* CAPT. CANN *and* MR. WINDER)[1]

PROPERLY speaking, the Acholi are not a Sudan tribe at all. The vast majority live across the frontier in Uganda and the so-called Acholi of Opari District, numbering 2,500, are in fact a mixture of many

[1] Most aspects are treated in much greater detail in *Pagan Tribes.*

THE ACHOLI

tribes, Latuka, Lokoiya, Anuak, Logiri, and include only some 700 true Acholi, outlying fringes of the tribes who used to live in the Ateppi valley but who were moved north to the foot of the hill in about 1924 for sleeping-sickness reasons. On the other hand, their neighbours have adopted their language and customs to a great extent, with the result that it is extremely difficult to be sure that any particular custom is Acholi at all.

Their language is of the Nilotic family, much closer to Anuak than to Shilluk and also closely allied to the Nilotic Kavirondo of Lake Victoria.

Our knowledge of their social structure is still very vague and many points remain to be cleared up.

Captain Cann believes their clans to be totemic, each clan having its own particular animal, but doubts whether it is believed that the clansman's spirit passes into the animal after death.

They have a well-defined system of age classes, initiated apparently at about ten-year intervals when the aspirants are about 15 years old. There thus appear to have been three fighting classes:

Up to 15 years of age, boys, uninitiated.
(1) Age 15–25. Junior class.
(2) ,, 25–35. Warrior ,,
(3) ,, 34–45. Senior ,,
   ,, 45–55. Reservists.
   ,, 55.   Old men, non-combatant.

Each class has its own 'uniform' and its own name, e.g. *Lomariang* (elephant), *Lipitiro* (bush-pig). When the time is approaching for the new class to be initiated the aspirants approach the junior class with a present of a sheep or a goat. The junior class then set upon the novices with sticks and try to chase them away; if they acquit themselves manfully they are then formally accepted without further ceremony. The classes are probably on a village basis, but this requires confirmation.

The Acholi have a considerable hierarchy of tribal functionaries whose exact functions and inter-relations are not yet clear.

1. The village headman, *wan gang*: the founder of the village, or a descendant of the founder; presumably hereditary and perhaps in reality a clan head, though this requires confirmation.

He is assisted by the *jadonga* (sing. *jadwong*), counsellors whom he consults in all matters of importance and by whom all internal affairs are dealt with without reference to the (tribal) chief (*rwot*). These *jadonga*

146 OTHER TRIBES OF EASTERN MONGALLA

are apparently hereditary and are said to average about one per twenty families, but we are still ignorant of their origins and what they really represent. The tribal chief (*rwot*) apparently has his own *jadonga* who act as his council and hear disputes, referring their decisions to him for confirmation. They evidently have a magico-religious background, as it is they who decide who the 'rain wife' is to be and their presence is necessary at rain-making and hunting ceremonies.

2. The tribal chief, *rwot*.

3. The rain chief, *won kot*.

4. The land chief, *won ngom*.

The *rwot* may and frequently does combine in his own person all these functions, but where, as sometimes happens from sleeping sickness or other reasons, a community are not living on their own ancestral ground, their own *won ngom* cannot function and they must have recourse to the real 'land-owner'. The *rwot* has his hereditary spear, *tong ker*, sometimes with a double point, recalling the double-headed spear of the Latuka rain-maker. It has highly magical properties: oaths taken on it are particularly sacred, and water in which it has been dipped may be used in ordeal.

5. The war leader, *otega*: chosen apparently by the warriors of his village or tribe for known bravery and ability to command, though the decision to take up arms rested with the *wan gang* and his council, and the *otega* had no authority to engage in battle without his permission. He commanded all the age classes and decided the place and hour of attack. The senior class formed the first line, the second was formed by the middle class led by the *otega*, who encouraged his forces by chanting verses of songs which the warriors chorused; the junior class formed the third line, while the 'reservists' guarded the village.

At village war-dances the *otega* is a conspicuous figure leading the dance in full war-finery with an enormous 'busby' of ostrich feathers.

As amongst the Latuka, the rain chief must have rain powers from both father and mother, and hence to transmit his powers, his rain wife, *dak ker*, must be the daughter of a rain-maker. Although he may have other wives, he does not marry the rain wife until after his father's death. She is nominally abducted and the bride-price is paid, subsequently, by his people.

To-day the men all have a covering of some kind. In Baker's time they wore a skin mantle slung across the shoulders, but went naked to war, painted in horizontal stripes. They worked their hair into a long tail with up-turned end, which has entirely vanished to-day.

THE ACHOLI

147

The girls in Baker's time were practically naked, as is the case to-day; a single strand of very thin chain being a common dress, in strong contrast to the Nilo-Hamites.

A feature of the village life is the *o*, the men's sitting-place, rather like a club. There may be two or more in a village, with considerable rivalry between them. There are special sleeping-huts for bachelors (*otogo*).

Infant betrothal is not generally practised; after marriage the girl spends two or three months with her people, visiting her husband in the *otogo*.

Burial is just outside the hut, men to the right, women to the left, generally in a half-sitting position, but twins are buried flat. Chiefs are buried in a tunnel, half in and half out of the hut.

Chiefs generally abstain from eating elephant-meat.

The existence of God is believed in, but he is more or less inaccessible. He is called *Lubanga*, but this is said to be a missionary introduction from Uganda, the old word being *Juok*. He created not only man, but the *Jok*, independent spirits inhabiting streams, &c. After his death a man's spirit (*tipo*) continues to frequent his old haunts, and three months after his death the *kac* is built, a platform on four uprights, at which sacrifices are made. Another form is the *abila*, a miniature hut. Malignant spirits, *cen*, may also occur if a man dies angry.

In temperament the Acholi are cheerful, vivacious, and imitative, and perhaps superficial, in very strong contrast to the other Nilotics. They enlist freely in the army and police.

In one or two details they recall the Topotha: they practise the scarring of the shoulders to denote that the spear has been blooded, and at dances I have noticed the leather guard fitting closely to the edge of the spear-head so characteristic of the Topotha. It is interesting that the Labwor as described by Mr. Wayland (*J.R.A.I.* lxi), while in dress and appearance very similar to the Karamoja, speak a language almost identical with Acholi.

III. TRIBES OF THE ABYSSINIAN FRONTIER

THE following is a summary of our somewhat scanty knowledge of the Abyssinian frontier-tribes from Lake Rudolf northward to the Boma Plateau. The information about the Marille is derived from a report by Mr. Shackleton of the Kenya Political Service, supplemented by Capt. Whalley, H.B.M. Consul, Maji. The remaining notes are derived from Capts. Whalley and King. I am much obliged to Mr. Shackleton for permission to make use of his report.

1. MARILLE

THIS tribe call themselves Dathanaich or Dathanik. By the Turkana they are called Marille; by the Boran, Gelubba; by the Abyssinians, Gelab.

They are not to be confused with the Murule of the Boma Plateau.

They are a semi-nomadic tribe, part agriculturalist, part pastoral, whose centre is the Omo delta immediately north of Lake Rudolf, inhabiting the country north and east of the lake. Their cultivation is principally in the Omo delta. In the early rains they graze their cattle over the plains north of Mount Kaiserin and sometimes as far west as Makonnen Cherosh and Moru Akippi. In 1934 there were large numbers on the Kuron delta, and in former years they are known to have raided as far as Kathangor.

They are reported by Whalley to differ considerably from their western and northern neighbours, being yellower and having sharper features. With the exception of a few borrowings their language appears quite unlike the Turkana or the Nilo-Hamitic languages. Their name for God, *Wak*, is the same as the Galla, and we may suppose that they have at any rate a considerable Galla admixture.

They are a warlike and blood-thirsty tribe who, since their acquisition of firearms, have continuously raided the Turkana. They are on good terms with the Nyangatom, their neighbours to the north.

They are divided into five sections, the Shir, Ilele, Irantale, Oro, and Nkor. The two latter are very small. The Irantale include a family of highly unpleasant witch-doctors whose head is Tapo. Ato Masai, the chief of the Ilele, appears at one time to have been regarded almost as the paramount chief of the tribe. The Shir, whose chief is Lukwaithia, are the nearest to Kenya and the largest, numbering

MARILLE 149

over 1,000 men. They have two subsections, Nkoria and Ngarich, west of the lake.

There is a sacred grove at Natade, some five hours' march east from the head of the lake.

The Shir are divided into four exogamous clans:

Turunyerim.

Farogaro.

Galbur.

Ethe.

Men and women are circumcised, the former not until quite late in life, after marriage. Fighting age classes, based on circumcision, are formed; in 1932 there were six of these classes, only two or three men of the senior class being alive, which would give a class interval of about ten years. There are also believed to be sub-classes.

Diviners are important, Thirite being the best known among the Shir. They take the omens for a raid: before the expedition sets out an ox is speared, the warriors smeared with the stomach-contents and painted with white clay.

Until their acquisition of rifles, of which they now have considerable numbers, their chief weapon was the bow, with which they used a noticeably heavy arrow with an iron head. They did not use shields.

They have a well-developed fire-cult, Lukwaithia being the hereditary dispenser for the Shir. In an epidemic or before war all fires are extinguished and relighted with fire kindled by him. Before a raid a fire is lighted through the smoke of which all the warriors must pass (cp. Topotha). In times of sickness the people run through the village with lighted brands which they then throw towards the sunset.

In the villages only Lukwaithia's fire may be used: on a journey fire may be kindled, but for this purpose the clans take seniority in the order given: thus if a Farogaro and a Galbur man are travelling together, it is the former who makes the fire.

They worship the same sky-god, *Wak*, as the Galla: if rain is wanted a sacrifice is performed at some big tree, the burial-place of one of the big men of old, and *Wak* is called on to give rain.

Twins are considered lucky. In old days the first-born son—or indeed any sons born before the father had been circumcised—were sacrificed in the *Omo*, but this practice is said to have died out.

At burial the backbone of adults is broken and the body buried in a crouched position.

The Marille have large herds of cattle. Milking, into wooden vessels,

150 TRIBES OF THE ABYSSINIAN FRONTIER

is done by the women, though away from the village a man himself may milk. Cattle are always slaughtered by spearing, never by throat-cutting, though this method is employed for goats.

Each man has his personal bull whose praises he sings and on which he relies for bravery in battle. This bull must never be allowed to die of old age but is ceremoniously speared when old age comes upon it.

They also have large herds of camels, whose milk is drunk.

2. NYANGATOM (*called Donyiro by the Turkana and Marille, Bume by the Abyssinians*)

ESTIMATED adult men, 1,000.

There is no doubt that they are a branch of the Topotha, with whom they intermarry and whose language they speak.

Four sections are reported:

Nkapun	ch. Lothienya
Ilingakol	Lotem
Nithuakol	Lokwari
Ngiribao	Lokorio (? Agofari)

Their main habitat is on the Omo and Kibish rivers between 5°16 and 5°12, where they grow large durra-crops. They have large herds which are driven in the early rains past the Tapeisi or Donyiro Mountains as far west as Moruakipi, when they visit the Toposa Magoth at Kaliba.

3. NYIKOROMA (*called Mursia by the Marille;* AUSTIN *also mentions this name which is probably the origin of 'Musha' on our maps*)

THE Tirma are also reported to be called Makurma by the Topotha, Nitirmaka by the Jiye.

The name apparently includes the tribes of Tid and Tirma: the Tid are called Dolot by the Tirma. There seems no doubt that these people are a branch of the Kichepo of the Boma Plateau whose chief is highly respected by both Tirma and Tid.

The chief of the Tirma is Losob, and of the Tid Bitor.

They are agricultural and pastoral, but not normally nomadic: they move to Simbira and Kuroni.

Judging by the vocabulary supplied by Whalley, Driberg is in error in saying that they are of Didinga stock.

Estimated adult males: Tirma, 750.

      ,,   ,,   ,,   Tid, 500.

4. KICHEPO

THEY are called Thuri by the Epeita.

They inhabit the southern portion of the main Boma Plateau, their principal village being called Bejenu south of Mount Nyelichu.

The estimated number of adult males is 750.

They are stated by the Epeita to have reached their present habitat from the north-east, comparatively recently. This is supported by their hereditary enmity with the Anuak (local names for whom are Yambo, Nyoro). The Nyikoroma (Tirma, Tid) to the south are certainly a branch of the same tribe and are stated by the Kichepo to have moved south about forty years ago. Meino, on the east of the plateau, is the name of an area formerly inhabited by them and now deserted.

They are on friendly terms with the Jiye; there appears to be little love lost between them and the Epeita. They were very friendly to Captain King when he visited them in 1934.

Captain King's Didinga policemen could not converse with them. The following is a small Tirma vocabulary, collected by Captain Whalley.

Water	*ma*	Wood	*abire*	1	*atomon*
Milk	*una*	Tree	*kazo*	2	*naman*
Fire	*ago*	Blood	*koro*	3	*dizi*
Sun	*atunu*	Eye	*kabai*	4	*wush*
Moon	*tagisa*	Nose	*girong*	5	*aiena*
Rain	*gududak*	Head	*core*	6	*ille*
Bull	*are*	Stomach	*kengo*	7	*sabai*
Cow	*ngati*	Millet	*liva*	8	*ise*
Dog	*rosa*	Meat	*aju*	9	*sakal*
Egg	*kobi*	Man	*eramai*	10	*atomon*
Honey	*crete*	Woman	*teiru*		

Their principal chief is, or was, Losanga: he was carried off to Maji by the Abyssinians in 1934. His sons are Parikaman and Mulibuthi.

The men wear their hair in rats' tails and frequently carry a long quarterstaff, some 5 feet 6 inches long.

The elders wear a big ivory bracelet on the left wrist. The women distort the lower lip, inserting a disk which may be as large as a saucer, and seemed to Captain King very self-conscious about them.

They are very good agriculturalists with abundance of durra, maize, beans, and tobacco; they make hives from tree-trunks.

5. EPEITA

A VARIANT name is Kapeita. They are called Murule by the Kichepo, the second vowel being very lightly sounded.

They inhabit the western edge of the Boma Plateau, around Mount Towoth, north of the Kichepo. Captains Whalley and King estimate them at from 400 to 700 adult males. Their principal chief (1934) is Lokerinkole, whose village is called Nugunuk.

According to Topotha accounts, when the Topotha emerged from Karamoja they found the Beir and Epeita living in the present Topotha country and drove them out. We may guess that the Longarim were driven on to their present hills at the same time. Lokerinkole stated that—possibly two generations ago—they were around Kathangor and moved thence on to the plateau, preceding the Kichepo. Until recently they were on good terms with the Jiye, but in 1933 and 1934 there were open hostilities over grazing and fishing on the Kengen.

There is no doubt that they are a part of the Beir (Ajiba) tribe; there is constant intercommunication and intermarriage. Their language, like that of the Beir, is practically identical with that of the Longarim (as compared with the related Didinga). The young men wear a similar head-dress to the Didinga, but neater and ornamented with beads. The hair is also sometimes worn felted over the nape of the neck with points at the sides.

Their round huts have a curious curved entrance-passage inside.

They are good agriculturalists and grow large crops; their stock is all kept on the plains, on the Kengen River.

They were very suspicious of Captain King in 1934, due perhaps to their hostilities with the Jiye.

IV. THE MORU-MADI GROUP

General.

THE Western or Moru-Madi group consists, on the west bank, of the following tribes: the Moru, the Avukaiya of the Meridi and Yei Districts, the so-called Kaliko of Yei District, with a few Lugbari, the bulk of whom are in Uganda. In Uganda also are the majority of the Madi, on both banks of the Nile, south of Nimule. In the Sudan the Madi of the Opari District extend the group to the east bank, while north again of them is the small and isolated Luluba tribe.

Physically, as shown in Dr. Seligman's statistics, the group has considerable homogeneity and contrasts sharply with the Nilo-Hamites, being noticeably shorter and rounder-headed. The considerable stature attributed to the Madi may be due to error.

Linguistically they are, in vocabulary at any rate, extremely similar. Madi and Moru are not mutually intelligible, but a Lugbari or Kaliko can converse with an Avukaiya with little difficulty. It is to be noticed that the Moru are sharply divided between two quite distinct language groups, the Moru Misa and kindred sections speaking a Madi dialect, while the Moru Kodo, Nyamusa, and Bite, like the Baka along the Nile–Congo Divide, belong to the same linguistic group as the Bongo. The Yei River seems to have been the boundary between these two Moru sections. In view of the tribal incoherence of the Moru it is strange that the Bongo-speaking Moru should always speak of themselves as Moru. For convenience' sake reference to the Baka will be made in this section, but linguistically they are outside the group.

Culturally they are far less homogeneous than the Nilo-Hamites, with whom, moreover, their principal characteristics are in sharp contrast. The Madi, about whom we so far know very little, appear in their general characteristics to stand somewhat outside the west-bank tribes.

To-day they are predominantly agriculturists, and are much better cultivators than the Nilo-Hamites. They are to-day in no sense pastoralists. Caution is, however, needed here; both the Moru and Baka are emphatic that in pre-Dervish and pre-Belgian days they possessed large herds of cattle, and relics of a cattle bride-price are said to survive in some of the Moru sections.

In contrast to the Nilo-Hamites the women go practically naked, with only a tiny apron or a bundle of leaves before and behind,

THE MORU-MADI GROUP

while the men cover the genitals; amongst the Moru, according to Dr. Fraser, they have always done so, and it is not the result of foreign influence. According to Dr. Seligman the men of the Madi formerly went naked.

All the west-bank tribes are bowmen: they use spears, but have never had shields. According to the Moru it was the possession of shields by the Zande which made them such formidable enemies. The Madi are said to have shields of the Acholi type.

The age-class system, so typical of the Nilo-Hamites, is entirely unknown amongst the west-bank tribes. On the other hand, the elder status has in many cases considerable importance. The Kaliko elders wear a special ivory bracelet and, according to Dr. Fraser, admission to the elder status was amongst the Moru a ceremonial affair and there were recognized heads of both elder and junior grades. Entry to the junior grade is signalized by the extraction of the four lower incisors, but this is done privately, not ceremonially. Amongst the Moru there was a period of probation before admission. The Madi, on the other hand, are said to have the age-class system.

Among the west-bank tribes none of the chiefs can trace back their pedigree for more than a very few generations. This raises a strong suspicion that the office of chief is a recent development consequent on contact with foreigners, and that formerly tribal management was in the hands of the elders. This is somewhat strengthened by the obvious anxiety of the present Moru chiefs to belittle the powers of the elders. Of the rain-making functions of the chief, there is, on the west bank, no trace at all. Rain-makers exist and among the Moru were extremely important, but the function was not exercised by the chief. The rain-making technique amongst the Moru is quite different from that of the Bari, and rain-stones are not used. The Bongo rain-stones are well known, but their kinsmen the Baka do not have them.

Here, again, the Madi afford a very sharp contrast. The Madi chief is *par excellence* the rain-maker and employs rain-stones.

They have the usual exogamous clan-system: among the Moru and Baka this is definitely totemistic, each clan having its particular animal into which the spirit of the clansman is believed to pass at death. Dr. Seligman suggests that the Madi clan-system is totemistic, but there is no indication of this in Father Molinaro's study of this tribe's beliefs.

A feature common to all west-bank tribes is that of recess burial, that is to say, at the bottom of the grave-shaft a recess is cut away

THE MORU

into which the body is placed: the recess is then partitioned off so that none of the earth with which the grave is filled can fall on the body. Alternatively a platform is made in the shaft over the body with the same object. In one form or the other this custom is practised by the Moru, Baka, Avukaiya, Kaliko, Lugbari, Madi, and, according to Dr. Evans Pritchard, by the Bongo. Moreover—and here lies a point of particular interest—it is also in use amongst the Fajulu, and is the custom for the Kuku and Bari rain-makers. Whether it is done for Kuku commoners is not clear; but the Bari commoner is buried in a different type of grave. Its association with the rain chiefs of the Kuku and Bari seems to support Dr. Seligman's theory of a western influence on the Bari.

The historical memory of these tribes is very short, partly, no doubt, owing to the disturbances to which they have been recently subjected. The Zande and Manbette expansion taxed them severely, the Zande penetrating into what is now the heart of the Moru country. The early days of the Belgian régime also had a very disintegrating effect. The pedigree of the principal Madi chief goes back many generations, and this tribe seems to have been in its present habitat for at least 200 years, and to have no recollection of having immigrated there.

The west-bank tribes have definite, if vague, memories of movement. The Moru say that they come from the south or south-east: the Avakaiya have similar ideas, while the Kaliko say they only emerged from the Congo to their present habitat comparatively recently. Thus, they all seem to have come from the Congo. Now Junker describes the home of the Amadi, with whom he clearly associates the Moru, as being in the big bend of the Welle, in which the name Amadi is shown on the present-day maps. It is at least possible that the Moru, Avukaiya, and Kaliko came to their present areas as a result of dispersion from that centre; and in this connexion it is significant that the Kaliko call themselves Madi, while the same name occurs frequently among the Moru sections.

MORU. (MR. MYNORS, DR. FRASER, MAJOR BROWN)

ALTHOUGH both sections, curiously enough, call themselves Moru with some emphasis, the Moru are sharply divided linguistically and probably racially into two distinct, mutually unintelligible, parts, with the Yei River as an approximate boundary. East of the river are the Moru proper, consisting, roughly from north to south, of the following

THE MORU-MADI GROUP

sections: Moru Kediru (Chiefs Ruba and Walla); Moru Misa (Chiefs Inderago and Agangwa); Öndri (Chiefs Wago and Ngeri) and Ögi. Closely allied to them are the Avukaiya of Meridi and Yei. The Böliba in the extreme east (Chief Jambo) are a small branch of the Öndri, the word meaning 'Easterner'.

In the following account this group are regarded as the Moru proper.

The other group consists of the Moru Kodo (Chief Madreggi of Meridi and Chief Hassan) and north of them the Nyemusa and Wira (Chief Dokolo). These are linguistically related to the Baka to the south and the Bongo to the north. Mr. Mynors, who is informed by Dr. Tucker that he finds certain resemblances between the Baka and Mangbettu languages, is convinced that the Baka came from the south-east, from south of Dungu, and suggests that they may have become separated from the Bongo by a north-westerly thrust of the Moru and Avukaiya.

In the past few years the distribution of the Moru has been com-pletely altered; they now live along the roads, instead of along the river-banks as formerly. This and still more the invasions of the last seventy years have almost completely erased any memories of the more distant past. They have no memory of any connexion with the Madi (the name occurs among them as a group-name). One very old man told Mr. Mynors that they were originally akin to the Lugbari; but he was certainly over 75 years old, and lives on the exact site of his grandfather's village, so it may be taken that they have been in their present location for at least 120 years, and probably much more.

They suffered badly during the invasions of the Zande, who penetrated beyond Amadi and are said to have killed a thousand of them, whom they penned without water on Mindri Hill near Lui. They also deported numbers, Madreggi's people in particular, into Zande country. Dislike of the Zande still continues: otherwise they are on good terms with their neighbours. The Böliba intermarry largely with their Nyangwara neighbours, as do the eastern Kediru. The Kediru (Chiefs Ruba and Kalaki) also have a curiously close con-nexion with the Mandari, even the clans appearing to be common to both. The Nyemusa are on close terms with the Jur and with the Atwot. They seem to have been always a very incoherent tribe, prone to intersectional war. There are still traces of hostility between the Moru, especially the Kediru, and the Kodo who were fighting at the beginning of our occupation. Intermarriage is more common than

THE MORU

formerly and is now practically unrestricted, except that the Kediru are rather looked down on. The Moru marry Kodo wives more often than the reverse, which is significant, and the Kodo are in general despised.

The Öndri are often referred to simply as Moru; the other sub-tribes are usually referred to by their individual names, always with the prefix 'Moru': Moru Misa, Moru Kodo. The customs described in the following pages are generally, unless otherwise specified, those of the Moru Misa.

In the Egyptian days Amadi was an important district head-quarters; they disliked the Belgian régime greatly and seem to have frequently rebelled against it.

The Chiefs.

Chiefship is now hereditary: such pedigrees as we have show a tendency for brother to succeed brother. It is said that if the heir had not attained elder grade a regent would probably be appointed who might function till he had.

None of the chiefs can trace their pedigrees back more than three or four generations, which raises the suspicion that they may owe their origins to Egyptian or Belgian appointments, and that any executive functions were in the hands of the elders whom the chiefs to-day try to belittle. The rain-maker also had very great power.

Tokporo, an uncle of Chief Hassan, was a well-known leader against the Zande and was killed by them. He was succeeded by his brother Nyare, who died about 1900 and who fought in living memory with Chiefs Waringwa, Walla, and Girima.

In former days quarrels and disputes, if not settled by violence or witchcraft, were adjudicated by some individual of repute in such matters—*vureba*, case-men, or *ta-opaba*, word-tellers—acknowledged for the wisdom of his words. Although he would take the lead, it was a family matter and any one could come and speak. The village courts are to a large extent a return to this idea.

Blood-money is commonly demanded, for a man rather less than for a woman.

The Clans.

Their system of clans is totemic, each clan having a totem animal into which the soul (*kaliba*) of the deceased passes at death. The Baka hold the same belief, but apparently no other tribe of the Moru-Madi group. Most have secondary totems (*karo*), and there are even split

THE MORU-MADI GROUP

totems where only part of the animal is taken, e.g. the neck, blood, breast, &c., It is into the principal totem animal that the soul passes at death. The sub-totem may be those which at some time befriended the family; a hartebeest, for example, covered up the tracks of a fugitive ancestor, thus effecting his escape: the hartebeest became a sub-totem. The system is extremely complex; minor totems comprise mice, lizards, small reptiles, insects.

If the friends and relations are wailing loudly at the moment the soul passes, it is believed then and there to become the clan animal which can be heard moving away; if, on the other hand, the usual dead silence is observed the soul passes quietly out and finds its own way into the totem.

The spirits (*tori*) of deceased relations may nevertheless appear in personal form in dreams. (*Kaliba* or *lendri* = the soul in the living body; *tori* = the spirit after death.)

The totem animal may be killed—though the weapon would be abandoned—but may not be eaten. There is a general prohibition against eating snakes, and if a python is killed its skin is hung on a pole and a dance performed to avert damage to the killer's crops. There is also a general prohibition on the flesh of the carnivora.

Mr. Mynors writes as follows: 'Clan totems appear to be principally of two kinds, viz. those creatures into whose forms members of the clan are believed to transmigrate at death, and those animals which are sacrosanct because of some incident in the mythical past history of the clan. The various insects and reptiles which are also called totem (*karo*) (a better translation would perhaps be 'taboo') appear to belong to the latter class, but little seemed to be understood about them, and, in general, the traditions about *karo* are little understood: in particular I found some confusion of thought on the subject of the transmigration of a soul or spirit (*lendri* or *kaliba*) into an animal after death. Accounts differ as to how this actually takes place; whether at the time of death the animal is to be seen or heard lurking near by— and it has to be reconciled with the idea that the dead shades (*lendri*) revisit us in dreams (*tori*). I think one may conclude that the idea is never developed very fully and that the general belief tends to identify the totem beast only with the vague community of "ancestors" (*diamba*), not with individuals, but how clearly the close relationship of man and animals is sometimes felt to exist is shown by the number of stories of monstrous births, of how one of twin babies has changed in a flash into a beast and run off into the bush—stories related as of happenings

THE MORU

159

in historical times or even the present day and reputed to be practically first-hand information.'

The clans are very numerous indeed, sometimes not numbering more than five or ten persons. Owing largely to foreign invasions and modern displacements they are often split, but are not dispersed, i.e. a given clan may be found in one or more places; but the inhabitants of any one locality will be in the main of one clan. The place-name is synonymous with the clan-name. They live, not in villages, but in scattered homesteads. Each clan is controlled by its own head, who retains his definite position and importance. Without his permission no outsider may cultivate ground belonging to the clan, and he is responsible for upholding the tribe customs (*labi*).

As Mr. Mynors writes: 'The clan is the basis of Moru society: a child automatically belongs to its father's clan, except in the rare case of a child born out of wedlock whose father fails to redeem it by paying the demands of the girl's father (usually half to two-thirds full bride-price) and leaves it to be brought up in the mother's family as a *labi aku* (devoid of clan customs). A woman is considered to pass into her husband's clan when she has borne him a child, whilst from that date the husband ceases to eat the totem, *karo*, of her clan: otherwise, should she die, I believe that her body is returned to her clan home for burial, but I have also heard that a childless wife of long standing and good character may ultimately come to be regarded as of the husband's clan.

'The clan appears to be one of the very few Moru institutions which survived the troubles of the days before British rule almost unharmed, although of course many of them seem to be far smaller in numbers of members than heretofore, and the present multiplicity of clans may well be explained by considering that they once did duty for a far larger total population—of course a few clans may have died out entirely. Most Moru institutions seem to be somewhat nebulous, to lack clearly defined traditions and to be capable of great local modifications, and to this rule the clan is no exception. It is primarily an abstract conception.'

Age Grades.

No age-class system exists.

Until recently the age-grade system was well marked and important. After the extraction of the teeth, done privately, there was a period of probation before entry into the junior grade, when new names were

160 THE MORU-MADI GROUP

taken by both girls and boys, the girls generally taking boys' names. Long ago there were initiation ceremonies, contests with bows and special arrows, the old men acting as umpires. At dances or in the hunt the junior grade wore special beads and feathers. The senior grade wore a strip of leopard skin round the forehead. There was definite admission into the senior grade also, a stupid or feeble man being passed over. The candidate was produced and first of all blessed by some of the old mens' grade who laid their hands on his head and stomach, and put earth on his feet, adjuring him henceforth to conduct himself suitably. The same ritual was then done by some members of the senior grade, after which there was a feast. There was also the senile grade as well. There were corresponding grades for the women.

The system remains, but with the wide dispersion of tribe as police and other Government servants it is losing its hold. Little importance attaches to the initiation ceremonies; there is a growing tendency among the young not to have their teeth extracted. The value of the grades was to make bonds of brotherhood and mutual equality between the members and to discipline the young. To-day the growing lack of discipline is often lamented by the elders. But hospitality still remains a bond, and it is difficult for one age-fellow to refuse a loan to another. Assistance in agriculture, in payment of fines, and in payment of the bride-price is still expected and the latter help is not regarded as a loan. In marriage arrangements the age-fellow is the natural go-between; and his claim to a portion of game shot by his 'brother' is never disputed.

The Rain-maker ('Böri).

Unlike the Bari rain chief, the Moru rain-maker is more a magician, and a black magician, than a 'priest'. For this reason Government influence has been against him; he now keeps in the background and his prestige is much diminished.

The Kediru have none, but obtain their ministrations from those of other sections. There are one or two among the Misa, but they are found chiefly among the Öndri, who have a rain-making clan, the Vora.

The rain ceremony is one of propitiation and averting evil influences. Rain-stones are not used: the essence of the ceremony is the sprinkling of oil and water which have been mixed in a pot. The fertility of the soil also depends on the rain-maker, who receives gifts for his services. He has assistants (*kamari*) who go round the villages

THE MORU

and officiate on his behalf. It is they who inaugurate the new dance appropriate to the particular cultivation-period.

The central idea on which his power and the fear he inspires depend is that he has the power of turning into a leopard, in which form he will wreak vengeance not only on his own enemies but for those who solicit and obtain his services. To this the alleged powers of the Madi chiefs afford a parallel. He has a spirit-house (*ramu*), a grass shelter behind his house at which he appears at new and full moon to curse his own or his clients' enemies. Anything left in the precincts is safe, no one will dare to touch it.

He is said by Dr. Fraser to have a special stool, the size of an ordinary stool with a human figure carved on the front, on which only the reigning rain-maker may sit.

His successor is chosen from among the *kamari* (assistants), and the office is therefore apparently not necessarily hereditary. A male goat is tethered in the presence of the dying rain-maker; the assistants are led up one by one and place their hands on its back; when the 'chosen one' touches it, it drops down dead, and he is then placed on the stool and blessed. This ceremony is said to have been performed in 1930.

The terror the rain-maker inspires is reflected at his burial. He is buried at night, without mourning or lamentation, in dead silence lest he turn into a leopard which will prey upon the living. At the burial the other rain-makers smear their bodies with oil or red powder to imitate leopards. A grass roof is set up over the grave, at which a great dance is held subsequently. The striking similarity of these customs with those of some Kakwa sections is noted elsewhere.

Since writing the above I am informed by Mr. Mynors that after discussion with the leading rain-makers and others, he has formed the opinion that originally rain-making was not a specialized 'profession', but was practised by the heads of households as and when required, and that the present specialists owe their pre-eminence to comparatively recent contact with the east. The Bari rain-maker, Fitia Lugör, was specifically mentioned, as was the fact that the ancestor of a present rain-maker had brought back magic spears from the Nile. This specialization is clearly focused in the Öndri, and the monopolization and its attempted extrusion provoke definite jealousy in other sections.

The following is Mr. Mynors's account of Moru rain-making.

'The Moru have commonly been described as having a system of rain-making applicable to the whole area, but on close inspection it

THE MORU-MADI GROUP

becomes apparent that practically the whole of the clans from whose members the rain-makers (*'Böri*) are drawn, are in a small area or near the River Yei in the south of the district: the clans are distinguished by the addition of the term *'Böri* to the clan name, and they are all of the Öndri subsection. One or two have settled a little way from the main body, but I discovered a very considerable latent antagonism to their activities, particularly, of course, amongst the chiefs, who violently oppose any rival to their authority. This explains much of the secretiveness of the rain-makers, for since Government chiefs were appointed, rain-making has been officially discouraged, but I have the best reasons for believing that much is also due to a fear that they may be discredited if their ritual is too closely scrutinized in the light of modern scepticism.

'In areas remote from the true home of the *'Böri* their influence is acknowledged nowadays by giving presents to their representatives when touring the country, and by waiting for the word to be given by them denoting 'officially' the change of seasons. But at the same time methods of tackling independently the evil influences which withhold the rain are found all over the country. Thus the Misa and Kediru, if rain falls, hold a big dance and sacrifice chickens under some big tree, for throughout the district—amongst Kodo and Nyamusa also—big trees are considered to be intimately connected with rain. If no rain falls, after a few days the people go *en masse* to a thicket (*koci*) and run about it crying, dancing, and beating drums to see if the rain can be aroused from there. Others also sacrifice black goats or chickens by some never-failing well. Near Chief Jambo is a wood named Woria and a special pool, Buda. According to the 'Böliba (who, although akin to the Öndri, appear to have no *'Böri* clan) a monorchid (*mulu alo*) is taken and thrown several times into water to see if he is withholding the rain. If all else fails, all the menfolk gather round some big *kileku* tree in the vicinity (it slightly resembles a plane and has very striking clusters of flowers and fruit in the autumn) and shoot at the stem with the old-fashioned arrows tipped with ebony (*pai*), the arrows being left sticking in the trunk. Refusal to join in this is considered a sign that a man wishes ill to his neighbours, and it is commonly believed that a man can hold back the rain by taking one of the large snail-shells which abound (*toslobo*), filled with rain-water, and burying it beside his hearth: formerly a man found doing this would have been killed out of hand, and the aids of divination were called in to discover who might be the culprit. It is believed that if a durra-leaf be carried from one part

THE MORU

of the country to another, no rain will fall in the place where it is thrown down unless or until it is thrown into water.

'The oldest of the *'Böri* rain-makers at present alive is an old man named Labi at Chief Wajo, now almost in his dotage, childishly proud of his pre-eminence and jealously insistent on the observance of a respect and awe which appears a little ridiculous even to some of the natives themselves. He is an impressive figure, with loud voice and flashing eyes, tall in stature and incredibly old, but his methods may be gauged when I relate that one hot afternoon I walked a mile or so with him at a brisk pace, and he, being clad as always in a long, heavy, police-pattern overcoat, began to sweat profusely, whilst I was untouched. "See", he said, "how my body turns to water, unlike yours: to-night it will rain." Heavy clouds were gathering at the time and a very light shower fell before morning. Many are the stories told about him, how he catches snakes in his hand and kills them by biting them on the back of the neck (I have never found any one who has actually seen this): how, when a road-making party cut down the big tree under which he used to live, a giant snake came every day to his new village, terrifying the inhabitants out of their lives, until Labi took it and cast it into a near-by stream. His present home is under the shade of the biggest tree in the neighbourhood.

'Labi gives the following genealogical tree:

'According to his somewhat rambling account, the family had at first no rain-powers until Ozuongo went one day to the Nile (Cupiri) to see his sister, who was married to a man there (? Bari). Ozuongo refused to accept any of the customary courtesy gifts, but finally took

5 spears and 2 knives, which he brought away home with him. One of these spears developed a habit of going about by itself, and when any one lied in a case before the rain-maker it would go to the liar's village and he would promptly fall into a sickness only to be cured when the rain-maker's assistant (*kamari*) had sacrificed a black goat on his behalf. This power of causing sickness is (or was) one of the chief attributes of the '*Böri*, but Labi's story never made clear how the rain-making properties of the spear became known. The original spear apparently returned to its donor, but the other four remained and were shared out in the family. All were lost in the confusion of the Mahdist times and the present spear (apparently only one) was made in imitation.

'This account allows for this particular clan to have found powers of rain-making, whereas by another tradition the Vora clan (who are the rain-makers *par excellence*) were the originators, and the powers have spread from it by marriage, for it is commonly believed that rain-making can descend through the female line, although there are no female '*Böri*. There are now quite a number of clans containing '*Böri*, usually closely connected, though not always, as, for instance, the '*Böri* Moresal at Sub-Chief Bili, who claims that all his ancestors were also '*Böri*, viz.:

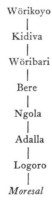

'The grave of Wöribari is still to be seen in the bush near K. Musa, that of Kidiva also is said, though no longer visible, to be at Chief Jambo, whither he had fled from invaders from the west. This clan gave up burying their dead with slab graves of Miza type because the Mahdists used to dig them up and throw the contents about. It is extremely curious that a number of '*Böri* are said to exist among the Nyangwara of Chief Soro Kenyi: an important one died there recently named

THE MORU

Jorobe, and another named Wöri Modöco at Chief Fataki, whose son is carrying on the tradition. There is a tradition amongst the Böliba that the original Vora came from the country of Pitia Lugör (Shindiru), to whom even now they owe allegiance. Lastly, one may add that the word '*böri* is apparently used in the Öndri as an adjective meaning "great, big", though I am uncertain whether there is any connexion.

'Rain-making powers are inheritable, but usually every member of a family does not inherit them: the father usually chooses his successor from among his sons, two methods being known. According to the first all the candidates place their hands ceremonially in order on a black goat, which is supposed to fall dead when the '*Böri*-to-be touches it. A better-known method is the severing of a piece of stone (*lopa*) with a blade of grass, a feat which only the destined magician can perform. Frequently the immanence of divine power is shown after (or sometimes before) this ceremony by the appearance of swelling on the body, or a kind of low sickness inexplicable on ordinary grounds. Thus also it was a portent that Ozuongo was born with a tail, and on the morning after birth was found by his mother crawling about on all fours: when she tried to flee he held her back by force and made her give him suck until, after five days, he became a normal child. Labi related with evident satisfaction that his father, uncle, and grandson were all born with teeth and embryo tails about 2 to 3 inches long—subsequently cut off for convenience. Other sons of the '*Böri* usually become assistants (*kamari*) to the new one, helping with ceremonies, taking information or orders round the country, and collecting presents on the same principles as an American racketeer.

'The installation of a new '*Böri* does not seem to be attended by any remarkable ceremonial beyond the usual gathering, speeches, and sacrifice, and though he may take his seat ceremonially on his father's stools, this does not seem to have any intrinsic value, except in so far as it is one of the family heirlooms. These stools are the old three-legged stools of cattle-owning days (also used as a headrest for their elaborate coiffures), resembling those still to be found amongst the Madi, but now almost extinct owing to the competition of the bamboo stool of Zande origin.

'Funerals were conducted in great state, at night, the other '*Böri* adorning themselves to represent leopards.

'The '*Böri* had two functions, of which only the latter remains. First, he could punish or kill people either by turning into a leopard

166 THE MORU-MADI GROUP

and attacking them, or by afflicting them with illness, and this he would do either to uphold his own prestige or at the request of a private person (presumably for reward) just like any other magician. A magic whistle (*mila*) would usually be employed for this purpose, as in the Baka *ruru*. Second, he could intercede at the public request if the Divine power withheld rain. I could obtain no single account of how this is done. Labi showed me with great secrecy some ordinary small earthenware pots lying in the shade behind his hut in disarray, and admitted that they were fairly new made as his first lot were accidentally lost in the burning of a hut in his cultivation, where they were usually kept so as to be out of harm's way, e.g. damage from children. He also produced from his hut his ceremonial spear, said to have been made to replace those lost in the Mahdia and resembling a light fish-spear with barbs on the neck of the blade and a thin iron shaft. It is called *Ngingi*. According to his account the spear is taken to a stream, rubbed with oil, and has a chicken sacrificed over it, after which it is immersed in the water: the chicken is supposed to expire in its final struggle near the person who is holding up the rain and who is thereupon sprinkled with a mixture of raw oil and pounded *kono*-creeper. On the other hand, other *'Böri* say that the spear is purely a private elaboration of Labi's family on the standard ritual which consists in putting *kono*-creeper on the neck and bathing in water: oil is used for anointing the sick and may also be mixed with water in a pot and sprinkled in the rain ceremony, but not necessarily.

'One of the chief functions at which the *'Böri* presides, and in which his authority receives its widest recognition, is the ceremonial dance which is held to denote the opening of a new season of the year. It usually begins with a gathering in the morning at which speeches are made on any subjects of particular local importance, and a dance follows in the evening, till in the early hours of the morning the *kamari* starts beating the rhythm of the new season's dance and all the people join in. News of these big dances, which used to be terrific orgies but are now shorn of much of their importance, is carried to other communities where there is no *'Böri*. When Labi presides at such a ceremony his magic spear is laid on the ground beside him.

'To sum up, one may hazard the conjecture (the evidence is insufficient for more) that the normal Moru method of rain-making was a purely local affair of propitiating some local spirit: in this they resemble their neighbours of the Bongo-Mittu group to a very large extent, who also have no rain-stones or magicians (unlike the Bongo

THE MORU 167

themselves), and one may guess that the Moru with their well-known fondness for adopting foreign customs probably adopted some of their neighbours' magical technique. The *'Böri* rain-maker has little that is peculiar in technique, but has secondary attributes as an ordinary black magician which are difficult to parallel in the locality: in any case this idea of individual power is to a great extent a foreign importation of comparatively recent date, and owes its importance to fear and blackmail rather than to admiration and respect.'

Doctors and Diviners.

The doctors (*kwoso* or *kozo*) are beneficent. They minister to bodily and spiritual ills, and their ministrations, even though sometimes fraught with harm, are in intention good. There are more women than men doctors, and generally speaking they have a common principal totem.

In contradistinction to them there are several practitioners of black magic such as the diviner or sorcerer, *odraba*, who kills by black magic or occasionally by the actual application of medicine. Similar to him is the *mböröju*, who closely resembles the Baka *ruru* in his blackmailing activities. These two are definitely feared and most antisocial, and the former at any rate not so uncommon as could be wished. The *milaba* is primarily a purveyor of charms (*mila*) for love, hunting, sickness, &c., which take the form of two little bits of wood hung on the belt or wrist, but he is also said to be able to make a whistle which has fatal powers when blown.

Individual Life.

Twins were not killed, but there is a belief that if they are of opposite sexes one will shortly die. There is evidently supposed to be a close connexion between them: if one twin has to be punished the other must be lightly chastised; if a man marries a twin he must pay a trifle towards her sister's marriage.

It is said that until recently a first-born son was often killed, from a belief that the father would not survive its adolescence.

Marriage.

Marriage must be preceded not only by payment of part of the bride-price, which is paid by instalments, but by work for the bride's people, cultivation, house-building, or looking after beehives. Complexity of relationship under the clan-system causes difficulties, and not

THE MORU-MADI GROUP

infrequently an inverted pot is seen stuck on a pole on the roof of a hut. This signifies that the blood-relationship of the couple was challenged at their marriage, but that it is agreed by all that they are not related.

After a sufficient part of the bride-price has been paid, the girl begins to visit her husband, but at first stays with him only for a night or two, and does not eat at his house. Unless she conceives, when she is handed over at once, it may be up to two years before she feels she can settle down, when she is formally handed over by a retinue of her clan.

Payment of the bride-price does not complete the husband's obligations. A present is expected from him when the first child is born, and the demands for presents and assistance continue almost indefinitely. (Apparently it is not until she has had a child that a woman is considered to have passed to her husband's clan.) The relationship of 'in-laws' (*adro*) is considered to be a very close bond.

Infant betrothal, formerly very common, is becoming rarer with the (Government) enforcement of the girl's right to refuse a distasteful marriage. In general the freedom of women in marriage matters is much greater than of old, and is in danger, in the eyes of the elders, of becoming licence. There is an unruliness amongst the girls, who do not want the laborious life of the village and wish to marry only soldiers, police, or lorry-drivers. Hence one cause of breaking betrothals made in infancy, which used to be considered disgraceful.

The inheritance of the widows is normally arranged by the dying husband. They are never passed to the brother next in age to himself. One each, never more, goes to the other brothers and the remainder, if any, to other relatives. The practice of bequeathing the youngest wife to his son is disliked. A wife he dislikes may be returned by the dying husband to her parents and the bride-price repaid.

A widow is not forced to live with the man to whom she has been bequeathed. Should she desire to make an independent choice she has her hair shaved over her husband's grave and the man she wishes to marry does likewise.

If a wife is barren or dies childless the husband has no right to demand another in her place, though in the latter case if relations between the families are friendly he might be given another girl without payment of bride-price; or part of the bride-price may be returned.

A woman with good cause may run away back to her parents and after she has done so two or three times, public opinion will give her her freedom, on return of half the bride-price. If she runs away by

THE MORU

night and is killed by a leopard or a snake half the bride-price must be returned.

For adultery in old days the man might be killed, and the abolition of this danger of sudden death is regretted as being responsible for serious laxity of morals. Similarly with pre-marital intercourse. Formerly it was practically unknown for an unmarried girl to have a child: even now it is not common. Ordinarily, if a child is born the seducer marries the girl, unless her parents oppose the marriage. If marriage does not take place he pays a fine which entitles him to take the child, which he would normally do owing to the clan-system: otherwise the child would be tainted as *labi aku*—not brought up in *labi*, custom, of its proper clan. The girl, even if there is no child, will lose in reputation, and if she has several such affairs may have to be content with a husband much her senior. One gathers, however, that before puberty eroticism by the children is little regarded.

Burial.

The grave is normally made in the middle of the homestead, and is of the recessed type. The Öndri seal the recess with stakes, and by all it is considered repugnant for earth to fall on the body except by the Kediru, who will throw earth directly on the corpse. By the Avukaiya, as the Zande, the grave is dug in an anthill. Chiefs and rich men are buried on *angaribs* wrapped in clothes or blankets; for the poor, mats will suffice. According to Major Brown, in the case of important men the body is smeared with ashes and oil and occasionally with longitudinal stripes of white ash and is kept under a shelter for two days surrounded by fires of aromatic wood. The burial position is on the right side, facing the sunrise for men, or the left side facing the sunset for women: a string (*kinju*) is tied to the little finger of the upper arm, led out through the grave and tied to a pole placed on it. This is believed to bring prosperity to the descendants. Pots and a little food are often placed in the grave; if there are no children to inherit, all the household pots will be so buried. It is a usual practice for two of the nearest relatives of the deceased, say brother and sister, to advance backwards to the grave-side and each cast three handfuls of earth on the corpse without looking at it, after which the other relatives fill in the grave. If death took place in a hut, the interior is sometimes fanned throughout with a winnowing basket (*kubi*) to ensure that the soul has found its way out.

Among the Öndri the grave is marked by a small conical mound for

THE MORU-MADI GROUP

a distinguished man with a small thatched roof over it to keep off rain. The lack of any stone monument may be due to the rarity of stone in their country, but Mr. Mynors suspects that it may be connected with rain-making. He states that he has not been able to hear of any tradition relating the origin of these graves, but it is believed that on occasion of making a new rain-maker all kinds of creatures can come pouring out of the grave of a rain-maker, the principal being white ants, for there is a relationship (not difficult to comprehend in view of the ants' habits) believed to exist between the white ant and the rain-maker.

The Misa have megalithic monuments, cairns of big fire-stones with a large slab of stone resting at forty-five degrees against it. For first-born children they make a 'cromlech', a small stone table on three or more stone supports. It has been suggested that the number of feet denotes the sex of the inmate, but neither Dr. Fraser nor Mr. Mynors can find warrant for this.

The Kediru have practically no stone, and their graves, like those of the neighbouring Mandari, are marked either by a 'wigwam' of small poles or by a tripod of three forked poles, often carved very schematically to represent a human figure. These are contributed by various relatives. Where possible, lumps of ironstone or granite are heaped over the grave.

The carved grave-post (*lusi*), specially characteristic of the Avukaiya, is invariably made by the Kodo and Nyemusa, and partially by the Ögi and the neighbouring Misa. It is very diagrammatically carved to represent the human body, and in the case of a hunter the shape of the notches show what animals he killed, square notches indicating buffalo and other game, pointed notches denoting elephant, in which case streamers of bark are usually affixed to the post. The stakes may also be fashioned to represent the horns of smaller game, two or three being erected, and the actual trophies, especially buffalo horns, will be placed round the grave of a great hunter.

On the subject of these posts Mr. Mynors gives the following information:

'One more phenomenon requiring explanation is the carved post (*lusi*) erected by the grave either with or without a heap of stones, usually with a deeply notched top. One receives a definite impression that this technique is a product of the Yei and Naam river valleys, the home of a section of the great Bongo-Mittu Group, upon whom the Moru surged up from the south. These posts seem to be found in

THE MORU

all sections of the group surviving in the locality (except the Baka who are in many respects peculiar), and one is irresistibly led to the conclusion that the technique passed from them to the Moru. At present it is found principally amongst the Ögi, who used to be in close contact with the Kodo (Bongo Group), and is only now spreading slowly in the other parts.

'The posts are of very hard wood (usually *were*) and thus last almost as long as the Miza megaliths: they often are carved on the side with patterns or crude human figures and are notched at the top with square or pointed grooves to denote the deceased's bag of the biggest game (or, if a woman, I believe it is customary to put the husband's record). Strings of *manja* fibre are attached to the post (4 for woman, 3 for man) and renewed in later years as a votive offering by members of the family, e.g. before going hunting. The Ojila practise the technique very extensively, and a small post about a foot high is often erected beside a big one, on which are poured offerings of beer or other substances. A man will tie new *manja* strings to the *lusi* holding his bow in his left hand, and a chicken is sacrificed over the piled-up weapons of the hunting party near by. Children usually have no posts. Two rude human figures are carved on the sides of the post for a woman, three for a man. The top is specially notched for a mother of many children, and I once saw a remarkable grave beside which was a tall pole and hanging from the pole were about a dozen miniature winnowing baskets, some 6 inches square. It appeared that the deceased was a woman noted for upright character and great industry and these had been offered by her friends as a tribute. Just before the post is erected it is the custom for those who have married daughters of the deceased each to shoot an arrow into the top of the post: these are left there for ever and pay silent testimony to the deceased's fertility. Sometimes the true sons may do this if there are no sons-in-law.'

As mentioned above, rain-makers are buried at night, and the same was true of particularly important chiefs. Major Brown was informed that lepers are buried away from the homestead; that no wailing or lamentation is allowed and all the village fires are extinguished.

Mourning is denoted by smearing the body with ashes for three days and, as in the case of sickness, by allowing the hair to grow long. This applies to all near relatives, even children. The head is ceremonially shaved a year later: a dance then takes place at the grave, and perhaps a grave-post or flag is erected.

THE MORU-MADI GROUP

A death is almost invariably followed by divination to discover the guilty party. A circle is made of stones, pegs, or bunches of leaves, each representing a locality—one is generally placed for 'God' also, allowing for a verdict of 'natural causes': a chicken tethered in the centre has its throat cut, the place where it collapses denoting the guilty party. For more particular inquiries resort is made to the diviner (*londriba*), who works by throwing little twigs on the ground. The guilty party discovered, the next step in the old days, if he were alive—it might be a spirit who was found responsible—would be to go and kill him; and even to-day the roots of the belief are deep in the faith of many of the old people and often throw light on motives for murder. Among the Baka much trouble is caused in this way. The *teba* or poison ordeal was formerly a very common method of dealing with suspected persons, especially women. Four beans of the *teba*-tree were administered separately with copious draughts of water: the accused either vomited up the beans with no ill effects—a sign of innocence, and the accusers had to pay a fine—or retained them and died.

If the respective families agree to make peace over a killing in a quarrel, there is a special rite. The killer is shut up alone in a hut for three days and allowed only uncooked red durra and water. He is then brought out into the midst of the people, the lethal weapon, with a piece of special wood tied to it, being placed on the ground. An animal is then killed (? with this weapon), and the relations eat together of the uncooked liver: the killer's head is shaved and his forehead marked with charcoal. Strict exogamy is henceforward observed by the two families making the pact.

Religious Beliefs.

Remote ancestors are forgotten, but the cult of those recently dead is at the very core of tribal life: their spirits (*tori*) exert a paramount influence in cultivation, hunting, &c., and must be placated. Misfortune or their appearance in dreams denotes their displeasure. The method employed is by dancing and by sacrifice over the grave; merissa beer is poured and chickens or goats sacrificed. Sometimes, for blessing a poor cultivation or when no ancestral grave is handy, little notched pegs are driven into the ground on the spot and the sacrifice made over them. For hunting, the weapons of the hunters are piled in a heap and a chicken sacrificed over them.

God (*Lu*) is the general creator of all things, lives in the earth and is

THE MORU 173

unknowable. His aid may be invoked, for instance in a search for water, by placing the juice of the wild vine-stem (*kono*) and perhaps some honey as an offering. If a man is struck by lightning but not killed, an offering of *kono*-juice and eggs is made for his recovery.

A *Lu* oracle cult is of frequent recurrence, though it is said to have first been practised only at the beginning of the Belgian régime. Some individual, with no hereditary pretensions, announces that *Lu* has come to him: a large hole is dug in the ground and covered over, leaving only a small aperture; a small hut is erected over it, and all those who make a suitable offering will hear the voice of *Lu* answering and advising them.

The practice seems quite unjustified by tradition, but some practitioners have amassed great wealth by it. It is generally directed against the chiefs and is much disliked by them.

Mr. Mynors gives the following account:

'In contrast to the vague conception of Universal Being, the Moru have very definite ideas about the influence exerted on affairs by the spirits of departed relatives. As has been mentioned in discussing totems, the exact metaphysical position of these spirits is rather vaguely conceived, but they appear to be watching every act, to be able to exert influence on material objects and to appear in dreams as a portent. When malign influence is suspected, e.g. of causing persistent illness, frequent deaths, infertility of woman or field, recourse is usually had to divination to ascertain the party responsible, or it is elucidated by the heads of the clan, or else the requisite sacrifice is offered generally to several deceased. The following description is of a fertility ceremony witnessed in Nyamusa country (Bongo-Mittu group), but several Moru who were with me stated that the ceremony was identical with that of the Moru, as, indeed, is most of their magico-religious practice.

'I was at the time engaged on a lightning trek, undertaken without warning, through country on the west bank of the River Yei, north of the Nyamusa and nominally uninhabited, though in practice the constant haunt of a number of "wild men". It was observable, as I approached this group of homesteads, that whilst most of the inhabitants began to flee in panic (expecting to be arrested), those who were engaged in the ceremony stood their ground. It appeared, on inquiry, that the local chief had been married to his second wife for about three years without having any children by her, although he had had several by his first wife. Her family cast around to see who

THE MORU-MADI GROUP

could be thus exerting evil influence upon her, and it came to mind that at her betrothal and marriage little notice had been taken of her father, who had died whilst she was in infancy: doubtless he was jealous of enforcing respect to his memory, so it was decided to hold a service of exorcism in his name.

'Before the two or three huts comprising the homestead was gathered in a small semicircle an assembly of the family and near relatives, with a handful of neighbours, squatting on the ground. Each one—the mother, uncles, aunts, cousins of the girl—arose in turn and spoke for periods ranging from three to ten minutes, lauding the present spirit of family concord, and praising the dead man and his achievements, exhorting his spirit not to injure the girl but to accept the tribute of the sacrifice about to be offered. Much of the harangue was also devoted to a long argument with one of the aunts who was said not to have had anything to do with the family for several years (i.e. she also might be ill-wishing them) and who had had to provide the fine black billy-goat which was destined for the sacrifice. An altercation developed and she finally retired in dudgeon behind the huts so that she might not see the death of her favourite goat. As each one spoke, he (or she) took hold of a half-gourd filled with *merissa* flour, a little of which he sprinkled in the air round the door of the principal hut whilst speaking, and at the conclusion of the speech rubbed a little on the back of the goat.

'When all the speakers were finished, the previous general atmosphere of lethargy disappeared. The principal uncle, owner of the homestead and head of the family, now took the half-gourd and proceeded to anoint with the *merissa* flour the breasts and insteps of all members of the family and some of the onlookers who were close friends. The rest of the audience was sprinkled lightly with the flour *en masse* (myself included), and a pot of beer passed round. Meanwhile, the girl herself, dressed in her best clothes, stood looking on and chatting to her friends a little way off: her husband should have been present and only Government business had kept him away.

'Interest now shifted to the goat which some youths were leading round and round to try to overcome the obstinate refusal it had shown for some hours to urinate. The assembly began to punch it in the ribs as it came by until at last the desired event occurred: immediately there was a wild rush to catch every drop in the cupped hand and even to scrape up the sand where a few drops had fallen. The urine was treated as the *merissa* flour, smeared on the relatives and sprinkled at

THE MORU

175

random over the crowd. The goat was then seized by four strong men, pinioned and thrown to the ground: the uncle took each member of the family in turn and bumped them solemnly three times on the flanks of the recumbent goat, the girl herself coming last, in order that the evil in them might pass into the goat. The four strong men then seized the animal, raised it three times at arms' length, to declare the ceremony to the world, and the goat was killed and cut up, to be eaten by the family.'

There are no secret societies: various attempts to introduce the *Bili* cult have not succeeded, possibly, Mr. Mynors suggests, because Moru society is essentially communal as opposed to the extremely individualistic Zande. The Zande custom of blood brotherhood is also unknown.

Festivals.

For the dead at the time of death there is three days' sitting round the grave in ashes, during which time no one enters the house. Six months later there is a big feast when the big stone slab is put in place; thereafter there are other feasts and dances at unstated intervals from one to two years.

There are minor festivals in November at the beginning of the grass-burning. Goats are sacrificed and requests made for all unfriendly spirits and other impending evils to pass on with the old year.

The rain-maker or his assistant comes once a year to minister and receive his first-fruits: this is a big celebration which may last for two or three days.

Drumming is closely connected with cultivation. The Moru have six drums: one very large, two different medium, and three different small and high pitched. Their year is divided into three periods, dry weather, sowing, and harvest: each period has its own particular dance and restrictions as to the drums which may be used in it. In the dry-weather period one medium and two small drums are used: and the dance is called *ruma*, the name of the second drum (though the Misa and Kediru, who do not commonly use this drum but play the big *diy'e*, call their dance *mure*).

In the second period all the drums are used and the dance is called *di-ago*, ancestors, a significant name. The dance of the third period is called *nyolu*. Each dance is differentiated by special steps and special rhythm.

Amongst those who have no rain-makers, especially the Kediru, the

THE MORU-MADI GROUP

moment for the change is decreed by some elder. Where there is a rain-making clan, such as the Vora of the Moru Öndri, the change used to be the occasion for a tremendous festival and dance, people coming from near and far. Early in the morning, about 4 a.m., the rain-maker's assistant who was leading the song would change the tempo to that of the new period, all the people following his lead. With the declining importance of the rain-maker this is being virtually abandoned, people merely awaiting the rain-maker's decree.

The fact that the large number of drums is used during the ripening period, presumably when the favourable influence of the ancestors is particularly necessary, is in striking contrast to the practice of the eastern tribes, amongst whom at this period any drumming is taboo.

The narrow tube-shaped drum found amongst the Madi which is beaten by women is unknown here, and as a rule it is considered very shocking for a woman to beat a drum.

The Rainbow.

The rainbow is believed to be the belched-forth breath of a gigantic python which lives under the ground. To be caught in its path is one of the worst of omens, and if it is pointed at the offending hand will be smitten with leprosy.

Land-Tenure.

There is no private 'ownership' of land: the land belongs to the clan, and one of its members may cultivate anywhere he wishes on the clan land providing he does not encroach on any one else. He might also occasionally be allowed to cultivate on his mother's clan's land. The head of the clan (*bödriba*) is the authority, and can forbid cultivation or occupation of specified areas, and a stranger can only cultivate with his permission. The clan boundaries are known to every one. The streams also belong to the clan, and permission would have to be obtained before strangers could water cattle or draw water. Similarly trees, fruits, roots, and firewood could not be gathered or cut from another clan's land without permission, but there would be no question of payment. Cattle similarly must only be grazed in the clan territory.

As there is a superfluity of land compared with the population disputes seldom or never occur.

The individual merely has the usage of the plots he cultivates. If he abandons them, e.g. to change his cultivation, they revert to the clan and anything left growing on them may be taken by any

THE MORU

one in the clan. When he dies, his widows, if they marry his brothers, as is normal, continue to cultivate their old plots; but a widow returning to her own people or marrying outside her husband's clan may take half the contents of her grain-store with her unless she has children, when all must be left behind. The same thing applies to a wife who is divorced. An elder son can claim the whole of the land cultivated by his dead father (subject, presumably, to the rights of the widows). If the man dies childless the land will be taken by the nearest male relative, the father, if alive, having the prior claim.

Economic Life.

Live Stock. Though practically no cattle are now left it seems certain that they originally existed all over the Moru district, even among the Baka. Traces of a cattle bride-price are said still to survive among the Moru. Amongst the Misa, where the caves and fissures of the Odo Hills afforded hiding, a large number survived the Zande, Egyptians and Dervishes, but insurgence against the Belgians brought about practical extermination, and to-day only the Kilaba, Gölia, and Moröliba clans—who submitted to the Belgians—possess them. There is also a small herd at Chief Walla's. Owing to the intervening fly-belts the introduction of new stock is most difficult.

Milking (of cattle) might not be done by women of child-bearing age, though young girls and old women might do it. Now it is done by the men only. For the milking the cow is put in a 'pen' (*abari*) consisting merely of four posts: its head is then loosely bound in the crutch of another forked post.

Goat-houses are often raised on legs, a hollow segment of tree-trunk serving as a ladder. The buying and selling of goats is a complicated business. If a male is exchanged for a female, the male may be eaten; but the female and all its offspring except the first young female remain the property of the seller. The same thing applies to a female bought for money.

Chickens are kept and eaten, but no one except very old men and women eat eggs. The exception is that a young child must eat the yolk of an egg before it is allowed to drink water and thereafter occasionally for a year or two.

Agriculture. When ground has to be cleared the man puts in a few days' initial work, then collects his neighbours, whom he feeds, to help him.

His fields are apportioned amongst his wives, whom he assists in

THE MORU-MADI GROUP

rotation. He does the initial tilling and sowing, the women the cleaning. Each wife is responsible for her own plot, and nothing is more certain to bring a wife into disrepute with the community than a badly kept field. Each woman has her own grain store, but she may not dispose of the produce without her husband's consent.

The long-handled straight hoe (*kebu*) is the only tool used.

There is much neighbourliness in lending a helping hand if a man is ill. Working for money is a new thing and a few are doing it, but it is not popular.

Iron-working and smelting was formerly a very important industry: some of the old iron-workings were quite deep and had branching passages at the bottom. Smelting has now entirely died out, but the blacksmith (*tokaba*) remains an important person. He is frequently a Moru Kodo: the profession is not specially related to any particular totem group.

The Moru are skilful bee-keepers: they remove the comb from the hive at night with the aid of smoke without destroying or driving out the swarm.

A common industry is the extraction of a saline solution from the ashes of certain grasses and reeds.

Great ingenuity is shown in the construction of children's toys: humming-tops, rattles, toy guns shooting a grass stalk, imitation motor-cars and aeroplanes, hoops.

They are musical and have a number of harps and lyres of different kinds, even cut out of durra stalks.

According to Mr. Mynors: 'Whistles are still much used by herd-boys and also in hunting, where the "Cekuze" (Tesiku K.) both summons the hunters and announces on their return what luck they have had, playing a different tune according to the animal killed. Every man, also, has a special private call which he gives on his pipe to make himself known to his family or friends when approaching the village or passing through thick bush. Similar to this is the *ciri*, a peculiar cry or call, sometimes peculiar to an individual, sometimes passed from father to son: it enables discrimination to be made between friend and foe, and is used as a call for help when lost in the bush. It is kept a jealously guarded secret from strangers: sometimes its use may be a matter of life and death, and use is never made of it lightly— indeed many people are utterly refused to reveal their *ciri* to me, apparently for that reason.

'No one can be long in Moru country without realizing that the

THE MORU

Moru are great singers, for not merely do they sing to themselves as they walk along the road, or nowadays play incessantly the little metal harp (*kudi*) which has replaced the spear as a vital item of luggage—to the great disgust of the elders—but in every village the shrill voices of women and children are to be heard, singing as they sway mechanically back and forth over the grindstone, grinding simsim oil or flour for the daily meal. In the centre of every dance is to be found the *longgoba*, or song leader, a position of eminence much prized: the tunes appear to be more or less traditional but the songs are always new—topical and personal, related to the events of the moment, and responsible for many a quarrel. It is remarkable that there are virtually no traditional songs at all (except for a few which are used in games), while to sing a démodé song even of this year's date is as bad as playing an out-of-date foxtrot.'

Dress, Ornaments, and Weapons.

The typical tribal marking is the 'feathered arrow' on the sides of the forehead.

The men cover the genitals: this is apparently not a modern fashion but has always been the practice.

Young girls wear a fringe apron of cotton string stained with brown clay from a belt of bright-coloured beads. This is a modern fashion: formerly they wore a string of goats' hoofs till adolescence, than beads and bells. A bunch of nuts is now sometimes worn in place of the fringe. Older women wear a bunch of leaves in front and behind.

The bow is the typical Moru weapon: it is very stiff and a special type of hand-guard is used to draw it. They have never had shields, and in their fighting with the Zande regarded the shields of the latter as a most unfair advantage.

Hunting and Village Life.

Fully to appreciate the life of the Moru, writes Mr. Mynors, one must take account of their intense love of hunting, which occupies so much of their time and energy, to a varying extent in different parts of the country, but often treated as of equal importance with agriculture. In the east, where the soil is light and sandy and the annual rainfall somewhat uncertain, the Kediru have few root crops and plant mainly a shallow-rooting, quick-maturing grain, which may be harvested in November and December: they then abandon themselves to hunting (and dancing) for a clear space of nearly five months.

THE MORU-MADI GROUP

This country is mostly covered with thorny scrub, with numerous flat, grassy plains (*toic*): elephants were formerly to be found but now the game is mostly small. It follows, therefore, that the people are bowmen and the spear practically unknown—although they constantly suffer from its absence when attacked by leopards or other infuriated animals. The hunt is conducted usually in large drives, without the use of nets. The Kediru are also very devoted to fishing, and during the dry season the whole village will often move *en masse* to sit for days beside their chosen pool in the river Tapari, or its tributaries, which they systematically fish with spears or with two kinds of basket-work trap: such fish as they cannot eat on the spot are smoke-dried and taken home, and the pool is usually thoroughly cleaned out. The central part of the country invites somewhat different treatment, for the country is on the whole more thickly wooded, elephants are not uncommon and the rivers are larger, often with perennial flow, harbouring hippopotamus and more difficult to fish: for this purpose poison may be spread on the surface of pool (usually one which blinds the fish) or traps placed where the water flows in narrow channels or cascades. The spear is more often to be seen and nets are sometimes used as an aid when a game drive is being made. To the west the country becomes very thickly wooded, so that the bow is almost entirely replaced by the spear or only a compact type with short, light arrows is used. Hunting parties cover small areas only at a time, and nets have to be extensively used as the thick cover greatly aids the animals in their flight. Hunting goes on desultorily over a large part of the year and parties following elephants may be absent from home for months on end during the dry season. But there is little worry over the question of food supply, for they have good root crops and a heavy yielding grain.

Generally speaking, hunts are of two kinds, a drive throughout the bush towards a line of armed men—often assisted by nets blocking clear passages through the bush—which is known as *fafa*; or a general drive (resembling 'walking up' in England), which is known as *mara* and is the more common because it requires the least preparation. The hunts do not usually set out till the sun is high in the heavens, for the common course is to follow up the track of some beast returning from water to the thick cover where it proposes to spend the day, and there surround it. In a *mara* bows and arrows are usually employed —but in a *fafa* the spear almost exclusively, for there is some danger at such close quarters of shooting into the line of hunters: when such

THE MORU

181

an accident happens—as it does not infrequently owing to an animal passing through the line, there is usually no question of compensation or punishment provided that there is no suspicion of foul play. In both these kinds of hunt, passers-by or strangers unknown to the organizer may usually join at will, when they hear the drum announcing it—beaten as for death, viz. *bilibilibilibili-bilibilibilibili* &c., a double beat four times repeated.

There is also a third type of hunt, known as *lendi*: this word appears to designate in its original meaning the low-lying swampy plains covered with rank grass sometimes to a height of 8 or 9 feet, which are such a feature of all parts of the country. These remain green longer than the surrounding country, and when the bush is burnt off great care is taken to leave these open spaces intact. Each one is claimed by some individual as his perquisite and he arranges his own party of hunters for the time when he proposes to set fire to the grass, having due regard to any recent fires in the vicinity which might affect the amount of game seeking refuge in his *lendi*—as yet untouched sanctuary. Hence arises the secondary meaning of *lendi*, viz. fire circle: in pre-Government days these grassy plains were always fired all round simultaneously (this practice was also followed in firing the ordinary bush, whenever possible), with the result that none of the game escaped and sometimes whole herds of elephants would be trapped. To increase the effect, especially against elephants, it appears that some sort of 'bomb' made of the oil of the wild aromatic sesame (*kino*) was ignited in the middle of the grass. Firing thus in a circle is theoretically forbidden, but a *lendi* is still the chief event in the hunting world: special preparation is usually made, only unseasoned *lidi* (broth) is eaten by the hunters, who sleep outside their huts (to avert evil?) and any stranger who ventured to join the hunt uninvited would find himself very unpopular.

Magic, of course, plays a considerable part in hunting. Charms are provided by the Milaba to avert ill luck (these can be used as whistles to attract the game). Sacrifice is offered to the spirits of the departed, usually by piling the weapons of the hunters in a heap over which a chicken is sacrificed by the Kamari, if present, or else by the chief wife of the organizer, in which case it is usually done at the door of her hut, probably at the foot of the *paranda* (*kataka* K.) if any. This is a small well-branched sapling, usually about the height of a man, set in the ground near a hut: on it are placed the skull and/or horns of all animals killed—perhaps sometimes even snake skins. This kind of

THE MORU-MADI GROUP

shrine is commonest amongst the Avukaia and Baka, but is also found amongst the Moru of all parts. Usually the *paranda* is taken at the beginning of each hunting season and burned together with its crop of skulls, no other firewood being used. It was commonly believed that it was necessary to obtain special magic before elephants would be killed, and sometimes also other of the larger beasts, such as buffalo. The magic used to be confined to a few families, but everybody now-adays thinks that they have it: it usually takes the form of concoction of one of the many bulbous herbs in the bush, which is either swallowed or externally applied. After the killing of a carnivore (man, lion, leopard) the blood shed can be expiated by tying a piece of *manja* bark to the bow—this led to the identification of a murderer in 1931. When a leopard is killed its skin is usually kept inside a hut for a con-siderable period, as much as a year, and is then ceremonially exposed, this being the occasion for a big dance which usually degenerates into an orgy, lasting for some days.

Various myths and stories are current. The *ogidango* is a mysterious animal like an enormous cow, white on one side, red on the other, which appears in the mist rising off the river: it joins a herd of cattle and causes them to stampede, whilst a human being who sees it will surely die. Far more circumstantial is the account of the *ndilu*, a creature which figures in more than one story of suspiciously non-Moru appearance, but which seems actually to have appeared in the flesh within living memory. In bulk equal to the hippopotamus, though different in shape, it had the form of a lion and caused great havoc amongst both herds and men, for it would penetrate into villages without fear and devour the inhabitants. It appears that this creature is not unique but a species, for they are said to have appeared at in-tervals, coming up out of the thick forest to the south. The last to appear was in the time of the Belgian occupation and it was killed with a gun by a certain *'Böri* named Lebari Abdalla who died at Chief Ngegi's village as recently as 1928. Can one suppose it was just a large man-eating lion? On a different level are the tales of an animal, to which nevertheless some mystery attaches, which appears to be some sort of forest hog or red hog, judging from the solitary skin which I have seen. It is known variously as *ngöröngöro* (Miza), *manyisili* (Ondri), or *kidimbi* (Ojila) and is described as having a long snout, dropping ears, tusks protruding, oily skin, and extremely bad temper: it lives in the bamboo groves on the hills and feeds on roots, and is apparently to be found mostly to the south-west, towards the Olo Hills, but only

THE MORU

a handful of Moru seems ever actually to have seen it and it is but rarely caught in traps.

Miscellaneous.

The Moru hut is small, round, and almost hermetically sealed. Thatching is of the ridged type.

Men and women never eat together: the boys feed with the father, the girls with the mother. After years of married life the first wife may eat near her husband, but never with him.

THE KALIKO (MAJOR GRAY)

THIS tribe call themselves Madi; Kaliko appears to be a foreign name, probably Zande, connoting 'wild man'. They inhabit the high country south of Yei. They are shown in Junker's map rather south of this, on the upper waters of the Kibali, and the Yei Kaliko say that they only moved into their present area comparatively recently.

They are generally on good terms with their neighbours. They formerly fought with the western Kakwa, and say that they were attacked by the Mangbettu at Belgian instigation. They were mercilessly ravaged by the Egyptian Government.

The Kaliko and Avukaiya scar their foreheads with four rows of horizontal dots, the Lugbari with three. This is also highly characteristic of the Fajulu and Niangwara, but is not practised by Bari or Moru. The characteristic tribal marking of the latter is a 'feathered arrow' outside each eye.

They appear to have the usual clan system, but no details are known. They state that their clans are not totemistic. There are certain general food taboos, snakes, frogs, and the carnivora being forbidden.

They are emphatic that they have no rain-makers, having no need of them. The existence of the *monyekak* has not been traced; but there is a planting ceremony at which the feathers of a sacrificed chicken are planted in the ground, probably by the local head of the clan.

There are no age classes, but considerable emphasis on the elders (*Baka*) grade: elders wear the iron or ivory bracelet and do not have to render labour to the chief. Tooth extraction, performed privately, is a preliminary to entrance into the junior grade: the elders are said to instruct the juniors in their duties. Disputes are settled by the chief sitting with his elders.

184 THE MORU-MADI GROUP

There is a dependent class called *Batonge*, 'strangers', Kaliko who through poverty have had to become the clients of wealthier men in other sections. There are also the *Okwako*, 'bachelors', men who through physical appearance or deformity have failed to obtain wives and are attached to their married relations in a menial position.

Burial is in a recessed grave inside the hut which is kept in repair. Offerings of beer are placed in it and drunk by the relatives the following day.

Formerly they were cattle-owners on a large scale, but owing to the depredations of the Egyptian Government there are now very few. Junker describes an expedition which took 4,000 head from them. Milking is normally done only by the men, preferably by men of the *Baka* grade. Sheep and goats' milk is not drunk by the women, who also may not eat their flesh, nor eggs.

THE AVUKAIYA (MAJOR GRAY)

THIS tribe inhabits part of the Maridi and Yei Districts. They are divided into two distinct sections, the Avukaiya Azila and the Avukaiya Ajiga. The former are mostly in the Sudan; most of the Ajiga are in the Belgian Congo near Dungu. They are shown in Junker's map in approximately their present positions.

Their language strongly resembles that of the Moru-Misa, by whom they can be understood with little difficulty.

They have no age classes, but age grades exist. They state that their clans are not totemistic.

They have no rain-makers in the Bari sense, but there are individuals who may be accused of withholding the rain and who are then tied up till it comes.

It is regarded as important that twins should eat together, and that food should be given not to one but to both.

Burial is in an ant-heap in the 'platform' variant of the recessed grave: a notched grave stake (*lishi*) is erected over the grave and arrows are shot into it by the relatives (cp. Evans Pritchard's description of Bongo burials quoted by Seligman, *Pagan Tribes*).

God, *Ovaré*, has two aspects; *ovaré*, beneficent and *ovaré-onjé*, malignant: offerings of beer and fowls are made to *Ovaré* at seed-time, harvest, and for blessing the hunting-nets. But caution is needed here; as in Moru *Ovore* means simply 'luck'.

THE MORU-MADI GROUP

THE BAKA (MAJOR BROWN, MAJOR GRAY)

LINGUISTICALLY at any rate the Baka are outside the Moru-Madi group, their language being closely allied to that of the Moru Kodo and Bongo, but owing to their close geographical and cultural relationship with their Madi-speaking neighbours a reference to them is convenient here.

They inhabit a strip of country along the Nile Congo watershed and are divided between the Meridi and Yei Districts. They are shown in Junker's map in very much their present position. Their original home may have been towards Mvolo; but they were much worried by the Zande, who are said to have eaten all the brothers of Balali, Chief Senambia's father, and a large section seems to have been driven into the Congo near Dungu whence they were again driven north to their present position.

Their clans have animals associated with them, and it is practically certain that these are totems and that the spirit of the deceased is believed to pass into the animal at death. Sub-totems appear to exist: thus for the Dobo clan the warina, lizard, eland, and kite may not be killed; and if a warina is accidentally killed the head must be shaved—the usual sign of mourning. Other Maridi clans are the Modu (bustard), Miri (cobra), Marakaiya (fish). In the Yei District the chiefly clan are the Kungu.

Chiefship is hereditary: cases are heard by the chief with his counsellors: in Maridi it is said that the chief's senior wife hears petty cases. In the old days if murder was committed a girl had to be handed over in restitution.

They have private rain-makers called *Gi-ini* who bring the rain by burying some roots in an earthenware bowl under a *solo* tree and then blowing upon wooden whistles: they can also stop excessive rain by passing a torch of old thatching grass round the bowl. They know of the Bongo rain-stones, but do not use stones themselves. If the rains do not come the *Gi-ini* are liable to be tied up and ducked until they do.

The function of *monyekak* (*nkana*) is known and is generally exercised by the chief, who in Maridi District performs a fertility ceremony by placing branches of the *solo* tree on the different plots.

Twins must be punished together and if girls must be married at the same time.

A recessed grave is used, surmounted by a cairn of stones.

186   THE MORU-MADI GROUP

Planting and harvest ceremonies are recorded in the Yei District. At seed-time grass cups of durra porridge are carried round in a procession headed by the chief who places a cup on each plot as an offering to the ancestral spirits (*Lomé*): at harvest he similarly sprinkles beer as a thank-offering.

Cultivation is semi-communal in that though the families have individual plots they are all in the same cleared area. They are apportioned by the *nkana*.

They formerly had large numbers of cattle but now have none at all.

They eat both eggs and chickens.

If dogged by misfortune small round huts are constructed, *nichilomé*, in which offerings are placed, subsequently consumed by the family's maternal uncle or nephew.

THE MADI

THE Madi of the Opari District are so mixed that it is extremely difficult to be certain which of their practices are indigenous and which are acquired. They can only be studied properly in Uganda. Many of our so-called Madi are Fajulu or Kakwa: while they have for a long time been exposed to Acholi influence and seem to have borrowed a number of their customs.

I am indebted to Mgr. Zambonardi for calling my attention to a valuable study of Madi beliefs by Father Molinaro, published in *La Nigrizia*, 1927, of which the following is a précis:

The Madi word for God is *Ori*; he is regarded as the creator, without body, all present, all knowing, but not interesting himself greatly in human affairs. He lives in the sky, where also man dwelt when he was created. At some time a man and a woman were for some offence expelled from heaven to earth in a shower of rain (or some say that they fell down accidentally) and increased and multiplied. The celestials afterwards made a rope of cows' hide by which communication was kept up, each side going from time to time to dance with the others, until the hyena bit through the rope. The men thereafter tried to reach the sky by building a tower of bamboo, but after they had built it very high it collapsed.

The word *Ori* is also used as meaning spirit. When a man dies his spirit hangs about the house until the *abila* is built, a miniature grass hut just outside the door of the house for the spirit to live in: sacrifices

THE MADI

187

are made for it from time to time. If a man dies at a distance the medicine man (*ojoggo*) performs a ceremony to induce it to come and enter the *abila*.

In the spirit life two stages are distinguished.

In the first, as long as the spirit is remembered and mentioned and receives sacrifices it lives in the *abila*: the sum total of spirits in this condition are called *ba-bu-garee*. Sometimes, in the case of very distinguished people, the *abila* is rebuilt with flat stones which, when the village is moved, the people will take with them.

The second stage is when the *abila* has been allowed to fall down, sacrifices are no longer made and the spirit is forgotten. These spirits then go out into the forest where they shelter in certain sacred bushes which may not be touched or cut.

Other forms of spirits are the *Ei-ori* or *Ero-ori*, the domestic *lares*. One lives under the eaves of the house in a shelter made of cane, over which water is poured to promote the health of the children. Or instead of the cane, a certain climber (*aseleu*) may be planted. The other resides in a pot which is kept under the granary.

No Madi will eat or drink anything without throwing on the ground a little for the spirits.

In the case of a quarrel, an offering may be made to the *Ero-ori*.

If a man accidentally or purposely kills one of his own people, he has to pay a number of animals as compensation. A white animal is then driven round the culprit several times and then thrown, when he and his kindred have to kick it with the right foot. After it is killed some of the blood is smeared on their forehead and chest, and a piece of the skin placed on their feet. The carcass is not eaten.

When a village is moved the chief first sacrifices a goat and a chicken on the new site.

The chief (*opi*), who is assisted by the elders (*amba*), is regarded as the father of his people and has very great powers and is greatly feared. He has a special spirit, the *opi-ori*, to which his great prestige is due because he can send it to bring harm or illness to those who have displeased him. If a man does not own such a spirit by inheritance he may buy one. Each chief's spirit is called by its own particular name. The most famous is *Orio* belonging to Chief Onzi of Paratzele in Uganda, which has sometimes been seen in the form of a serpent with a human head: it also acted as an oracle.

Towards the end of the harvest, a special hunting sacrifice is made by the chief. Notice is sent out in advance, and on the appointed day

THE MORU-MADI GROUP

every one must stay in their villages and no work must be done. A goat is sacrificed on the sacred stone which stands at the entrance to the chief's village, and after a few days there is a communal hunt in which all take part.

Rain sacrifices are made in the Rudu, the sacred grove, where chiefs and very distinguished men are buried. An altar (*kidori*), a flat stone supported on six or ten small piles of stones, is built over the tomb; all present are first sprinkled with water into which the chief has spat; a bull is then speared and blood sprinkled on the *kidori*, and the chief invokes the spirits of the ancestors to help them with rain. The flesh of the bull is cooked and eaten.

They believe in a future life, but not in punishment or reward.

If a man falls ill, and the cause cannot be otherwise traced, he is invited to confess his misdeeds and to make compensation to any one he has wronged.

Spells are made by killing a snake, lizard, or toad and throwing it into house, cattle enclosure, or granary.

It is always hoped that the first-born child will be a daughter.

Twins are not well looked on: they are called *Leju* or *Rubanga*. *Rubanga* is one of the *ori* that presides over reproduction; but in this case the word means 'mysterious, marvellous', and at times of disaster the cause may be placed by the witch-doctor on a twin who should be killed.

A child is given two names, one the name chosen by the mother, the other picked by lot from the many names suggested by the relatives.

THE LULUBA (MR. BEATON)

THE Luluba, called by the Lokoiya Ondoe, inhabit the hills of the same name south of Liria. Their language is in vocabulary very similar to Madi. According to tradition they dwelt originally in the plains near Shindiru, were driven out by the Bari, and took to their present hills about twelve generations ago; and later, possibly 120 years ago, welcomed an immigration of Fajulu from Lukulu in the Yei River District and owing to their possession of rain powers accepted them as their chiefs.

The main indigenous clan is the Kokajin. The Fajulu chiefly clan is the Korsak. There are five clans of Bari origin, two of Lokoiya, one of Latuka, and six others which are presumably also aboriginal.

The chief is a rain chief and owns rain-stones; there is a *monyekak*

THE LULUBA

(*osivori*) of the presumably indigenous Okure clan who performs a fertility ceremony by sprinkling a little sesame oil on the ground; also a *monye mere*, father of the hill, who ceremonially reaps a few heads before harvesting is permitted and also takes the lead in firing the grass.

Disputes are settled by the chief and elders in council; every one has a right of free speech except the *opi*, a servile class said to be of the same descent as the *dupi*: they are nowadays mostly working on their own. The smiths are also a despised caste—and the only people who may eat baboons.

In former days a girl had to be handed over as blood-price for a murder.

There is an age-class system, the names corresponding closely to those of the Lokoiya. Unmarried youths live by classes in separate houses.

Twins were not killed, but a goat was sacrificed to preserve the mother's life.

The bridegroom is expected to work each year for his relations-in-law until the first child is born.

Burial is in a small round grave, just outside the hut, in the embryonic position. The following points were noted at the burial of a male child about 10 years old.

The grave was dug by the clansmen; the body anointed with oil and lying on a bull skin was revolved three times over the mouth of the grave before being lowered, with the object of averting the return of death to the household. After the senior clansmen present had thrown a handful of earth on to the body six men filled in the grave. A circular mound was raised over it on which a gourd of water was placed, in which those concerned with the actual interment washed their hands and legs. The six men who had worked on the grave then smashed under foot two *Ioruco* fruit (a green runner rather like a cucumber) and standing in pairs back to back round the grave, each man anointed his navel and the small of his back with the seeds. The object of this ceremony was to avert the contamination of the dead.

Lamentation of the wildest kind then broke out in the immediate family. When this had quietened down a drum was produced on which the senior clansman beat gently six slow, three quick, and again six slow beats and then put it back in the mother's hut. Twice a clansman brought a spear from his house and brandished it in anger over the grave.

190   THE MORU-MADI GROUP

On the following evening a goat would be killed and eaten and a little beer drunk.

The mother and immediate relatives will shave their heads and smear them with ashes for two or three months, but the clan will do this for a month only.

Ancestor worship is practised spasmodically generally only in times of misfortune. There are no spirit houses.

Milking is done by young boys, never by women: the milker must not drink from the vessel himself.

The hills have a big industry in the manufacture of *pulala* (red ochre.)

The Luluba had the reputation of being truculent and formidable fighters. They were armed with shield and spears as well as bows. Even to-day strangers are somewhat chary of venturing into their hills.

Land Tenure.

The ownership of the land is vested in the clan; the clan land has well-defined and well-known boundaries, generally natural features, but stones are used if these are missing. There are land-owning and non-land-owning clans. The arrangement and division of the land as between land-owning clans is in the hands of the *Osivori* (*monyekak*). Thus if a village moves to a new site it is his duty to divide the new area among the land-owning clans; but he cannot allot even new lands to a non-land-owning clan, and once that primary division has been made the disposal of land to individuals inside the clan and the admission of strangers is entirely in the hands of the clan head without reference to the *monyekak*, except in his own clan where these functions are performed by him. It is to be noted that not every land-owning clan has a *monyekak*; and that the *monyekak* of a new village continues to exercise his functions in the new site even though it could in no way be regarded as originally his.

Once the individual clansman has received his plot it remains his and his sons' until the male issue dies out, when the son of the senior clanswoman would be likely to inherit it.

As usual each wife has her own portion of her husband's area; if he dies her inheritor inherits her portion with her. A male child on reaching manhood inherits his mother's plot only, unless he at that moment or later inherits an ex-wife of his father.

Should a man be dissatisfied with his land, or should his plot become too small for his many wives, he may acquire additional land, if avail-

THE LULUBA

able, from the clan head, otherwise he must either move off into un-owned bush or purchase a portion from a neighbouring clan. For a goat he would acquire a portion ample to support a woman and her children. This wife will have her home built on this plot and not in her husband's old enclosure.

An immigrant stranger would apply to the clan head of some one he knows in the village, particularly of his *mananye* (mother's brother). If he intends to settle down permanently he will buy a plot of land for a cow; if only a temporary resident he will be given hoeing rights with-out charge, though he will probably make a gift to the clan head.

Clan ownership includes wood-cutting, fruit-gathering, grazing, watering, and hunting, but unless there is ill feeling a certain latitude is allowed, providing stock do no damage to crops and the clan head receives the right foreleg of any game killed on his land by outsiders.

V. BARI-SPEAKING WEST BANK GROUP

THIS group consists of the Nyangwara, Fajulu, Kakwa, Kuku, and Nyefu. The Liggi mentioned by Emin and Junker have become scattered and assimilated with the Kakwa, Fajulu, and Nyangwara and have lost their tribal identity.

The group presents special problems. Unlike the other groups its tribes have quite definite memories of movement. It seems quite certain that they have moved up from the Nile Valley, probably in the order given above originally, though there was later overlapping.

All speak Bari dialects and are mutually intelligible. In varying degrees they all exhibit elements of Bari culture, weakest in the Nyangwara, increasing progressively through the Fajulu and Kakwa to the Kuku.

Physically, according to Dr. Seligman's figures, they occupy an intermediate position between the tall, long-headed Nilo-Hamites and the shorter, rounder-headed Moru-Madi, and in the following particulars approximate rather to the latter.

1. The typical women's dress of bunches of leaves which is completely foreign to the Bari and the east bank tribes. The men of the Fajulu and Nyangwara cover the genitals: to judge from Junker they have always done so and it is not merely a modern borrowing. The Kuku men, on the other hand, until recently went naked.

2. The absence of the age-class system which is such a definite feature of the Nilo-Hamites.

3. Amongst the Nyangwara, Fajulu, and Kakwa the roles of the chief, rain-maker, and *monyekak* are quite different from those of the Bari. The rain-maker exists; but he is not the chief. The chief is generally the descendant of an original migration leader: he is frequently styled *monyekak*, but has no fertility functions or powers. The Kuku, however, are typically Bari in this respect, their chiefs being rain-makers *par excellence*.

4. In common with the Moru, Avukaiya, &c., they all (except the Nyangwara) use the recessed type of grave, which is not used east of the Nile except, oddly enough, for the Bari rain-maker.

5. The striking similarity between the burial of the Kakwa and Moru rain-makers. The Moru custom of tying a string to the finger of the corpse and leading it out of the grave is also practised in certain circumstances by the Kakwa.

BARI-SPEAKING WEST BANK GROUP 193

These resemblances might be due to borrowing or actual fusion between the two groups. But taken together they seem too strong to be accounted for by borrowing; and the possibility that they have been caused by the amalgamation of the two groups is strengthened by the strong suspicion that amongst the Kuku the *monyekak* clans represent a pre-existing Madi population which was absorbed by incoming Bari speakers, the present Kasura clans who have the rain. It is also curious that while amongst the Kakwa most of the rain-makers use the Bari rain-stone technique, there are clans and groups, e.g. the Böri, who have a completely different ritual.

There is a third possibility also. Bari tradition is definite that formerly the Fajulu and Luluba dwelt together around Shindiru among the Bari, and that when, about twelve generations ago, the Bari drove them out the Luluba fled to their present hills while the Fajulu moved across the river. The Nyangwara and Fajulu have vague traditions that the Luluba are their brothers. But the Luluba are a Moru-Madi speaking tribe and it seems permissible to suggest, very tentatively, the hypothesis that the Nyangwara and some of the Fajulu may have been originally Moru-Madi elements occupying the Nile Valley.

THE NYANGWARA. (*Information from* MR. BEATON)

They call themselves Yangwara and are called Nyangwara by other tribes.

They generally describe themselves as autochthonous in the country round the Miri Hills. They also sometimes relate that the ancestors of themselves, the Luluba and the Bari, were three brothers, who separated and went their several ways at Gori, Baker's stone at Rejaf. But in general they seem to regard themselves as different from the Bari.

Lotome, the first remembered ancestor of the Gwokorongo chiefs, lived at Dogeleng near the Koda River seven generations ago; Kodipon, the oldest known of the original Rokon chiefs, was living at Kworsak ten generations ago.

Fajulu pressure from the south led to hostilities and long-drawn out enmity which still persists.

There has been, and still is, a lot of intermarriage with the Moru, and to the casual eye the Nyangwara living nearest to the Moru appear to resemble them strongly.

o

BARI-SPEAKING WEST BANK GROUP

They have absorbed a position of the old Liggi tribe.

The men scarify their foreheads with diagonal lines.

There are no subdivisions of the tribe.

Their clans are generally speaking localized and not dispersed. The only clan prohibition observed is that the Bora clan may not eat elephant, to account for which they have the following story: 'Once upon a time a man came down from heaven and slept with the daughter of Kaya. When she was big with child her father asked how this came to be, whereupon she showed the reason of it, saying "If you come to my house by night you will find him with me." Which he did and found the man from heaven who said, "You do me wrong to come on me thus, but I will do you a benefit, cover me with a mat." And when he covered him he vanished into heaven. Thereafter he sent down the bride-price from the clouds. But when the daughter of Kaya gave birth, both she and her son were made into elephants and went out into the forest: wherefore the Bora eat not of elephant flesh to this day.'

In the case of an interclan marriage having taken place the Nyang-wara, like the Fajulu and Bari, dramatize the splitting of the clan by cutting a goat in half lengthwise, one half for the man, the other for the girl, after which the two have a mock fight with sticks.

They have no age classes. The children have their teeth extracted by batches in public, but without any ceremony.

Chiefship is hereditary, descending to brother, son, or nephew according to age and reputation. In default of one of these the chief might appoint his sister's son to take over his functions. Normally the chief appoints his successor before his death; otherwise this would be done by the council of elders.

In the council the speaker must hold the talking-stick; the elders arrive at their verdict, which they then submit to their chief.

Their oaths and ordeals are of the usual nature.

The chiefs are not rain chiefs. There are two rain-makers, who have one rain-stone between them. They are said to be in origin Bari of the Bekat rain-making clan, but have been adopted into the Bora. They also perform fertility rites by stirring the baskets of seed-corn before it is sown, receiving an arrow from each family and a hoe from the headman. The rain-maker's grave must be kept clean of grass by his family. If it is burnt there will be a failure of the rain.

There are no other *komonyekak*. There are no *dupi* and smiths are free.

THE NYANGWARA

Twins were not apparently killed or exposed. The father may sacrifice a goat.

The usual bride-price is 30 goats and 30 sheep. There is no obligation for the bridegroom to work for the girl's family, but a poor man may do so.

If a wife dies childless a man may call on his father-in-law for another for a reduced bride-price.

Chiefs and commoners are buried in front of their mother's hut, in a long grave not apparently of the recessed type. If the dead man has children, the free arm is propped upright in the grave.

They do not make spirit houses.

The ancestral spirit resides in a small pot (*sape*), kept in the house. When the new crop is harvested and the first food has been cooked from it, at dusk a libation for this spirit is poured into the pot and eaten by the young children the next day.

An evil spirit also inhabits small khors waiting for some one to cross when it pounces on him and causes him to fall sick.

The cultivation divisions of labour correspond to those of other tribes.

The Nyangwara have lost practically all their cattle. It is unusual for women to milk, and milk is never drunk direct out of the milking gourd. Butter is made and cheese is pressed in a hollow bamboo. Both sexes will eat eggs, but women do not eat chickens.

Their huts are very distinctive in two respects. The grass of the roof, which is generally ridged, is extended to form a 'skirt', which almost touches the ground; and the doorway is protected by a large projecting porch, which is used as a sitting-place by the family.

THE FAJULU. (*Information from* MR. GIFF, *supplemented by* MR. BEATON)

THE tribe call themselves Fajulu and are so called by their neighbours. They intermarry largely with the Bari and to some extent with the Kakwa, but do not claim relationship with these tribes or with the Nyangwara. In the old days they used to raid the Lugbari. Like the Nyangwara, they have Liggi elements incorporated with them.

The bulk of the evidence points to their having come originally from the Nile. Fourteen generations ago Nyokadi, the ancestor of Chief Lomeling (Muresuk clan), led a migration from Korobe Hill.

BARI-SPEAKING WEST BANK GROUP

Seven generations ago Julu, the ancestor of Chief Walakai (Niaga clan), led a movement from Mayat Hill. The Malari family believe that their ancestor Kanki more than seven generations ago lived near Shindiru in the Bari country, and that one of them married a daughter of the big Bekat rain-makers. The advance northward to Mount Tali from the Loka area took place eight generations ago under Wörlimö (Rensuk clan: the ancestor of the present Chief Gindilang). This brought them into conflict with the Nyangwara, an agelong feud which still persists.

There are no intertribal sections, but they are divided into a number of patrilineal clans. Marriage into the mother's clan is barred, the reason given being that a man's maternal uncle (*merenye*) belongs to this clan and that a man cannot marry into the clan of his *merenye*. These clans are on the whole territorial and not dispersed; clan members assist each other in cultivation and share game killed.

Should an interclan marriage take place a goat is cut lengthwise, one half for the man, the other for the woman, to symbolize the splitting of the clan (cf. Bari, Nyangwara).

There is no age-class system, except that the Fajulu in the extreme north, around Tijor, have traces of it, borrowed possibly from the Mandari. The initiatory extraction of the four lower teeth is done privately. It is tending to fall into neglect. There are no drum-houses.

Chiefship is hereditary. The chief is entitled to one tusk of every animal killed and to a foreleg of all game. He can call on his people to cultivate or build his house, repaying the workers with a feast. He appears to hold his authority as the descendant of a migration leader and not from any supernatural claim.

Justice is administered by the chief, assisted by the elders (*temejek*). In the old days a girl was handed over as blood-ransom if a man had been killed. Ordeals are taken by stabbing the *kir* tree, by breaking the feather of the *kongo* bird, or by drinking powdered ivory. If the accused survives the ordeal, his accuser must pay compensation.

Rain-makers, with the Bari rain-stone technique, exist, but with the exception of Chief Laila are private individuals. The powers are hereditary and can be transmitted through a daughter to her son only if she has a brother. The rain-maker also fertilizes the seed-grain, collecting it in a heap before sowing and performing a fertilization rite over it. Chief Gindilang has two rain-stones, but does not use them, and does not claim to be a rain chief. He can, however, call the wind.

THE FAJULU

A black ram or chicken is sacrificed and its stomach contents smeared on a stick of *dolongi* wood with which he beats the waters of a pool near Mount Tali, saying: 'O father, see your sons are dying of hunger, send us rain.' The rain wind is then supposed to blow.

The *monyekak* does not seem to exist. As noted above, fertility rites are performed by the rain-makers. The chiefs are called *komonyekak* of the areas they administer, apparently as the descendants of the original migration leader and of the first cultivator. They do not perform fertility rites.

There are a very few *dupi* who presumably assist the rain-makers, though this is not absolutely clear. In the Malari clan the eldest son is the rain-maker and the next in age manipulates the stones. The *dupi* marry amongst themselves, but the class is becoming extinct. Smiths may have been a separate class, but are now becoming ordinary freemen and may contract ordinary marriages with 'free' girls.

There is also a category called *dupi wuri*. These are either foreigners or freemen who from poverty or misfortune have been obliged to attach themselves in a menial capacity to wealthier men. They have none of the mystical properties of the true *dupi*.

Twins are regarded as unlucky and used to be exposed for a night in the forest. If either or both were spared by the wild animals they were kept.

Bride-price varies according to the means of the individual. In these days cash is becoming equated with the traditional payment in live stock, a cow being reckoned at £2, a bull at £1, a goat at Pt. 20. The prospective bridegroom hoes for his bride's family and repairs the houses of her mother and brothers. After she has borne a child, he makes a present to her father and her whole family will look to him for occasional presents.

The girl's ceremonial consent is necessary to her marriage. On the other hand, infant betrothal is not uncommon, and if the bridegroom is in a position to pay the bride-price at once the girl will go to live with his mother or sister until she is marriageable. If a wife dies childless or with only one child the husband may claim part of the bride-price to be returned, or might be given another girl if the father had 'eaten' the original bride-price.

The same arrangement prevails if she is divorced or runs away.

If the husband dies, his wife or wives are normally inherited by his brothers, though the sons may take them. If there are no brothers and the sons are small, the widows return home, but hand over

198

BARI-SPEAKING WEST BANK GROUP

part of the household furniture to the childrens' guardian in trust for them.

Premarital intercourse is frowned upon but illegitimate children are common. It is said that in the old days if the seducer of an unmarried girl refused to marry her, her brothers would kill all his live stock so as to make it impossible for him to marry. Nowadays practice varies. Mr. Giff cites two examples:

(*a*) An unmarried girl A., living with her father B., bore a child by C. B. called on C. for compensation. He paid 2 cows and 20 goats, and when the child is weaned will take it to be brought up with his own children. The child will be known as his *wuri* but its *luitot* (free) status will not be affected. A. will probably command a reduced bride-price, not necessarily because she is 'second hand' but perhaps because she has already given out something akin to life force.

(*b*) An unmarried girl A., living with her father B., bore a child by C. She did not wish to marry C., and she and her child lived with B., the child being known as B.'s *wuri*, but his tribal status will not be affected. A. later married for a reduced bride-price.

Adultery, according to Mr. Giff, is regarded not only as 'theft' from the husband for which compensation must be paid, but as a punishable offence against society for which the offender may be beaten. Sometimes the husband will repudiate the wife, in which case the seducer will either marry her, or, in one case quoted by Mr. Giff, the man having refused to marry her, the wife and her child live with the husband's father. The child is always known as a *wuri*, but eventual status is not prejudiced.

Burial is just outside the house in a grave of the recessed type. In the old days a slave is said to have been buried with the chief.

The following points are taken from the detailed account of a man's burial by Mr. Giff. The men who attended were all armed: the deceased had moved his house not long before, and when it was seen that he was *in extremis* his household goods were removed to his old house; the body was received into the grave by his sons; the recess was fenced off with stakes (this was also done in the case of an infant burial) and sealed with clay; in filling the grave a little earth was first pushed into it by persons facing outwards, with their elbows; after burial all concerned washed their hands and limbs from a pot placed on the grave; a mock assault on the grave by the men merged into a dance in which the women joined; the sister of the dead man took a prominent part in all the dancing, and with the two daughters for a time lay

THE FAJULU

prostrate on the grave; a man constituted himself a defence, pursuing and retreating before an imaginary enemy; animals were sacrificed on the grave; the heads of the children and wives were shaved and the hair deposited in the forest; some of the man's possessions were placed on the grave, near to which the sons slept till the next full moon to protect it from the *karubanit* (ghoul).

Dancing continues at intervals according to the means of the family: any one failing to attend is suspected of being a *karubanit*.

In the case of a child, there was no dancing over the grave, but the mother continued to mourn at the grave for two months. In that case the father's head was not shaved, because he was angry with his wife for 'killing' her children; the mother's head also was not shaved because she was angry with the spirit (*mulukötyö*) for killing her children.

In cultivation, the heavy work in clearing is done by the men, cleaning up and burning the grass by the women; friends help and are rewarded. The seed is sown by the women, who also do the harvesting. The same is true of ground-nuts, but the cultivation of sweet potatoes and cassava is exclusively men's work.

There is a feeling in the minds of some against drumming between seed-time and harvest.

When the first durra is harvested there is an offering of first-fruits to the spirit of the householder's mother. The family stand in a circle; the father sprinkles a little grain round them and then presents some to the spirit in the *lubanga* (*v. infra*, p. 202). The spirit is asked to give health and long life to the family.

Dances are held at the *kima* harvest in June and the *laiut* harvest in October which seem to have a religious significance.

The two sexes eat separately, the children with their fathers or mothers according to sex.

They do not now possess many cattle, and do not venerate them. They are not commonly eaten—the same applies to sheep and goats— except at festivals, funeral ceremonies, as a reward for help rendered, or often sacrifice to the spirit. Only males are so killed. As cattle are becoming equated with cash they are not particularly averse to selling them. Castration is practised.

Milking is done by the older boys or men, not by childbearing women. No particular vessel is used; the milker washes his hands and mouth before beginning. Milk is drunk fresh, mixed in cooking with

BARI-SPEAKING WEST BANK GROUP

porridge, or soured. It is not now mixed with cows' urine. Blood is remembered as a famine food in old days.

Eggs are eaten by males only.

Their weapons are the bow and arrow and spears. They seem never to have had shields.

The 'feathered arrow' is the typical Fajulu marking (cp. the Moru), but those living near the Kakwa frequently have the Kakwa 'speckled band' of four rows of dots (the same thing is done by the Nyangwara, Kaliko, Avukaiya, and Lugbari (3 rows)). A longish 'tail' of white fibre is typical of the Fajulu women's dress. The old women substitute a large piece of cow skin.

Their smiths are very expert, but no longer smelt their own iron. The women make and sell pottery, building the pots up in rings. After firing they are finished by being smeared inside and out with the sap of the *dini* tree. The maker cooks porridge in the pot once.

Fishing is done by experts (*kabitak*) with hook and line, and by the women with baskets. Poison is also used. The *kabitak* are not a special social class. The religious and supernatural beliefs of the Fajulu are described by Mr. Giff as follows:

Their conception of the deity seems to be divided into two separate entities.

The creator is *Ngun lo ki* (god in the sky). His work or creation is perfected, but he still appears to have vague, undefined functions. He is not wholly an absentee God.

The conception of the god in the earth (*Ngun lo kak*) is bound up with that of the Ancestral Spirits (*Mulökö*). I have not yet been able to decide the exact relationship. Provisionally, and greatly daring, I suggest that he is the sum total of the beneficent spirits, who become merged in a unity without losing their identity. One does not hear much reference to *Ngun lo kak* in everyday conversation. The spirits of deceased father, mother, brother, or child, on the other hand, form a subject of almost normal conversation.

Long, long ago the two gods were in communication by means of a rope of cow-skin which hung between earth and sky.

The inhabitants of both places were constantly going to and fro. Dances were arranged and the inhabitants of either place were called to these festivities by the sound of the drum; this happy state of affairs was terminated when a hyena cut the rope.

There appears to be a belief that every man has two spirits. One is

THE FAJULU

beneficent; the other is malignant. When a man dies the bad spirit is ever on the watch to find means of harming the family of the deceased householder. The good spirit has power to bring to naught the activities of his harmful rival. But he only exercises this power as a reward for attentions to him; any blot on the family honour, or neglect of his necessities (for however spiritual he may be he is subject to hunger and thirst), is visited by allowing the bad spirit free scope. To ward off evil from the house a small grass shade, like the roof of a miniature hut, is placed on a pole in front of the dwelling and tilted so that its base is towards the hut. This is not a spirit house.

The powers of the spirit (and hereafter we shall use the word 'spirit' to denote the good spirit) are exercised from the family home. When the ground is left special arrangements must be made if he is to be helpful. People who have recently been moved to new sites by the District Officer sacrifice to the spirit in the old home. One instance which came to my notice will help to illustrate this, while at the same time giving some idea of the technique of sacrifice. I quote from my journal: 'went to Lemi's *rubo* (old home). Just missed a sacrifice to Wani's father. The goat had been killed on the west side of the grave, remote from the old house. Blood still wet on the grave. Fire still smouldering on the ground some 10 feet away, on south side. In the *tongbo* (small pot) were some hair of the goat, and a little blood. The bones of the goat lay under the old *gugu* (grainstore), where the people had eaten their portion. Deceased's chair, or rather the broken pieces which constituted what was left of it, lay on the grave. P.... says that the spirit sits on the chair, looks into the pot, and eats what has been put therein. Rope by which the goat was led was left on the grave. P.... says this is always done.'

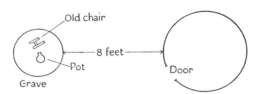

It may be noted that Wani's new home is about two miles from the resting-place of his father's bones.

Should circumstances prevent the burial of a man in the customary place outside his hut, there is an observance which apparently does equal honour to the *Mulökötyö*, and allows his powers to be efficacious.

202   BARI-SPEAKING WEST BANK GROUP

Some two months ago a Government engineer was accompanied to the Kaya Valley by Fajulu porters, one of whom fell from a tree while collecting honey, and died of his injuries in Yei Hospital. The body was buried in Yei, but a piece of *junguli* tree was cut down, and buried outside the man's house exactly as if the real body had been buried there. A *tongbo* was placed on the grave in the usual way.

Informants tell me that there is another application of this practice. If a man for any reason becomes unconscious and is believed to be dead, but later returns to consciousness, a piece of *junguli* is treated with the customary formality. Why? Was there a duality, and has one spirit left the body of the man?

But such instances are exceptional. We must return to normal conditions. There are no spirit houses. A tree or shrub grows in front of the house, or a little to one side of it. This is called *muluet*, and is inhabited by the *Mulökötyö* of the householder's father. From this vantage ground the spirit can guard the door of the house and drive away evil. Offerings of beer are placed at the foot of the tree.

The *Mulökötyö* of the householder's mother is venerated with a respect equal to that paid to the spirit of the father. She (or perhaps he) lives in a special house in which the man sleeps when he does not cohabit with his wife. The significance of this house (*lubanga*) may be the better appreciated if a concrete example is given. An old man, Latio, owns the house concerning which I took the following text:

'He has built the house of his mother because his mother has died. He has built it so that his mother may leave him to live a long time, because those spirits [note the plural] are in the mother's house there. When he has cut a goat, he brings a foreleg to the house of the mother there, so that the mother may leave him a long time. Anything which he has found [presumably while hunting] he brings to the house of the mother there and divides with his wife, and the wife goes to cook the food in the other house [that is, her own house]. When she has cooked the food then she puts it in a pot and makes an offering (*lolongakindi*) to the spirits in the mother's house there. When it had sat for a little while he goes and eats the food, because it has been offered to the mother. And he lives in that house always, so that his body may be very well. If he has cows he calls one of them after the name of his mother, and he does not beat the cow because it is called after the name of his mother. He supplicates that cow thus: "Mother, leave these my children so that their bodies may be well." '

More difficult to investigate is the conception of the spirits of children. On this subject native belief does not seem to have been formulated so exhaustively or with such precision. In one instance which came to my notice the illness of a child was attributed to the spirit of its dead brother. I found, too, that men were afraid to give me the names of their dead children. The spirits of the children would be angry. They would not object to talk about them; only the mention of their names is dangerous.

It has been hinted that the spirit is a moody being, who jealously exacts all the attention due to him. In many of the instances in which he visited with wrath the inattention of his people they are completely ignorant of having offended. Here may be introduced the medicine man ('*bunit*).

His primary function is the divination of causes of the anger of men's *mulökö*, and advising on how such breaches may be healed. One '*bunit* with whom I am on terms of friendship has a forked stick (see diagram) which he uses as his instrument of divination.

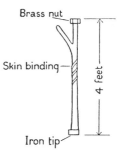

Another of my acquaintance has permitted me to see something of his art. His instrument consists of two short pieces of wood attached to a ring. This he places flat on the ground and takes up a squatting position about 2 feet from it. He produces from amongst the oddments of his profession four pieces of leather. He throws these on the ground so that they will fall on edge, and rebounding roll in the direction of the instrument. His object is to ascertain, from the position in which they come to rest relative to the instrument, the cause of the client's misfortune. By this means he seeks out the causes of illness, domestic unhappiness, unrequited love, conjugal disharmony, and sterility.

Before dealing with his treatments it is necessary to outline the other departments of his activity. The '*bunit* is not only a priest; he is also a magician and a doctor. As a magician he had to deal with undefined forces of the spirit world—forces which he has failed to rationalize. So, along with propitiation and cajoling of known spirits goes the charming of unknown evil; in other words, the practice of magic. Add to this the '*bunit*'s purely medical office, and we form some idea of his social importance in making for cohesion, and in giving confidence and mental stability.

As priest he opens a consultation by rattling his gourd to make

BARI-SPEAKING WEST BANK GROUP

contact with his *mulökö*. Then he may prescribe the necessary sacrifice to be made to the *mulökö* of his client. As doctor he gives medicines, the raw materials of which he may grow round his house to save himself repeated journeys to the forest. Thus my friend to whom reference has already been made treats yaws by asking the patient to chew the leaf of the *nungguli* plant, and then to rub it on the affected parts. If a man is disappointed in love the *'bunit* makes him chew a leaf of a *lo'yet*, and rub it over his forehead. If a wife fails to bear children the *'bunit* tells the husband to send for the male members of his own family, and to make a feast for them. They are then asked to spit over his body, and the saliva is rubbed in. As magician the *'bunit* may advise the wearing of armlets, necklaces, or wristlets in addition to either or both of the other treatments.

We may now turn our attention to certain anti-social beings believed to exist in the flesh.

The *'demanit*, or *yemanit*, is the man or woman who has powers of giving the evil eye. He or she works by entering inside the *zariba* of the intended victim and casting the evil eye on the house or the food which he is eating. The actions of the *'demanit* are inspired by jealousy of another's well-being; one who suspects a visitor of such intention will do well to give him a present.

A person accused of having given the evil eye is brought before the chief. If the accusation is denied accused is made to drink a potion made from the sap of the *kulutet* tree. Guilt is proved by the death of the accused. If innocence is upheld the accuser must give ample compensation.

The work of the *karubanit* may be summed up thus:

When all have retired for the night the *karubanit* comes out. He dances in front of the house which he has chosen. If he finds a grave he falls down on it; he puts out his tongue, spits blood, and works himself into a frenzy. The householder, if he is fortunate to find him in this condition, may make void his efforts by cutting off the sorcerer's ears. But as none of my acquaintances have yet seen a *karubanit* at work I have not heard of one losing his ears. If the sorcerer goes unchallenged the victim becomes ill and dies.

The administration of poison is the work of the *kasumanit*—a woman who, either to gain private ends or acting in a professional capacity, is able to give snake poison. It is prepared by killing a snake, hanging its head downwards, and collecting the venom. The *kasumanit* finds means of mixing her *kisum* with the victim's food or beer.

THE FAJULU

To track down the poisoner and bring her to justice two methods are employed.

The first has the virtue of simplicity, being a form of ordeal used when one particular person is strongly suspected. She is made to interlock the fingers of both hands, and an egg is placed in the palms, in such a manner that when it is squeezed the compression will be along the major axis of the egg. If she breaks it she is considered guilty.

If a number of persons are suspected a corresponding number of stones are collected and placed on the ground so as to form a circle. A stake is driven into the ground at its centre. To the stake a chicken is tied by a wing, by means of a string the length of which equals the radius of the circle. The chicken's throat is cut. The locus of its dying movement is the circle made out by the stones. The stone on or beside which it dies represents the perpetrator of the crime.

The punishment of a convicted *karubanit* befits her crime. She is made to drink poison from which she dies.

Lightning (Pe'ya). Lightning lives in the clouds and comes to earth with them when it rains. It strikes a man who makes false accusation against you, or who breaks a promise. One gathers from the way in which it is spoken about that it has personal attributes. Thus, it hears the offence being committed; it returns to the sky after having done its work.

The *kasumanit* has power to bring the lightning to attack a man. A sergeant of the company which was formerly stationed at Loka was killed in this way. At midday he drank beer which had been poisoned by a *kasumanit*. In the late afternoon he was struck by lightning.

Lightning is not, so far as I can gather, an agent of *Ngun lo ki*.

The Rainbow (gori). The rainbow is the saliva ejected by a large snake (*maworo*) which lives in the Nile. If one were to go near it one would be burned.

It acts as a barrier against the rain. When the rain-clouds come it stretches itself across the sky, and holds back the storm.

In the case of accidental killing, while hunting for instance, a man kills one of his own people, he must shave his head, just as if it were one of his own relations, but no other purification ceremony is necessary, though the victim's children will be his special charge until they grow up. If a man accidentally kills a stranger or commits deliberate

206 BARI-SPEAKING WEST BANK GROUP

murder there is a different procedure, the *'bara* ceremony. After shaving his head, in the presence of his friends, he plunges his spear into the *kiruet* bush; every one then rushes home, the drum is beaten, every one shouts and takes his spear to repel an imaginary foe. If this is not done it is believed that leprosy will be contracted. The same thing is done if a leopard is killed.

THE KAKWA. (*Information from* MR. GIFF *supplemented by* MESSRS. GRAY and WINDER)

THE tribe call themselves Kakua or Kakuak; and are called Kakwa by the Bari and other tribes.

They claim to have come from the Nile and to have close affinities with the Bari. Korobe Hill, where they arrived subsequently to the Fajulu, was a big dispersion centre from which they pushed out west and south. They presumably made their way to Korobe via the Kiya and Kaiya valleys, as many clans can only trace their ancestry to settlements on those rivers.

Fighting with the Makaraka led to much movement backwards and forwards. They were greatly harried by the Dervishes and then again, early in the Belgian régime, by Könyi lo Bari's raids (the father of Morbe Könyi), whose attacks may account for those sections of the tribe now south of the Kuku in the Kajo Kaji District and in Uganda. As a result of all these disturbances their tribal history has become very confused.

Their dislike of the Makaraka persists until to-day. Formerly they were wont to raid the Lugbari, from whom they took quantities of cattle and women. But there is no ill feeling to-day, and they intermarry with the Lugbari as well as with the Kölikö.

There are large numbers of the Kakwa in the adjacent Belgian Congo territory.

The typical tribal marking consists of four rows of dots across the forehead.

As a result of recent administrative procedure they have become organized in certain territorial groups: but there are no real tribal sections or subdivisions. There are certain clan groups characterized by prefixing *pa-* to their names. These may be purely territorial as Panyome, or as in the case of Pamagara and Pawuri, the descendants of Magara and Wuri, may denote a common ancestor. The Kakwa clans are excessively numerous; at least 80 have been enumerated and the list is probably not complete. With a total population of

THE KAKWA

6,000 taxpayers it is clear that the average size of the clan must be small.

They are extremely confusing to investigate, but certain general outlines emerge from Mr. Winder's investigations.

They are localized and not dispersed. Under the various chiefs and sub-chiefs we find groups of clans; in some cases some members of the group may be mutually exogamous, suggesting the possibility that originally they were of common descent. In most cases, however, all memory of a common ancestor has been forgotten, but there are the following exceptions:

1. The Böri group of six clans, Gimunu, Minyore,[1] Mitika, Jensuk, Komiru,[1] Runyi, descended from a common ancestor Konyi, by his two wives Wuri and Magara, and divided accordingly into the Pawuri (Gimunu) and Pamagara (Minyore, &c.). Incidentally this is the only case which has come to light in the province so far of descent being traced from the mother. The Pamagara are mutually exogamous, but all of them may intermarry with Pawuri.

They are peculiar in having no tribal markings; their rain-making ritual is not of the Bari rain-stone type; and they have a peculiar form of burial for their rain-makers which will be subsequently described.

Mr. Giff has been given a different genealogy in which Bongari figures as the husband of Wuri and Magara.

2. The Abegi group, consisting amongst others of clans Abegi Logo, Kerube, Pokujon, Gobor, Megiri who are all descended from a common ancestor Surobongit and may not intermarry. Formerly they did not intermarry with the Goja (Chief Wai Wai) or the Yari, but they do not share a common genealogy with these, and the prohibition may have been due to ancient feuds.

In the Abegi is an important family of rain-makers, descendants of Remanshuk, represented to-day by Paipai Lua and Kinikashuk, whose technique is also not of the Bari rain-stone type.

No clan prohibitions have been recorded except that men of the Nyori clan may not normally eat or, apparently, hunt elephants though women and girls may: if they do so, their legs will swell up. If, however, they arm themselves with a plant called *lugoyi* which they buy from the *Liggo* (the professional caste of elephant and buffalo hunters) they will be enabled to hunt and kill elephants and eat the meat.

A man will share his kill with any one fellow clansman that he may

---

[1] *Komiru* = lion; *Nyori*, the woman's chain-apron.

208 BARI-SPEAKING WEST BANK GROUP

meet during his hunt, and should also do so with any old man, of whatever clan.

Inter-clan marriage would normally be regarded as incest, and would call down the wrath of the ancestral spirits upon the guilty pair and upon such relatives as attended the marriage feast. But such marriages occur and there is a special ritual for 'sanctifying' them, though differing entirely from the Bari ceremony described in Section II. 1.

The girl while growing up wears a ring and leg ornament given by her future father-in-law as a token of betrothal: 'when the people see that ring on her foot they are afraid to marry her'. (This presumably applies to normal marriages.) The man's father and kinsfolk visit the girls: the matter is talked over and a he-goat (called *luparate*) is sacrificed. After they have departed the girls' brothers and kinsfolk kill another he-goat (called *ruki*), part of which is cooked, and the kinsfolk spit into the cooking-pot, which is then placed outside the fence and left out all night. If it attracts a hyena or wild cat the marriage is dangerous and is broken off. Otherwise it is in order: the girl is washed in water into which the man's kinsfolk have spat, and in due course the bride is taken to her husband's house.

If nevertheless the pair are visited by misfortune they and their children lie down in the hut: a pot with a hole in it is put through the thatch at the apex of the roof, and a newly hatched chicken is killed over it, the blood drips through and splashes the inmates.

If, however, a marriage takes place between a man and a girl whose clans were formerly at enmity, a different ceremony is performed, symbolizing apparently the unification of the two clans. The following is a summary of the account given to Mr. Giff:

While the bride-price is being paid, the girl will work (for her fiancé) but is not given food or drink because she is *ajupe* (has in her veins the blood of people whom the other clan has killed in war; without this ceremony she will miscarry). When the bride-price is paid, the prospective husband is summoned by her father to 'tread the *ajupe*'. The relatives and big men assemble, the girl's paternal aunt bringing a hen: a hole is dug, filled with sticks gathered by the man's relatives, an egg is placed on top, and beer poured over all. The man and the girl sit down, each with their backs to their own home, facing the home of the other's family: the man's brothers fire four arrows into the ground by the girl, two on each side of her and vice versa. They then change places, the girl puts her foot on the egg, the man his foot

THE KAKWA

on hers, they press and break the egg. Then the brothers drive the girl towards the man's house which she enters, and her relatives drive the man towards their houses, throwing sticks at him. He then enters the house, and he and the girl eat together, after which he gives small presents to her relatives and they drink beer together.

Should a girl miscarry the old men are consulted, and should they remember bygone enmity between the clans this ceremony will be performed even though the couple have been long married.

As a result of administrative action certain 'dynasties' of chiefs are beginning to emerge: but these are a recent and artificial creation; formerly the heads of the innumerable groups were all independent.

Serious cases are traditionally heard and settled by the chief and the elders: blood-money was payable for wounds, but until recently murder was outside the scope of the council and could only be settled by the private killing of the murderer or one of his family.

If a man wounds another accidentally he must remain on the spot to render assistance. If he runs away it is a sign of guilty intention.

Rain-makers are numerous. They are not chiefs, but are important and were more so in old days.

The generic name for all rain-makers is *Bora* (or *Bura*). This is applied to the actual rain-maker only and not to his family. All the Kajo Kaji chiefs, who are also rain-makers, are known as *Bura*. It also occurs as a territorial name, e.g. the clan Lumuri, to which chief Baba belongs, is described as living on the land called Bora. Mr. Giff suggests that the word may have begun as the name of a clan or grouping the heads of which had rain powers and became extended to cover all rain-makers. It may be only a coincidence that amongst the Moru Ondri there is a rain-making clan called Vora; but in view of the remarkable similarity of the burial customs for the Kakwa and Moru rain-makers, it is worth mention.

The majority of the Kakwa rain-makers use the Bari-Kuku rain technique. That is to say, they have male and female rain-stones which often have personal names, kept on a rain hill where there is generally a sacred grove or sacred tree and the family burial-place. Water is brought to the hill from the rain stream and poured over the stones. But some rain-makers use a different procedure and there is an indication that the difference is not so much between individual rain-makers as between groups. Thus none of the Pawuri and Pamagara rain-makers have stones; and the same thing is true of the Abegi rain-makers. It is tempting to wonder whether in such cases their

P

BARI-SPEAKING WEST BANK GROUP

rain-making ceremonies have a non-Bari origin indicating that the Kakwa present a fusion of two different tribal families.

The rain-makers also perform fertility rites; they 'bless' the heaps of seed-corn by stirring the grain with an ancestral stick. Some of them also perform ceremonies to drive off locusts.

In these respects they approximate in part to the Bari *monyekak*. There are, however, instances where fertility ceremonies are performed by individuals who are not rain-makers. Moreover, in reply to the question 'Who is your *monyekak*?' the Kakwa will give the name of his 'political' chief, although these do not perform any fertility ritual whatever, in this case using the word merely to describe the descendant of the migration leader who first brought the party or clan to the locality and apportioned the land between them.

It is convenient to mention here certain outstandingly peculiar practices connected with the burial of rain-makers. It is not quite clear whether these apply to *all* rain-makers or whether some of these are buried on their rain hills. They certainly apply to the Bori and to other groups as well.

The *buraso* or rain-maker (pl. *bura*) is buried just outside his house: he is buried at night, in silence, with no wailing or lamentation because if the people wail or lament his spirit will become a bad spirit and going out into the forest will become a lion or a leopard, and kill the people's live stock. It is, however, possible to recall the spirit from the forest by drumming. A thatched roof is erected over the grave.

In the case of a rain-maker called Adi of the Panyana group (and the following details presumably apply to other rain-makers as well) a cutting of the *laruki* tree, taken from the similar tree growing over his father's grave, was planted over his grave. After the burial the people danced round the grave for four or six days, and then departed, leaving the rain-maker's sisters and married daughters at the grave, where they must remain for a month and can then only leave after they have been ransomed by their husbands with a goat which is killed over the grave and eaten by the clansmen. In addition to the thatched roof over Adi's grave a hut has been built near by which is used as a goat-house for a goat which used to belong to the dead rain-maker. This animal is treated with great veneration: it may trespass where it likes and must not be driven away. An iron neck-ring with a bell has been made for it, and on its right foreleg are two iron rings and some money, formerly Adi's. In time of drought it is taken out and led round the cultivation. (This recalls the 'sacred goat ... ornamented

THE KAKWA

with bracelets and ear ornaments' mentioned by Driberg in connexion with the Allah Water cult; *J.R.A.I.* lxi.)

It is impossible not to be struck by the similarity of the burial customs for the Kakwa and Moru rain-makers. Amongst the Moru, e.g. the Bora rain-makers of the Moru Ondri, the rain-maker is buried at night, in silence, and a thatched roof is erected over the grave, which again strengthens the suspicion that the Kakwa may represent the fusion of a Bari-speaking wave from the Nile with a pre-existing tribe of the Moru tribal family.

The status of the Kakwa *dupi* is difficult to define. The term is applied to people who from poverty, misfortune, or physical deformity have been obliged to accept a menial position in the household of chiefs or rich men; and also to war captives, especially Lugbari. In both cases they perform menial tasks and are dependent upon their patron not only for their maintenance and for the bride-price of their wives, who according to Major Gray remain, with their children, in the ownership of the patron. At the same time the wives so found for them are free-born Kakwa girls. Similarly, girls captured in raids might marry Kakwa freemen.

This class are also known as *Kajua*, and have none of the mystical association with the rain-maker which is the distinctive feature of the Bari *dupi*.

On the other hand, some rain-makers have assistants who manipulate the rain-stones and go down into the rain-maker's grave. They are called *kedi lo matat lo piong*: it is not absolutely certain that the term *dupi* is applied to them. The rain-maker calls them 'brother'. Paipai Lua insists that his *kedi* is a *bai* (freeman) and not a *dupiet*: that he is not a *bora* but that he would be buried at night.

The position of smiths is indeterminate, but they have acquired practically full status.

There is no age-class system and the Kakwa youths do not have their teeth extracted, but the girls do (Mr. Giff suspects this to be a borrowing); they are done in batches and remain in seclusion for a month attended by elder women who cook their food. But among some clans (e.g. Payawa, Longamere) the girl's teeth are not extracted and the tendency is for it to become a matter of individual taste.

Twins are unlucky, and formerly the last born, or the girl if they were of different sexes, was exposed.

Bride-price fluctuates greatly, 25 sheep being the average minimum

BARI-SPEAKING WEST BANK GROUP

and say 3 cows, a bull, and 8 sheep a typical average for a fairly well-to-do man. With the modern opportunities for earning money fathers are tending to drive hard bargains inconsistent with the suitor's status. If the wife dies, the bride-price (*torabo*) is returned, with deductions for one or two children; if three children have been born nothing will be repaid. Theoretically a girl's consent is necessary to her marriage; but infant betrothal is common and in such cases it will be difficult for the girl to mention a refusal.

In addition to the bride-price, the suitor must work in his father-in-law's cultivation, build his grain stores, &c. During this period he sleeps in a separate hut with his fiancée, but her sister sleeps there also as a 'chaperon'. When he has returned to his village and paid up the full bride-price the girl is anointed with simsim oil by her mother and escorted to her husband's house.

Wives are normally inherited by the sons, but may be inherited by brothers or nephews; and even though the natural inheritor may feel aggrieved he has little or no redress. A widow may also return to her father's house, but in that case the father must return the *torabo*, with customary deduction for children.

If a woman leaves her husband all the *torabo* must be returned. Any children remain with husband and are brought up by his mother, or brother's wife, or sister.

Burial is in the recessed type of grave, close to the house. The grave should be dug by the brothers; the maternal uncles supervise, decide whether it is deep enough and are hard to satisfy. The corpse after being washed is placed in a sitting position by the grave. The maternal uncles then arm themselves and must be given a she-goat before they will permit burial. Some of the dead man's property is placed by the grave, and if he has animals two or three goats are tethered near by. 'If these are here he will not return.' After the grave has been filled in the people dance round it.

The heads of the wives are shaved by the paternal aunt after eating a special meal (*kadunga*).

At the beginning of the dry season beer is prepared, the man's bows and arrows are given to the maternal uncles and the wives are divided up amongst their inheritors.

If a woman dies pregnant the abdomen is opened and the embryo, if sufficiently developed, is removed. If this is not done the husband will have no more children.

The mound of earth over a grave is called *gong lo moko* and is

THE KAKWA

believed to have a spirit inhabiting it or to have spiritual attributes (see also under religious belief).

If two brothers quarrel over their father's inheritance and the younger utters the formula 'I bind them by *gong lo muko*', neither brother can touch the inheritance: the ban may be removed by the elders bringing them together, killing a young chicken over their heads, and smearing their bellies with the blood.

They have the normal division of agricultural labour.

A family may sell grain either for money, which is taken by the husband, or for salt which is taken by the wife, or for labour when both benefit.

A man who is ill will be helped out by his brothers, or by his daughter's husband or his wife's brother. But if help is sought outside the family circle hospitality must be given in return.

There is no feeling against drumming during the cultivation season.

They have a fair amount of cattle: goats are plentiful, sheep, which have an equivalent value with goats, are rather scarce. Milking is not done by women. Young women will not eat chickens: after they have had a number of children they will do so. Men and women eat eggs except that among the Tokosang (a term for those in the west adjacent to the Kaliko) the women do not eat them (or sheep or goat's flesh).

Religious Beliefs.

Mr. Giff prepares his detailed account of the religious beliefs of the Kakwa by emphasizing how vague and unco-ordinated these are; and that unless this is remembered our methods of analysis and classification may produce an entirely wrong impression.

It is clear from his account that ritual plays a far greater part in their lives than one would suspect. The same is no doubt true of other tribes also.

The Bari conception of *Ngon lo ki*, God in the firmament, is termed by the Kakwa *Nguleso*. He is vaguely thought of as the Creator, and is said to have thrown a man down from heaven who taught mankind to cultivate. There is a vague feeling that he ought to assist mankind, as shown in a text quoted by Mr. Giff.

'Long ago some people did not know about *Nguleso* because lions and wild beasts came out to eat men. And they said, "If *Nguleso* exists why do these beasts eat us?" and some answered, "because you do not act well; therefore he sends these animals to devour the land". Then they thought over the

BARI-SPEAKING WEST BANK GROUP

death of these men: and they cried out, saying, "*Nguleso* has treated me badly: I have not taken another man's property: I have not entered the house of another man: so he troubles me for no reason." They called together the spirits (*Nguloki*) and called upon *Nguleso* in the sky.'

Contrasted with Nguleso and yet associated with him and even confused with him is the evil malignant spirit *Ngulete*:

'. . . and they say that the *Nguleso* who is evil, his name is *Ngulete*.' '*Ngulete* is a bad spirit. If you build your house near a river *Ngulete* comes and strikes you down with illness. If you think, something of *Nguleso* has caught me, you call the *bunit* . . . *Ngulete* finds a big tree and lives in it. If the *bunit* knows that *Ngulete* is in that tree he tells all the people not to walk near it.'

The *Ngulete* can be exorcised by an offering or, if obstinate, by drumming.

Ngulete is not one, but many, and male or female. They are all the children of mothers called *Jaguruba* who live in the rivers and give birth to their children whom they guard jealously.

'If women go to cut salt (i.e. the grass from which salt is made) they find the *Jaguruba* at the bottom of the salt (i.e. hidden in the grass). And she cries, do not cut the grass, you must not cut. If the woman cuts the grass she kills one of them. If she (*Janguruba*) does not kill you she chokes you . . . or makes you deaf.'

The parent of all the *Jaguruba* lives in the Nile.

Ngulete has dealings with the ancestral spirits. These, though preserving their identity, seem to be regarded as combining to form a family spirit. For instance, not every man has the spirit-house in his enclosure, but the father of the family, or the elder brother if the father is dead.

These spirit-houses, in the shape of a miniature hut, are built just outside the house door. There is also a pole (*angku*) stepped in the ground. When a man kills game the spirits of his clan know and come for a share. The animal is cut up and the bones hung on the *angku*; a portion of the entrails is cooked and some placed in the spirit-house for the ancestral spirits and some in the dwelling-house for the visiting spirits. The rest of the meat is then cooked for the family. Later on the small boys are given what is left in the spirit-house; their elders eat what is left in the dwelling-house.

At harvest some heads of the new grain are ground and placed in the spirit-house. Some more is cooked with a bean pottage and smeared

THE KAKWA   215

on the grainstore. When the first beer is brewed some is poured on the grainstore.

The ancestral spirits are potent for good or evil, but it appears that only two 'generations' of spirits have powers; the spirits of great-grandparents need not be taken into account. The wife must propitiate her husband's ancestors and also corresponding generations of her own; but her ancestors have apparently no power over her husband.

The spirits act for good or evil, but may help against one another; the spirits of a man's paternal connexions can help against visitations caused by his maternal relatives, but son will not fight against mother, i.e. if a man's paternal grandmother is sending trouble his father's spirit cannot assist. Similarly the spirits can help against the *Ngulete*.

The spirits of children also have powers for good or evil over their parents or brothers. A man is just as loath to mention his dead child's name as his dead wife's. The child may even afflict his mother with sterility; in this case the grave must be reopened and the bone of the little finger must be taken (from the right hand of a boy, from the left hand of a girl) and worn as an amulet by the mother. Or a string is attached to the finger and led outside the grave (cp. the similar Moru practice).

In the case of serious illness or misfortune the *'bunit* is called in to ascertain the source of the visitation. A circle of stones is made, each stone being named for the different ancestors, for known 'evil eyes' and for ghouls. (The *Ngulete* are presumably also represented.) A chicken is tethered by a string in the middle of the circle: its throat is cut, it flutters dying round the circle, and the stone against which it falls dead indicates the responsible spirit.)

Certain other spirits are mentioned by Mr. Giff. The mound of earth over the grave, *Gong lo muko*, is believed to have spiritual attributes and, as already mentioned, may be invoked to prevent inheritance of a man's property.

Another spirit is *Janggara lo muko*, i.e. *Janggara* of horizon, in some way associated with the *Ngulete*. In some accounts this spirit lives on the eastern sky-line; in others it is identical with *gong lo muko*. The belief is very vague, and the young generation know little about it.

The lightning (*Penga*) lives in the sky: he seems to have personal attributes, but physically is an animal with a calf's body and the face and teeth of a lion.

The rainbow is the saliva of a large snake living in the Nile whose

216 BARI-SPEAKING WEST BANK GROUP

children find their way into the other rivers. It holds back the rain but may be harmful to any one finding himself too near to it.

Apart from the graves where rain-makers are buried and the rain-hills, Lelwa Hill on the border of the Kakwa and Koliko country is regarded as sacred by both tribes; a man going to hunt leaves a small offering there. Hill Kidibo in Koliko country now, but formerly Kakwa, is peculiar. Mr. Giff quotes two cases where illness and frailty in children was held as being due to the sufferer's spirit having gone to live at Kidibo, and special ritual was made by the *'bunit* to induce it to return.

THE KUKU. (*Information from* MR. WINDER *supplemented by* MR. GIFF *and* BIMB. YUNUS' *article in Sudan Notes and Records, No. VI*)

THIS tribe inhabits the Kajo Kaji Plateau.

They call themselves Kuku and are known by that name to the surrounding tribes.

In the past they raided the Lugbari for women and cattle. At some time there was serious fighting with the Acholi and Madi, probably in the time of Mela the grandfather of the present Chief Dar. A strong dislike of the Acholi persists until to-day.

They say that they came originally from the north, but entered their present area from the south or west, and found and absorbed a Madi element, some of whose descendants are now under Chief Bosso.

Their chiefs are essentially rain-makers, using the Bari technique of male and female rain-stones. They have the same sacred groves (*rudu*) already mentioned in connexion with the Madi, and rain-hills on which the rain-making rites are performed. All four big chiefs belong to one main branch, the Kasura clan, subdivided as follows: Kasura Kimu, Chief Tete; Kasura Kajo Kaji; Kasura Akeri or Ledong, Chief Mollai; Kasura Miri, Chief Miji. According to Mr. Giff the ancestor of the clan was Leju.

Side by side with the Kasura are a great number of very small clans, of which the most important are the Kandaba, Kenyiba, and Kamia. These are local and not dispersed. It is extremely interesting to find that as far as our researches go at present these clans never have rain-powers, except by delegation from the Kasura, and that the *monyekak* invariably is the head of one of them.

The importance of the Kuku *monyekak* is emphasized by Stigand, who states that although he does not cut a prominent figure he may

THE KUKU

have as much influence as the chief. Lisaje, mentioned by Stigand, was of the Kandaba: Ferinala and Binya have inherited his power to-day. Pate and Wani Bolo are the important *komonyekak* of the Kenyiba. Bobolosuk is an important Kamia *monyekak* and probably Remediang also.

On the *monyekak* depends the fertility of the land, which he ensures by yearly rites. He also ensures success in hunting and is entitled to a hind leg of all animals killed. He concerns himself also with boundaries, as when the Church Missionary Society were given the land for their station.

The sharp distinction between the Kasura having rain-powers and the small clans having fertility powers gives rise to strong suspicion that the small clans may represent an original Madi stock who have been absorbed by the incoming Bari-speaking Kuku proper from the Nile Valley.

Mr. Winder considers that not only did incoming Kuku (and the same applies to the Kakwa and Nyefu) absorb a pre-existent Madi population, but that the intruders themselves came in more than one wave. He points out, as mentioned above, that all the rain-making clans of importance appear to 'own' no land but to live on land which is considered the dominion of another clan. He also draws attention to the singular difference, strongly drawn by Kuku themselves, between those people who eat salt with their *lubia* and those who do not. He believes that four strata can be recognized.

1. The pre-existent Madi, represented to-day by the Litoba, Lowo, and Padombek clans under Chiefs Buli and Bosso. They are sometimes spoken of, and call themselves Madi, and point out that they are redder than the Kuku proper. The Litoba are supposed to have come from the Loka direction, but this does not necessarily militate against a Madi origin.

These people eat their *lubia* with salt.

2. The Kanyiba and Kandaba clans under Chiefs Yenge and Teitei who to-day are the *komonyekak* of all the best land in the Kuku country. They do not know who they are or where they came from, but they are recognized as apart from the Kuku, and take salt with their *lubia*. Although it may be only an accidental resemblance, it is worth mention that in Moru the suffix *-ba* is a common locative termination for group names.

3. The first Kuku wave who settled on land not occupied by No. 2. Of these there are many small clans, such as (*a*) under Bosso, the group

218 BARI-SPEAKING WEST BANK GROUP

known as Limi, comprising the Shera, Lamia, Kiloloro, Ringajin; (b) under Yenge, the Lomora, Lajabo, Lobule, and Kokajin (but note that in the Luluba Hills the Kokajin are supposed to be an original 'Madi' clan); (c) under Buli, the Niolobe, Umbogu, Kudupi; (d) under Miji, the Wokai and Kuliemo.

These eat *lubia* without salt; 'own' land, and among the Kuliemo at least there are relics of considerable rain-making powers.

4. The Kasura, in whom the chieftainship now abides, marked by very important rain-powers and an equally definite lack of connexion with the soil. Their original centre may have been at Kikiji Hill. They have in at least one instance delegated their rain-powers to the Shera for the Limi country to the south-east (vide 3a above).

The position of the Kasura is complicated by the presence amongst them of some Bekat, the big Bari rain-making clan. Their most important representative was Jami, whose death in 1932 gave rise to the well-known ordeal murder of several women by the Madi spirit doctor Ajuko. They are supposed to have come from Belinian and have given rain to the Kasura. Jami lived in the rain chiefship of Yenge (Kikiji) on Kanyiba land (*Monyekak* Pata).

There are also some Bekat Lamora, mostly under Teitei on Kandaba land, but they are of no importance.

No association of animals with the clans has been observed.

No age classes have been observed.

The only form of initiation rite is the extraction of the four lower teeth: this is done to batches of boys and girls during the dry season. The boys' teeth are extracted first, and it is definitely regarded as a test of endurance. The patients are kept convalescent for a fortnight or so afterwards, during which the girls' lower lips are supported by a long chain of white beads which, held in position by the lip plug, passes over the two ears and is joined together to hang down the back.

Dupi are found corresponding to those of the Bari, a servile caste associated with the rain-maker, manipulating the rain-stones for him and playing a conspicuous part at his funeral. Smiths also form a caste apart with whom the ordinary people will not intermarry, and who from the part they play at funerals, seem to have a mystical significance.

The chief is entitled to the usual assistance in labour, and the usual share of game killed, one tusk of an elephant, the skin of a leopard, and the hind quarter of smaller game—the *monyekak* getting the other.

Justice is administered by the tribal council of the chief and the elders (*temejik*), sitting usually under a tree. To be 'in order' each

THE KUKU

speaker must hold the 'talking stick' in his hand and move backwards and forwards along a line a few yards in length. This stick (*puri*) is not solely for legal use, and is found also among the Bari and Kakwa. At a Kakwa feast an old man holds the stick while recounting stories of the past.

Twins are regarded as highly unlucky and were formerly exposed.

A proposal of marriage is made by the man asking the girl for tobacco, the refusal of which is definite.

The man must cultivate and build grain-bins for his prospective father-in-law both before and for a season or two after the marriage. If a wife dies childless the bride-price must be returned.

The first wife has a definitely privileged position.

Ordinary people are buried in a recessed grave, on the right or left of the hut door, according to the sex of the deceased: burial is said to have been originally inside the hut. Rich or important men may be buried underneath a grain-bin. In the preliminary dance the men are armed and carry out mimic warfare against an invisible foe. As soon as a grave is filled in green leaves are scattered over it and immediately picked up. The scattering of the leaves, according to Bimb. Yunus, is explained as a request to the spirit to rest quietly; the picking up as an utterance on the part of each of a wish that no harm will befall him.

The body is received into the grave by the smith, who is given the clothes of the dead man as his fee.

The widow is led out, before the burial, to an adjacent khor, preferably by the smith's wife: her head is shaved, and she does not return until the burial is over. She is then kept secluded for four days, waited on by the smith's wife. During the mourning period, which may be several months, her hair is allowed to grow, she must not use ochre and must wear necklace and waistlet of straw rope instead of the usual beads.

Spirit shrines are erected outside the house, either miniature huts with a thatched roof or small 'cromlechs' of stone. In these, offerings are placed for the spirit, especially at the beginning of harvest.

The household property, which is regarded as the property of the family rather than the individual, is divided by the elders (*losiso*), the eldest son getting the lion's share. A girl's iron rings pass back on her death to her father.

The rain-maker's funeral is of quite a different character and closely resembles the corresponding Bari ceremony. Special features

220 BARI-SPEAKING WEST BANK GROUP

mentioned by Bimb. Yunus in his description of Kajo Kaji's funeral are the silence in which the body was carried to the grave; the selection of a guard, presumably the *dupiet*, who with one of the chief's wives watched the body until it bursts, when the actual burial took place; the selection of a girl as wife for the guard; the selection of ten cattle which were kept close by the grave. The mourning period was to be eight years, during which the guard would live near the tomb and tend the cattle, which at the end of the period became his property.

The men ordinarily went naked; women wear a small apron of cotton, fibre, or chain, and a long 'tail' behind; round the waist and hips is worn a broad belt of bright-coloured beads. In old days these were made of ostrich egg or snail shell.

They have bows and arrows and spears, but no shields.

The Kuku pride themselves on being good cultivators and use a particularly heavy mattock.

They possess cattle, but are said to drink little milk, the majority of which is kept for the calves.

The word used for God is *Nguletet* or *Mulotet*: the conception seems to be that of the community of ancestral spirits below the earth, each one retaining its own character, emotions, and spiritual wants.

The construction of the small spirit-houses has already been mentioned. If a man dies without children or near relatives to build his spirit-house his spirit goes to live in a river-bed. This is the only positive statement so far recorded for the belief, which we may well suspect elsewhere, that children are a spiritual necessity.

According to Mr. Giff the spirit resides under the hut of the ancestor's wife. A long stick at the base of which water may be poured may be set up outside the house to ward off evil.

Fortune and success, unhappiness, disaster, illness, or sterility depend on the good or ill will of the ancestral spirits. To determine the spirit who is angry the spirit doctor, *'bunit*, is called in. These may be men or women: they live the ordinary village life. In addition to the usual pretence of removing foreign bodies from the affected part, they have some knowledge of medicine and psychology. They massage, assist childbirth with some skill, and may attribute misfortune to a quarrel which has not yet been made up. Sterility is sometimes ascribed to non-payment in full of the bride-price.

The *'bunit* is essentially beneficent, in contrast to the various practitioners of black magic. Amongst these is the *Kidemanit*, the evil eye, whose spell can be transmitted by drinking out of a gourd from which

THE KUKU

he has drunk; the *Karubanit*, the bogy (a similar belief is held by the Acholi and Didinga) who has snakes in his belly, and who dances by night outside the victim's hut. If the victim wakes all will be well; otherwise he will fall ill and die.

The *Karubanit* will also dig up and devour corpses. Most serious of all is the belief in the poisoner, apparently always a woman, who catches snakes and prepares poison from their venom which administered in food kills, or smeared in the wall of the hut brings down the lightning. The Kuku are almost hysterical in this belief: in an ordeal in 1932 about a hundred women were tested by being made to drink water from the witch-doctor's pot: if innocent they would vomit, if guilty die. Five died.

Bimbashi Yunus gives us some interesting mythological stories.

The dog is held in great honour. It is believed to have taught them the grinding of grain, the use of herbs for seasoning, and of fire with which to cook; and to have taught them the natural course of childbirth in substitution for their previous practice of cutting the child out of its mother's womb.

The sun returns at night unseen upon its daylight path: to see it so returning will bring death.

The moon not only behaves in like manner but comes down to earth to graze on the rich green grass.

THE NYEFU. (MR. WINDER)

The Nyefu are a small tribe living in the north of Kajo Kaji under Chief Murjan, whose pedigree is as follows:

Pitia
?
?
Monga
|
Shube
|
Loko
|
Rume
|
Lado Boya
|
Murjan

222 BARI-SPEAKING WEST BANK GROUP

There are two current versions of their origin, one that they are Fajulu, the other that they are Bari. The implication is presumably that they are of mixed origin. They probably have no connexion with the Kuku, with whom they squabble continually; they were friendly with the Bari until about 1900, when Bari invasions led to enmity.

As amongst the Kuku there is a sharp distinction between the rain clan to which the chief belongs and a number of other clans who may have land rights, but have no rain.

The rain clan is the Relli, subdivided into four under Murjan (the Relli Fakanyi) and sub-chief Loro, Shula, Bulongo, and Gogonia. The other clans are the Yebur, Keipi, Rongat, *Nyureu*, *Nyore*, Simsim, Rigo, *Moiji*, *Deupet*, Kangaba, Yonkwaji, of which those italicized have land rights and were, it is said, *in situ* before the arrival of the others. These all intermarry: the heads of the Relli branches do not, but there seems to be intermarriage of the rank and file.

No clan totemism has been observed; the women do not drink milk or eat fish.

The rain-makers, always of the Relli clan, have rain-stones; *dupi* exist, but their status and functions have not been investigated. Smiths are said to be of any clan, but may not marry non-smith girls. Similarly, young men will not marry the daughters of smiths though old men may do so.

There are age classes: initiation is confined to extraction of the four lower incisors. But Murjan was particularly told by his father not to have his teeth extracted, presumably as being a rain chief. Teeth are not extracted after death as amongst the Kuku. The grave is of the recessed type, the body being protected by stakes from earth falling upon it: chiefs and *komonyekak* must be carefully buried, otherwise the spirit will turn into a beast of prey which will plunder the living.

There are now practically no cattle left; in the old days when they were plentiful the bride-price was 5 cows on betrothal and 5 on marriage; now 10 sheep or about £2 is usual.

The man must work for his father-in-law, cultivate, build *gugu*s, &c.; if he kills meat he must give him a portion. After marriage he will do the same for a year or two and thereafter occasionally.

The *langet*, the band of companions of an older man, is found as amongst the Bari.

VI. OTHER MISCELLANEOUS TRIBES

MAKARAKA. (MAJOR GRAY)

THE Makaraka appear to have been far more numerous 100 years ago than they are to-day. In the Egyptian days they furnished a large number of the local soldiery, overseers, &c., and thus obtained a position of great importance. Stigand quotes Junker for a population of 1,500. To-day they do not number more than 500 adult males, divided between Yei and Meridi Districts, and appear to be a dwindling race, with a very high sterility rate due perhaps to the precocity and notorious immorality of their women, combined with a high venereal disease rate. They are of little importance in the province, but are anthropologically interesting as representing a culture in many ways completely different from that of the other tribes.

Known to the other tribes as Makaraka, they call themselves Odiu; they speak Zande and are almost certainly part of the Zande race, with whom, however, they were constantly at war owing, from their own account, to their dislike of the Avungara despotism and cannibalism which they claim never to have practised. They were driven south by the Zande attacks to their present location north of Yei. They are on good terms with their neighbours.

They have the usual exogamous clan system. In the Yei District twelve clans are enumerated, each confined to its own area. These appear not to be totemic; there are said to be no food or killing prohibitions.

They have no age classes. In their initiation customs they differ completely from all the other tribes in that they do not extract the teeth but do practise circumcision. Candidates are collected in a special hut (*basa*) in the chief's village when the grain is in the ear, each with his male attendant (*samba*) of the *paranga* (circumcised) grade, who when the operation takes place sits at his back covering the boy's eyes. The operator receives a fee for each boy. After the operation they don a fibre skirt (*madada*) and remain in the *basa* in seclusion until the wounds heal, waited on by their *samba* to whom the women hand their food. Meat and certain vegetables are forbidden, and if they hear a demand for fire they may not eat that meal. A feast and a dance marks their emergence; each parent pays a considerable fee to his son's *samba* and the *madada* is hung on a post outside the

224 OTHER MISCELLANEOUS TRIBES

samba's house. The first game killed thereafter by the boy is given to his *samba*. The grades are infants (*foguli*), small boys (*kumbagudi*), circumcised youths (*paranga*), grown men (*kuroboro*), counsellors (*bakumba*), and lastly the very old men.

The rain-maker (*bairamai*) is a private individual of no importance who appears to act merely as a whipping-boy, being beaten or ducked if the rain is delayed. The father of the land (*bairasende*) is invariably the chief (or more probably the clan head), who exhorts the people not to quarrel during the cultivation season.

Twins are regarded as lucky.

Payment of bride-price is spread over several years; if the wife dies in the meantime the husband must make a compensatory payment to his father-in-law.

If a man has a child by an unmarried girl and does not marry her he must pay compensation to the girl's father, whose property the child then becomes for good and all. The seducer cannot acquire it even by payment.

Ordinary people are buried in a recessed grave above which a hut-like shelter is built and left till it falls to pieces. A chief is buried in a rectangular grave; a 'roof' is made in the shaft above the body and the earth filled in upon that. A properly made hut is erected above it, decorated with elaborate coloured designs, and permanently kept up.

After a death the women relatives take off their clothes and smear their bodies with ashes (nowadays they are nearly all clothed). The hair is dressed in a peak on the top of the head. After three days they wash and resume their clothes, but the mourning head-dressing is retained for three months. If a woman dies, her husband strips, except for a loin cloth and covers his body with earth.

There is an annual festival for burning the grass and blessing the hunting-nets; and a harvest festival is held at which first-fruit offerings are made.

There is no prejudice about drumming while the grain is growing.

In agriculture the men sow the seed, but otherwise whereas in other tribes the men cultivate assisted by the women, among the Makaraka the women cultivate assisted by the men. They use the bent mattock. They have very few goats and no other live stock. Chickens are kept, and these and eggs are eaten by both sexes.

They are skilful craftsmen, making wooden mortars and bowls, stools, and pots. They used to spin and weave, but with the advent of shops

MAKARAKA

these arts are dying out. They roof their houses with straw ropes spiralled round the bamboos.

In the old days war captives (*jogo*) were set to work in their captor's houses and were provided with wives by their masters. But they frequently acquired full status and were often even made their master's heir in preference to his sons.

Religious Belief.

God (*Mböli*) is regarded as the embodiment of, and almost indistinguishable from, the Ancestral Spirits (*Atoro*). He is vaguely considered the author of good or bad fortune. The spirits inhabit the heads of streams. The Makaraka have no spirit-houses but erect a three-pronged stake outside their huts on which the first-fruits are placed. Similarly, in case of illness the sufferer is placed near the stake and a goat is slaughtered, some of the meat hung on the stake, and some of the blood smeared on the patient's face and breast.

The heads of streams are inhabited not only by the spirits but by the rainbow (*Wangu*), believed to be a large python living in an ant-hill. The rain-maker is its attendant in this capacity; he is known as *bairamangu* and must keep it supplied with small animals for food so that the rain may not stop. He is even believed to sacrifice his own relative's children to the snake.

If everything else has failed to produce rain the people assemble bearing baskets of grain and move in a procession towards the head of the stream, the children scattering grain on the ground and into the stream. All the people sing a chant calling on *Mböli* to send down the rain. One such chant is as follows:

> *Eh, eh, Maziga, yo*
> *Kumba a ti ali yo* (a man fell down from the sky)
> *Nduko a kiti*   (His leg was broken)
> *Eh, eh, Maziga yo.*

This is called the *Maziga* ceremony.

For accidental killing there is no purification ceremony necessary, but for murder or killing in battle the man must shave his head and tie round it a strip of *kau* bark. For three days he must wear this and have no intercourse with his wife. Then a dance is given, a goat sacrificed, and some blood smeared over his heart. He then washes his body and removes the bark.

Their oaths and ordeals are of the usual type. They also practise the *benge* oracle of the Zande.

MUNDU. (MAJOR GRAY)

THIS tribe is found along the Nile-Congo Divide in the Yei and Meridi areas. Major Gray believes their language to be practically identical with that of the big Congo tribe of Abangba, and probably the more southerly Baijo and Mabodo also. He notes the following particulars concerning them:

They have (in Yei District) four main clans, but apparently no clan animals nor food prohibitions.

Twins are regarded as lucky.

They have no feeling against the beating of drums in the cultivation season.

The grave is of the recessed type; a hut is erected over it which is kept in repair and into which offerings of beer are periodically placed.

They have or had a 'servile' class of war captives known as *ganjibara*; little disability attached to the status, indeed they might obtain a position of considerable importance.

In front of their houses they erect a three-pronged branch (*kanga*) on which hunting trophies and first-fruits of the harvest are hung after the father of the household and his wife had eaten a small portion of the former.

They have the following blood-purification ceremony: the elders and women strike the killer's legs with sticks three times for a man killed, four times for a woman; a dance is then held at which food is brought in baskets and offered to the killer; after he has eaten a little the dancers snatch it away from him and eat it; the dance lasts three days, after which the slayer for three days must wear a bark fillet tied round his head.

INDEX

Only the chief references are indexed. After the entries for the more important subjects and tribes the words 'and *passim*' may be taken as read.

abari, cattle pen, 177.
abila, spirit-house, 32, 33.
Acholi tribe, the, 4 ff., 144–7.
Adiemani, evil-eye sorcerer, 38–40, 103.
Adultery, practices in regard to, 75, 76 (Topotha), 109–10 (Latuka), 169 (Moru), 198 (Fajulu).
Age-class and age-grade system, the, 7, 11, 18–21, 67, 69–74 (Topotha), 91–7 (Latuka), 116 (Lokoiya), 126–8 (Bari), 145 (Acholi), 159–60 (Moru).
Agricultural tribes, the, 7, 54–6, 79 (Topotha), 112 (Latuka), 117 (Lokoiya), 138 (Bari), 177–9 (Moru), 199 (Fajulu).
Aiyirri tribe, the, 82.
akala malamamuk, strips of leather, 75.
Alia tribe, the, 82.
Allah Water cult, the, 41–2.
ama, locusts, 97, 99.
amba, elders, 187.
amoka, overdrinking, 93.
amothing, rhinoceros, 66.
anaget, age classes, 70.
Ancestral spirits, 32–3.
Andragi-anyisi, the sky god, 32.
Andragi-onje, the earth god, 32.
angku, pole, 214.
Anuak or Berri tribe, the, 4 ff., 144.
apotir, wart-hog, 20, 93.
Apur Mana, 40.
Arber, H. B., on the Lango, 113–14; the Latuka, 36, 82–113.
Arts and crafts, 55–6, 80–1.
atoro, ancestral spirits, 225.
Avukaiya tribe, the, 4 ff., 184.

bai, freeman, 211.
bairamai, rain-makers, 224.
bairasende, father of the land, 224.
Baka tribe, the, 185–6.
baka, elders, 183.
bakumba, counsellors, 224.
balia, bachelor houses, 116, 127.
Bari-speaking tribes, the, 4 ff., 118–39, 192–222.
basa, hut, 223.
Basket-making, 56.

batonge, war captives, 27, strangers, 184.
Beaton, A. C., on the Bari, 16, 28–30, 46, 57, 118–39; Fajulu, 28–9, 195–206; Lokoiya, 23, 114–18; Luluba, 28; Mandari, 139–41; Nyangwara, 29, 193–5.
Bee-keeping, 55.
Beir tribe, the, 4.
ber kwe, my age fellows, 126.
Berri (Anuak) tribe, the, 4 ff., 144.
Birth beliefs and practices, 50–1, 76 (Topotha), 117 (Lokoiya), 133 (Bari).
Black, Major, cited, 41.
Blood-money, practices in regard to, 43–5, 75 (Topotha), 115 (Lokoiya), 132 (Bari).
—purification, 37–8, 131–2, 226.
bömöntio, pl. *bömön*, commoner, 122.
Bretherton, Mr., on the Latuka, 23.
Bride-price, the, 47–50, 76 (Topotha), 134 (Bari), 167–8 (Moru), 197 (Fajulu), 208, 212 (Kakwa).
Brown, Major L. N., on the Moru, 155–83.
Building, types of, 80.
Bull classes in the age-class system, 72–4.
'bunit, spirit doctor, 29, 30, 38, 75, 132, 203–4, 215.
bura or *bora*, *buraso*, pl. *bura* (*bora*, *'böri*), rain-makers, 12, 160–7, 209–10.
Burial, beliefs and practices, 8, 11, 12, 33, 51, 76–7 (Topotha), 112 (Latuka), 117 (Lokoiya), 135–7 (Bari), 169–72 (Moru), 189–90 (Luluba), 198–9, 201–2 (Fajulu), 212–13 (Kakwa), 219–20 (Kuku).
buru, 30.

Calendar, the native, 110–12.
camidok, ophthalmia, 111.
Cann, Capt. G. N., on the Acholi, 144–7.
Castration of cattle, the, 53, 76.
Cattle and other live stock, 53–4, 78, 137–8, 177.
cen, malignant spirits, 34, 147.
Change, evidence of, 59–62.

INDEX

228

Chiefs and chiefship, 7, 11–12, 21–7, 74, 75 (Topotha), 86 ff. (Latuka), 115 (Lokoiya), 122–6 (Bari), 140 (Mandari), 145–6 (Acholi), 157 ff. (Moru), 196 (Fajulu).

Circumcision, 19 and *n.* 1, 149.

Clan, the organization of the, 15–17, 68–9 (Topotha), 86–8 (Latuka), 114–15 (Lokoiya), 120–2 (Bari), 157–9 (Moru), 194 (Nyangwara), 196 (Fajulu), 207–8 (Kakwa).

Crafts, arts and, 55–6, 80–1.

Creation legend, a, 81.

Crime and punishment, 43–5, 74–5.

Cultural differences of the province, the, 7–13 and *passim.*

dak ker, rain wife, 146.

Dancing beliefs, 81.

— costumes, 20–1.

Dead, spirits of the, the belief in, 130–1.

Death and burial, beliefs and practices in regard to, 8, 11, 12, 33, 51, 76–7 (Topotha), 134–6 (Bari), 169–72 (Moru), 189–90 (Luluba), 198–9, 201–2 (Fajulu), 212–13 (Kakwa), 219–20 (Kuku).

demanit, evil-eye sorcerer, 39, 132–3, 204.

di-ago, ancestors, 36, 175.

diamba, ancestors, 158.

Didinga tribe, the, 4 ff., 142–4.

Diet, 58.

dili, elephant spear, 29.

Divination, forms of, 39–40.

Divorce, 48, 109, 134.

Doctors, spirit, 38–40, 75 (Topotha), 103–4 (Latuka), 132 (Bari), 167 (Moru), 203–4 (Fajulu).

Dongotono tribe, the, 82, 113.

Dress, variations in, 7–8, 11, 77–8, 136–7, 179.

Driberg, 92; on the Allah Water cult, 41, 211; on the Didinga-Longarim, 142–4; on the Topotha, 74.

Drum beliefs and practices, 8, 35–6, 93 ff., 102–3.

dugutigi, master of the land, 26.

duje, big drum, 36.

dupiet (pl. *dupikana, dupi perma, dupi wuri*), serf, 11, 23, 27, 28, 122, 124, 128–30, 189, 197, 211, 218.

Durra, the cultivation of, 54.

Earth chief, the, 7, 11–12, 16, 25–7, 31, 116–17, 125–6, 146.

— god, the, 9, 32, 130, 200.

ebuni, a plant, 66.

Economic life, 53–6.

Elephant-hunters, professional, 13, 28–30.

emedot, a head-dress, 77.

Epeita (Murule) tribe, the, 4, 152.

etimat, a head-dress, 77.

Evil eye, the belief in the, 38–40, 75 (Topotha), 103 (Latuka), 132–3 (Bari), 204 (Fajulu).

Exogamous clans, 15–16, 149.

Fajulu tribe, the, 4 ff., 195–206.

feiti, grave stakes, 136.

Fertility ceremonial, 7, 11–12, 35–6.

Festivals, 175–6.

Fire-making cults and ritual, 20, 34–5, 69.

foguli, infants, 224.

Fraser, Dr. K., on the Moru, 15, 155–83.

ganjibara, slaves, 27, 226.

Geography of the province, the, 3.

Giff, Rev. W. L., 31; on the Fajulu, 24, 29–30, 33, 130, 195–206; the Kakwa, 12, 26, 27, 33, 38, 130, 206–16; the Kuku, 31, 216–21.

Gi-ini, rain-makers, 185.

Gods, beliefs relating to, 9, 12, 31–2, 81 (Topotha), 118 (Lokoiya), 130 (Bari), 147 (Acholi), 172–3 (Moru), 200 (Fajulu), 213–14 (Kakwa), 225 (Makaraka).

goma, mattock, 138.

Gong lo muko, a spiritual attribute, 34, 213, 215.

gori, rainbow, 205.

Gray, Major D. Logan, on the Kakwa, 206–16; the Makaraka, 223–5; the Mundu, 226.

Groves, Major, on the Acholi, 144–7.

Hamites, the, 4 ff., 65–141, and *passim.*

Harvest beliefs, 35–6.

History, the, of the tribes, 9–10, 13–14, 65–8 (Topotha), 84–6 (Latuka), 114 (Lokoiya), 119–20 (Bari).

Houses, native, 117.

Hunting practices, 179–83.

ibirokwan, overthrowing, 93.

ibwoy, lazy, 20, 93.

INDEX

229

ihuhumio naijok, to propitiate God, 90.
ijaxa, to spit out, 105.
Ikang, rain-queen, 23.
ikholo, heron, 20, 93.
ilyefu, cleaned up, 111.
imanye, paternal uncle, 107.
Inheritance, the rules of, 80.
Initiation practices, 19–21, 91–102 (Latuka), 127 (Bari), 218 (Kuku), 223–4 (Makaraka).
ipuxe, female bastard, 49, 117.
Iro tribe, the, 82.
Iron working, 55, 80–1.
isyar' imanyi xari, thirst, 111.
itadiraro, abduction of the bride, 106.
itayedo, putting with child, 109.
ituko, blind, 100–1.

jadwong, pl. *jadonga*, counsellor, 145–6.
Jaguruba, nature spirits, 34.
janggara lo muko, spirit of horizon, 215.
Janguruba, spirits, 214.
jogitat, snake, 131.
jogo, war captives, 27, 225.
Jok, stream spirits, 34.
Juba, the sacred rocks at, 34.

kac, platform, 147.
kadudwe, spirits of the dead, 131.
kajua, slave, 27.
kak, platform, 32 *n*.
kakepak, beaters (in elephant-hunting), 29, 30.
Kakwa tribe, the, 4 ff., 206–16.
kaliba, soul, 157–8.
Kaliko tribe, the, 4 ff., 183–4.
kalipinök, small children, 126.
kalogo, oriole, 122.
kamari, rain-makers' assistants, 160 ff.
kamuka, leather strips, 29.
kang, clan, 104–7.
karemak, spearman (in elephant-hunting), 29, 30.
karo, totems, 157–8.
karubanit, ghoul, 199, 204–5.
kasayanit, dentist, 127.
kasumanit, poisoner, 133, 204–5.
Kasura rain clan, the, 12, 18.
kedi lo matat lo kudu, the rain-makers' serfs, 28.
Kathingotore (or *Kwoto*), a sacred stone, 34, 81.
kebu, hoe, 178.
kheret, intestines, 99.

khima, grain, 20, 93.
Kichepo tribe, the, 151.
kidori, altar, 188.
King, Capt. G. R., on the Topotha, 65–82.
kir, mahogany, 131.
koci, thicket, 162.
kole, hoe, 138.
komonyekak, chief, 11–12, 197.
kongo bird, the, 40.
kono, vine-stem, 173.
köntio, pl. *kör*, rain-chief, 122.
Koriuk tribe, the, 82–3.
Kubi, basket, 169.
kudi, harp, 179.
Kuku tribe, the, 4 ff., 216–21.
kumari, rain-maker's assistant, 36.
kumbagudi, small boys, 224.
kuroboro, grown men, 224.
kwoso, healing sorcerer, 38, 167.
Kwoto (or *Kathingotore*), a sacred stone, 34, 81.

labaloni, father of village, 88 ff.
Labi, a rain-maker, 163–6.
labi, tribe customs, 159, 169.
labi aku (outside the custom), bastard, 50, 159, 169.
Ladofani, sorcerer, 38, 104.
laduri khorwong, boys behind, 92, 94 ff.
Lafit tribe, the, 82.
lamaurwak, old men, 92, 97.
Lamomolani, evil sorcerers, 38, 103–4.
lamonyedupa, father of the drums, 88.
lamonyefau, father of the land, 26, 88–91, 111.
lamonyekhari, father of the river, 26, 91.
lamonyemiji, father of the village, 88 ff.
lamuroni, female healers, 103.
Land tenure and cultivation, 7, 54–6, 79 (Topotha), 91, 112 (Latuka), 138–9 (Bari), 176–7 (Moru), 190–1 (Luluba).
langet, group of clients, 128, 222.
Lango tribe, the, 4 ff., 82, 113–14.
Latuka-speaking tribes, the, 4 ff., 82–113.
Leboni, healing sorcerer, 38, 103.
lelekoi, pl. *lelekoxa*, friend, 104–8.
lemanit, evil eye, 103.
lemye, lion, 93.
liggitot, pl. *liggo*, elephant-hunter, 13, 28–30, 207.
Lightning, the personification of, 34.
Lilley, Lieut.-Col., on the Lango, 113–14; the Latuka, 38, 82–113.

230 INDEX

Linguistic characteristics of the province, the, 5–7, and *passim.*
lipitiro, bush-pig, 145.
liri tree, the, 122.
lishi, grave stake, 184.
loceleli, rain-maker, 93.
Logiri tribe, the, 82, 113.
logobe, grinding stone, 93.
Lokoiya (or Oghoriok) tribe, the, 4 ff., 82, 114–18.
lolong, sun, 111.
lolongakindi, offering, 202.
lomariang, elephant, 145.
lomé, ancestral spirits, 186.
lomiang, male bastard, 49, 117.
Lomini clan, the, 86.
lomomo, sausage tree, 111.
lomukudit, very numerous, 119.
londriba, diviner, 172.
Longarim tribe, the, 4 ff., 142–4.
Longgoba, song leader, 179.
longorony, dirty mouth, 111.
losiso, elders, 219.
lotole, hare, 139.
loyama, marriage, 99.
Lu, God, 40, 172–3.
lubang, 30.
Lubanga, god, 34, 147.
Lugbari tribe, the, 4 ff.
lugöyi, a plant, 30.
lui, freemen, 28, 122.
lukokönyumi tree, the, 122.
Luluba tribe, the, 4 ff., 188–91.
lungaser, my brother, 126.
lupudyet, youths, 126.
lusi, grave-post, 170–1.
luto, pl. *lutojin*, peg shrine, 118.

madada, skirt, 223.
Madi tribe, the, 4 ff., 186–8.
Magic, the belief in, 38–40, 75 (Topotha), 103–4 (Latuka), 132–3 (Bari), 167 (Moru), 203–4 (Fajulu).
Makaraka tribe, the, 223–5.
Mandari tribe, the, 4 ff., 139–41.
mananye, mother's brother, 191.
Marike tribe, the, 148–50.
Marriage beliefs and practices, 46–50, 68, 76 (Topotha), 104–9 (Latuka), 117 (Lokoiya), 133–4 (Bari), 167–9 (Moru), 196–7 (Fajulu), 208–9 (Kakwa).
matat lo gela, the foreigners' chief, 22, 123.
Mböli, God, 225.

mböröju, sorcerer, 167.
merenye, maternal uncle, 196.
mila, magic whistle, 166, 167.
milaba, sorcerer, 167.
Molinaro, Father, on the Madi, 31, 33, 186–8.
Monyedupa, the, 96, 100.
monyekak (or *monyekurök*), earth chief, 7, 11–12, 16, 25–7, 31, 116–17, 125–6, 138, 140, 185, 188–90, 216–17.
monyemiji, protectors of the village, 21, 35–6, 92 ff., 111, 115, 116.
monye wati, father of the people, 90.
moru, rat, 121.
Moru tribe, the, 4 ff.
Moru-Madi tribes, the, 4 ff., 153–91, and *passim.*
mulukötyö, pl. *mulökö*, spirit of the dead, 131, 199 ff.
mulökötyo lo kinyo, spirit of food, 130.
mulu alo, monorchid, 162.
Mundu tribe, the, 226.
Murder, practices in regard to, 43–5, 74–5 (Topotha).
Murray, G. W., on the Nilo-Hamitic languages, 6.
Mynors, W. H. B., on the Moru, 6, 10, 12, 155–83

nabakhala, cornstalk, 98.
naboro, sand, 20, 93, 97.
naburu, cheetah, 99.
naduya, drum house, 88, 91, 93 ff.
nakhesu, magical gourd, 104.
Nakwuge, God, 81.
nalam, new year hunt, 35–6, 88, 102, 110–11.
nalore, drum-poles, 98.
namangat, village quarters, 88, 91, 95 ff.
Names, personal, 76.
nametere, burial effigy, 51.
nanyim, simsim, 111.
naririk, fringe, 104–5.
nasanga, wooing, 104.
natat lo ber, chief of the class, 127.
nataxas, summer, 111.
natorit, dry-weather cultivation, 112.
natur, long trumpet, 35, 102, 110.
Nature spirits, 33–4.
nawi, cattle camps, 65.
nebuto (rape), compensation, 49, 110.
nekanga, trumpet, 110.
nemojit, token of receipt, 105.

INDEX

nengasa, daughter, 105; marriage payment, 106–7.
nengwok, fermented grain, 106.
netalixi fau, cooling-earth festival, 111.
neyemiti, marriage goods, 105–8.
ngokhe, hogs, 99.
ngote kinyo, mother of food, 131.
Nguleso, the sky god, 32, 33, 213–14.
Ngulete, a totality of malignant spirits, 32, 33–4, 214.
Ngun-lo-kak, the earth god, 32, 130, 136, 200.
Ngun-lo-ki, the sky god, 32, 119, 130, 200.
nichilomé, huts, 186.
Nilo-Hamitic tribes, the, 4 ff., 65–141, and *passim*.
nodwoti, maiden, 104.
nolobele, platform towers, 96, 97–8.
nongopira, fire ceremony, 35, 92, 95 ff.
nyamorum, healing sorcerer, 38.
Nyangatomo tribe, the, 150.
Nyangwara tribe, the, 4 ff., 193–5.
Nyefu tribe, the, 4 ff., 221–2.
nyidomei, fire-sticks, 69.
Nyikoroma tribe, the, 150.
Nyikuren, the fire-working clan, 69.
nyimarun, spirit-doctor, 75.
nyimong, bull, 66.
nyitakeri, clans, 68.
nyong, village, 20.
nyoringi, sister's son, 139.
nyorinyikö ti ngun, spirits of the dead, 131.

Oaths, the use of, 123.
Ochre, red, the production and use of, 8, 55–6, 81, 137.
ocoro or *otyoro*, a form of marriage, 108.
odesa, unlucky, 35, 98, 102.
odraba, sorcerer, 167.
ofilima, sweet grain, 111.
ojoggo, medicine man, 187.
okelipinok, boys, 116.
okwako, bachelors, 184.
olonyi lamwak (son of a whore), bastard, 49.
omarwok, old men, 115, 116.
opi, chief, 187, 189.
Ordeal, forms of the, 39–40, 115, 123.
Ori, God, 186.
Ornament, personal, variations in, 7–8, 11, 77–8, 136–7, 179.
osom, prostitute, 110.
otega, war leader, 146.

otogo, bachelors' hut, 147.
otyoro or *ocoro*, a form of marriage, 108.
Ovaré, God, 184.
owas, grain in the ear, 111.
owete, drying grass, 111.
oxobolo, elders, 115, 116.
oxobumiji, chief of the land, 116.

pai, ebony, 162.
paranga, circumcised youths, 223, 224.
Pastoral tribes, the, 7, 53–6, 78, 137–7, 177, 199–200.
Peg shrines, 118.
pena, foreign serfs, 129–30.
penga, lightning, 215.
pepe tree, the, 131.
perek, wanderers, 99.
pe'ya, lightning, 205.
Physical anthropology of the natives, 5, 57–8.
Platform towers, the, 97–8.
Polygamy, 46–7, 134.
Polygyny, 76.
Pottery, the manufacture of, 56, 80.
Pritchard, Dr. Evans, cited, 155.
Property and inheritance, 80.
pulalo, red ochre, 190.
Punishment, crime and, 43–5, 74–5.
Purification, blood, 37–8.
putet, council, 123.
pwara (central), dance floor, 96 ff., 105.
Python, belief regarding a gigantic, 34.

Raglan, Lord, cited, 88.
Rainbow, belief regarding the, 176, 215–16.
Rainfall, 3.
Rain-makers and rain-making, 7, 11–12, 18, 22–7, 75 (Topotha), 86 ff. (Latuka), 115 (Lokoiya), 124–5 (Bari), 146 (Acholi), 160–7 (Moru), 196–7 (Fajulu), 209–11 (Kakwa), 216–17 (Kuku).
ramu, spirit-house, 161.
Religious beliefs, 31–42, 81 (Topotha), 118 (Lokoiya), 130–2 (Bari), 172–5 (Moru), 213–16 (Kakwa), 225 (Makaraka).
Richardson, Mr., cited, 34, 116, 124, 125, 127, 138.
Rogers, Mr., on the Madi, 24.
Rope-making, 56.
rube, bogy, 133.
rubo, old home, 201.
rudu, sacred grove, 34.

INDEX

232

ruma dance, the, 175.
Running-the-gauntlet ritual, 20, 73.
Ruru secret society, the, 40, 167.
rwot, tribal chief, 145–6.

salesi, fire-stones, 131.
samba, attendant, 223.
Secret societies, 40.
Sections, the, in tribal organization, 17–18.
Seduction, 108–9.
Seligman, Dr. C. G., cited, 7, 9, 88, 91, 112, 118, 119, 122, 124, 130, 134, 135; on the Bambara, 26; the Bari, 10–11, 32, 192; the Hamites, 5–6; the *Lamonyemiji*, 88, 90; language groups, 6; the Lomini clan, 86; the *monyekak*, 26; the Moru-Madi group, 153–5; rain-making, 23–5, 88.
Servile classes, 27–8, 128–30.
Sexual beliefs and practices, 46–50, 76.
Shackleton, Mr., on the Marille, 35, 148–50.
Sky god, the, 9, 32, 130, 200.
Slavery, 27–8.
Smith, Castle, cited, 41.
Societies, secret, 40.
Song, elephant, 30.
Sorcerers, 38–40, 75 (Topotha), 103–4 (Latuka), 132–3 (Bari), 167 (Moru).
Spears, sacred, 124, 166.
Spagnolo, Father, cited, 119, 126, 131, 135.
Spirit doctors, 38–40, 75, 103–4, 132, 167, 203–4.
Spirits, the belief in, 32–4, 130–1, 186–7, 200–4, 214–15.
Statistics, vital, 57–8.
Stigand on the Kuku, 25–6, 216.
Stone cults, 34.
Suicide, 51–2.

ta-opaba, word-tellers, 157.
temejik, elders, 126, 196, 218.
teton, warriors, 126.
tin'dana lord of the land, 26–7.
tipo, spirit, 147.
tokaba, blacksmith, 178.
tomonok ti kare, fisherman, 122, 129.
tomonok ti yukit, blacksmiths, 122, 129.
tongbo, small pot, 201.
Tongkulya, a spirit doctor, 30.
Tooth extraction practices, 19 and *n*.2, 20.
Topotha tribe, the, 4 ff., 65–82.

tori, the spirits after death, 158, 172.
toslobo, snail-shells, 162.
Totemic clans, 16, 157–8.
Towers, the platform, 97–8.
Tree cults, 34.
Tribe, the structure of the, 15–30, 88–91, 145–6.
Tucker, Dr., cited or quoted, 6, 9, 114, 119.
Twins, beliefs relating to, 13, 50–1, 76 (Topotha), 117 (Lokoiya), 133 (Bari), 149 (Marille), 167, 188 (Moru), 197 (Fajulu).

Village, the nature of the, 17.
Vital statistics, 57–8.
Vora rain clan, the, 12.
vureba, case-men, 157.

Wak, God, 148, 149.
Wan gang, village headman, 145–6.
wangu, rainbow, 225.
Water cult, the Allah, 41–2.
Wayland, Mr., cited, 147.
Weapons, variations in the use of, 8, 11, 77–8, 117, 137, 179, 200.
Weber, Mr., on the Latuka, 82–113.
Werne on the Bari, 19 *n*. 2, 119.
Weland, E. J., cited, 65 *n*.
Whalley, Capt., on the tribes of the Abyssinian border, 148–52.
Whitehead, Mr., on the Bari, 28, 129–30, 136.
Winder, J., or the Acholi, 144–7; the Kakwa, 12, 206–16; the Kuku, 216–22; the Nyefu, 221–2.
Witchcraft, the belief in, 38–40, 75 (Topotha), 103–4 (Latuka), 132–3 (Bari), 167 (Moru), 203–4 (Fajulu).
won kot, rain chief, 146.
won ngom, land chief, 146.
Wood-work, 56, 80.
wuri, wind, 133.

xang, clans, 86.
xiromo, let them dig, 111.
xobu, pl. *xobok*, rain chief, 85, 86–7, 103.
xomongye, father-in-law, 106–7.

Yakang, the water of, 41.
yari, hunter, 122, 129.

Zambonardi, Mgr., 186.
Zande, the, 3 and *n*.
zeriba, the, 103.